Chris Orr

The Virgin

WINE
GUIDE

ACKNOWLEDGEMENTS

Thanks to Adrian Tempany for his help in fact checking.
Thanks also to the team at Virgin Books, particularly
Carolyn Thorne and Gareth Fletcher.

First published in Great Britain in 2004 by
Virgin Books Ltd, Thames Wharf Studios, Rainville Road, London w6 9HA

ISBN 0 7535 0913 X

Designed and typeset by Smith & Gilmour, London
Printed and bound in Great Britain by Bath Press

Contents

Preface

Wine is a fun, exciting, endlessly fascinating subject – but too many people who are passionate about it and write about it manage to transform it into an intimidating and overly complex affair. Lots of people want to know more about wine – and, given the fact that we're drinking more and more of the stuff than ever before, that's a pretty justifiable search for knowledge.

The key thing to grasp about wine, however, is fundamentally the most simple and yet most often overlooked, by both newcomers to the world of the grape and old hands alike. If you think back to those appalling mathematics lessons we probably all had to endure as children, you will no doubt remember that they were stuffed with lots of equations, some more complex than others. Well, I like to think of wine – and where it sits in our life – as a relatively simple collection of equations:

WINE + FRIENDS = FUN
WINE + FRIENDS + GREAT FOOD = DOUBLE FUN
WINE – FRIENDS – GREAT FOOD = GET A LIFE!

If you choose this book it's obviously because you want to know more about wine. Whether it's to impress your boss, feel more confident when you next find yourself in front of a shelf stacked with bottles, or because somehow, somewhere in between buying your first ever bottle of wine and reading this Foreword, you've caught the wine bug, I don't exactly know. But, if you *do* buy this book, I hope it's because you not only want to know more about the lovely juice you continue pouring into your wineglass, but, importantly, want to have a giggle, a laugh and a lot of fun in doing so. Wine is not meant to be boring, and I've tried to ensure this book makes that point in no uncertain terms. If this guide means one more wine bore has been added to the already crowded dinner tables of the UK, then I will have failed.

So, if you fancy learning more about wine without getting too heavy, then welcome to the party. I hope you brought a bottle.

Cheers

Chris Orr

Introduction
why another book on wine?

If you've read this far, then it probably means you've made the decision to learn more about wine. And presumably you've read the blurb and Foreword and know that this is a book dedicated to helping you to learn more about wine – and to have fun while you're doing it.

So, how was the first time for you? Everyone has a first experience of wine. My first sip of the lovely stuff came at the age of four, when my Uncle Max served Sunday lunch – and it was wonderful. Well, the first sip was. After that I can't remember. But, more than that was the general bonhomie: the laughter, the chat, the enjoyment everyone was having at lunch as they were drinking away. That's what I remember most – and that's what I always associate with wine.

Other people, it seems, don't always have such a positive experience – either because the first bottle they've had has proved to be less than wonderful, or more likely because they've had a horrible experience while trying to buy their first bottle. They've felt intimidated and ignorant, like an outsider – and no one wants to feel like an outsider.

What we want is to feel that asking questions is a *good* thing, that wanting to know more is a positive step, not an admission of stupidity. That is why we all pluck books like this off the shelf.

So, once you've taken the decision to learn more about wine, where do you go from there? Well, first things first. Wine is a very simple thing. Many would have us believe otherwise, but the truth is that it is as simple as can be. You buy a bottle of wine, you pull a cork from it, you drink it. If you like it, you buy the bottle again. After several of the same bottle, you may get bored with it, then decide to try something different. The something different you try may or may not make you happy – in which case you either go back to the first wine you tried or find a different wine to try.

Of course, like any subject matter with an infinite number of variables it can be complicated if you want it to be. There are literally thousands of different wines – actually hundreds of thousands. Most wines come from a specific region, within a specific country – each of which has a different climate – making variations almost infinite. And each year a new vintage, often very different from the last that is produced, appears on our shelves. Sometimes different vintages are blended together to make a non-vintage wine (as is the case with Champagne), adding yet more variations to the list. So, yes, the number of wines you might want to get your head around can be enormous.

But in my humble opinion there are only two reasons for wine to ever really get complicated:

REASON 1: YOU GOT SUCKED IN.

If this is the case, deal with it. It happens. Wine gets complicated when someone has taken it upon themselves to become an 'expert' – that is someone who acquires a considerable knowledge of wine, of its regions, of its grape varieties, vintages, winemaking methods and the minutiae that go into producing this wonderful and at times almost heavenly liquid. These people will buy increasingly larger books on the subject; they will spend increasing amounts of their income on buying rare bottles of wine, or discovering the 'latest' top-notch producer from a tiny little vineyard area in the back of beyond. Slowly but surely they begin to acquire wine and lose friends in the same proportion. Often their partners leave them, resulting in double the devastation for the new wine aficionado (but spouses remember that *half* the cellar is worth something, so take that too!).

For the majority of people, however, being an expert is not their reason for wanting to know about wine. Their reason is usually very simple: they want to drink less boring wine. They know there is a wealth of wines out there that they think they should be trying, but they're afraid to try them out. They lack confidence, and feel that a bit of basic knowledge will help them make those tough decisions as they stand in front of a supermarket's or wine merchant's bottle-laden shelf. This book is unashamedly about giving you that confidence and a knowledge of the basics only. If you want to take it further, that's entirely up to you.

REASON 2: SOMEONE'S OUT TO BAMBOOZLE YOU.

This is the most common reason why wine is complicated. It's a bit like buying a second-hand car. You often know only the basics, so, if a salesman wants to set you up and fleece you, all he has to do is throw in a few choice comments that will have you doubling your intended spend and worrying that even that is not enough. So it is with wine.

A lot of those involved with wine make a little knowledge go a long way in terms of humiliating the customer. It's not nice, it's not clever and it's actually not a very good sales technique, and yet so many spotty, bespectacled wine shop assistants insist on making you feel small, ill-informed and unwanted. What they don't get is that most people walk into a wine shop because they *don't know about wine* – but they don't *need* to know about wine, because that's the job of the person in the wine shop.

It's like having your pharmacist stare down at you and sneer, 'What do you mean you don't know the chemical makeup of hydrocortisone cream?' It's not your job to know. She's the one who spent five years studying pharmacology. Indeed, if I walked into a chemist and the pharmacist took that attitude, I'd take my nasty skin complaint elsewhere. And so it should be with wine – it's the wine assistant's job to know about wines. And it's the wine company's job to make sure he or she does. Your job simply amounts to telling the assistant how much you're willing to splash out and give a few clues on what thrills you or chills you.

This book is also, without repentance, about encouraging you to make the UK's wine merchants work for their money. If they don't know their subject, and don't know how to ensure you walk out of their store with a bottle of wine that will interest, excite and fulfil you, then they have no right being a wine merchant.

HOW DO I USE THIS BOOK?

Well, hopefully, it's not remotely like an Ikea flatpack instruction manual, in that it should be entertaining, and you can dip in and out of it, more or less wherever you like.

You'll find a pretty basic history of wine – one that you can easily memorise and impress your friends with, but it will take you no more than two and half minutes to read. You'll also find a quick-start guide to how you can easily make your enjoyment of wine better, from making sure you're drinking from a half-decent glass to ensuring you use all your senses to extract maximum value from the bottle of vino you have invested in.

There's also advice on *how* to buy and *where* to buy. It's commonsense advice more than anything else, but sometimes the obvious is worth stating. There's information on wine by style, and a runaround the world's principal wine-producing countries, not to mention a mini wine course designed to allow you and a few friends to learn a little as you get suitably hammered at the dinner table, then stagger off to bed to dream of yet more Pinot Noir.

And, best of all, there are a couple of cheat sheets. If you're remotely like me, i.e. terminally lazy, then there's just a chance that, once you've read through this first chapter, no matter how entertaining and erudite my writing is, you'll be thinking that it's a little bit like being in the English class at school: you *could* have read all of *Wuthering Heights*, as requested, over the Easter break, but then you would have missed out on (a) girls or (b) boys (delete as appropriate), which means you went out and bought the *How To Pass Your Exams in Two Easy Minutes* crammer book instead. There's always a risk that you could get caught by the English teacher, but that's the gamble you took. For those who are similarly minded, turn to Chapter 10 – I guarantee you'll stand a 70 per cent chance of blagging it through most awkward wine occasions and sleep soundly in your bed.

Mind you, I'd give reading the whole book a go – if nothing else, it would make me feel better.

chapter one
rip-off culture

Rip-off culture. It's the scourge of Britain if you believe what the tabloids say. When we fill up our overpriced cars with overpriced petrol, preferably not smoking our overpriced cigarettes or talking on our overpriced phones at the same time, it would seem that we're always getting a raw deal in comparison with our Continental cousins. Personally, I am not sure this is necessarily the case. But I haven't got any cast-iron proof, so I'm not going to attempt to persuade anybody one way or the other – except when it comes to wine. Because with wine I believe we definitely do get taken for a ride in Britain.

Every time you purchase a bottle of £3.99 wine in Great Britain (and in this case we'll reserve judgement on the Great bit), you pay just shy of £2 into the coffers of the Chancellor of the Exchequer. That's £1.30 in duty and 60 pence in VAT, to be precise. Now, bearing in mind that the average person in Britain spends slightly less than £3.99 on a bottle of wine, that means they're being taxed 50 per cent by the government every time they buy. Even City fat cats don't pay 50 per cent on their massive bonuses. So why should we on one of life's small pleasures?

Well, there are schools, higher education and the NHS to consider, I suppose. They all need to be paid for somehow. But it still seems an outrageous amount – especially as our cousins in the rest of the European Union all manage to skip such onerous duty charges.

Well, sadly, I can't do anything about the decision of the government of the day to keep duty on alcohol high. But I can illustrate why it means you should pay just that little bit more for your wine, and be rewarded with a significantly better glass of red or white to go with dinner.

DIG JUST A LITTLE DEEPER

I'm sure that, like me, you probably hate facts and figures. They're not much fun. But bear with me. On page 12, you'll see some illustrative wine bottles that show exactly where your money goes when you spend £3.99, £4.99, £5.99 and £6.99.

What's useful to know is that, when you buy a bottle of £3.99, on average you're probably getting 'juice', as they say in the trade, worth just 31 pence. Yes, 31 pence! However, spend a pound more and you'll find the juice is worth 74 pence. In other words, for just £1 more you're getting double the value of actual wine in your glass. Now, since it's wine we're talking about, that doesn't necessarily guarantee that you're getting double the quality, but it *will* give you a much better wine than what you buy at the £3.99 mark.

And so it goes on. With a £5.99 bottle, you get £1.15 worth of wine – that means 3.7 times the amount that you get in a £3.99 bottle. That's £2 more, yet almost four times the value of juice.

Sorry to labour this, but I think you can get the point. There is, of course, a point at which this progression begins to diminish. I think one can safely say that, above £9–10 for a bottle of still red or white, you are beginning to get to the level where the extra money spent doesn't give you any proportionately impressive improvements in taste or quality. Unless you know a bit about wine and have a fairly attuned palate, it could be a waste of money.

But in the lower brackets, particularly the £5–7 area, you really can find quite significant and amazing differences in quality for what is just a pound or two more.

BARGAIN WHAT?

As well as encouraging you to spend a few more pennies per bottle, however, the illustrations should also make you think a little harder about the so-called 'bargain buys' that always appear in the supermarkets' and wine merchants' aisles. Take a quick peek at the £4.99 bottle and you'll quickly see that the producer 'makes' £0.12 a bottle (though it can be more). The importer makes £0.15 a bottle, and the retailer makes £1.36. That's a big difference.

Now sometimes a retailer will knock some money off. Sometimes it comes out of the money they make. Sometimes it comes out of the money the producer or agent makes. Occasionally it comes out of the money all three of them make. But, if you knock a pound off the price of the bottle, you can barely fund that through the money they *all* make, let alone one of them. Retailers, importers and producers are generally all very nice people – but they're not charities. So where do you think some of the 'bargain' comes from? Often, it comes from the wine, or, in other words, when you get a £4.99 wine for £3.99, you're probably getting a wine that has nearer to £0.31 worth of juice in it than £0.74. Which means you're being ripped off.

Of course, there are no absolutes. Some people do manage to make a wine for £4.99, sell it at £3.99, deliver you a bargain and make money to boot. But it's always wise when shopping around to bear in mind the old adage that there's no such thing as a free lunch.

£3.99	What you get for	£4.99
£0.31	What you're actually drinking in value terms	£0.74
£0.10	Cost of bottle	£0.13
£0.23	Packaging and freight	£0.25
£0.07	What the producer makes	£0.12
£0.19	Shipping to UK	£0.19
£0.10	What the importer makes	£0.16
Duty £1.30 VAT £0.60	What the government makes	Duty £1.30 VAT £0.74
£1.09	What the retailer makes	£1.36

£5.99	What you get for	£6.99
£1.15	What you're actually drinking in value terms	£1.54
£0.15	Cost of bottle	£0.18
£0.28	Packaging and freight	£0.32
£0.18	What the producer makes	£0.23
£0.19	Shipping to UK	£0.19
£0.22	What the importer makes	£0.28
Duty £1.30 VAT £0.89	What the government makes	Duty £1.30 VAT £1.04
£1.63	What the retailer makes	£1.91

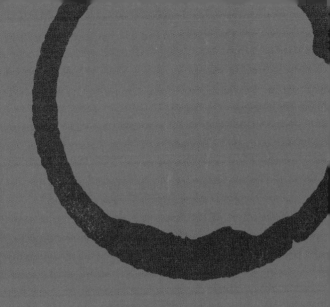

chapter two
how to buy

Where's the best place to buy your wine – and why?

The British wine drinker is among the luckiest in the world. Go to France and you'll find some 98 per cent of the wines on sale are French. Go to Australia and it's the same percentage of Australian wines on sale, with only a few imports. In Italy, I'd even go so far as to say that 99 per cent of all wines sold are Italian, with the other 1 per cent being made up of champagne – a drink the country's citizens seem unduly fond of.

In the UK, however, we have wines from virtually every country the world over. In part it's because we have a very small winemaking industry. There are some very good wineries in England, but you can count them on one hand. Bordeaux alone has over 13,000 producers – so why would someone living in Bordeaux need to buy anything other than the local stuff?

The UK also has one of the most clearly divided, and also accessible, ranges of wine retailers. From the supermarket, through the high street chains, via the Internet, down to the smallest independent, and even via the auction houses, there is a style of buying wine to suit everyone.

I'll now take you through each of these retailers and give you handy hints on working out which you should be choosing to bestow your hard-earned pennies on – and how to get the most out of them.

SUPERMARKETS

Supermarkets in Britain account for roughly 75 per cent of all wine sales, and Tesco is the largest wine retailer in the UK.

Supermarkets have done more to expand our drinking experience over the last two decades than any other area of the wine retail sector. More of us drink wine now than two decades ago, precisely because the supermarkets have done an excellent job of promoting the lovely liquid to their customers. Tesco, for example, has a wine list exceeding 800 lines and its average stores stock between 250 and 400 at any one time. And the story is the same with many of the others, even if the number of wines stocked varies.

This creates the perfect opportunity to experiment with different styles of wine, different grape varieties and different countries. Why? Well, it all comes down to simple economics of scale. Supermarkets get a good deal because they buy more and so can dictate terms to even the biggest of the world's producers.

However, the supermarkets are very brand-dominated. You'll find the likes of Jacob's Creek, Hardys, Mouton-Cadet and Lindemans taking up a large amount of shelf space, as well as a supermarket's own-brand produce.

WHY SHOULD YOU SHOP AT A SUPERMARKET?

Eighty-five per cent of all wine in the UK is sold under £5.99 – and most is sold in supermarkets. If you want great value and don't intend spending any more, then a supermarket is probably the best place to be.

They usually get the best offers. Independent merchants can't compete.

You'll find bigger discounts in supermarkets than anywhere else – though this doesn't always mean 'great value'.

WHY SHOULDN'T YOU SHOP AT A SUPERMARKET?

If you want advice, a supermarket is probably not the best place. Most supermarkets claim they have 'advisers' on hand in their major stores, but I have yet to see one when I have walked down the aisle.

If you want to experiment, remember that supermarkets are geared to the masses, and consequently miss out on a lot of the smaller, more interesting producers that make it over to the UK.

If you want to spend more than £5.99, you can still find great wines in supermarkets, but you won't always find the most exciting, or necessarily get the best value from them.

Make the most of: the great offers.

Don't be duped by: *all* of the great offers. For every wine that is really worth £6.99 but has been marked down to £3.99, there's another that's never been worth more than £3.99 and may not even be worth that. The best advice is to buy a bottle. If you like it and think it's worth it, *then* go back and buy twelve.

HIGH STREET MULTIPLES

The easiest way I can describe this sector is simply to tell you a few of the names that occupy it: Threshers, Oddbins, Unwins, Majestic, Nicolas – most of these names should be recognisable to you.

In the UK at present this sector has rather lost its way. Over the last decade many have lost their point of difference and instead have tried to compete head to head, offering promotion after promotion, and deal after deal – a lot of which are uneconomical for them, and consequently make it difficult for them to maintain profitability.

Some are turning to the convenience-store format to ensure their survival. But most are actually offering little more than your average corner shop when it comes to choice or value. And they miss out most, perhaps, when it comes to that simple, but oh-so-important factor that could easily set them apart from the supermarket and give them a specific point of difference: service.

Perhaps the best example of good service is with Majestic Wine Warehouses. It's one of the most successful, and possibly most profitable, of the major high street multiples for several reasons. It represents not only very good value but also offers great service. Pop into your local Majestic and you'll often find it run by someone young, enthusiastic, well trained and personable – and someone who wants to help you find the wine you want.

WHY SHOULD YOU SHOP AT A HIGH STREET MULTIPLE?

Convenience is the chief factory, but remember that often comes at a price.

WHY SHOULDN'T YOU SHOP AT A HIGH STREET MULTIPLE?

With the odd exception, they don't offer the value that supermarkets do, and few supply the service that would make it worthwhile paying the extra pennies for a bottle.

Make the most of: the champagne deals. They use them to lure you in and away from the supermarkets but they're usually good.

Don't be duped by: big-brand discounts. Take a peek around your supermarket before you bulk-buy – often the same brands will be on sale for less at Tesco or Sainsbury's, again because of simple economics of scale.

INDEPENDENT WINE MERCHANTS

The definition of an independent wine merchant is fairly straightforward. There are often only one or two shops as part of the offering, rarely more, and they are truly independent, buying their products from a broad range of agents and suppliers. They also source small parcels of wines that are too uneconomical for the supermarkets or multiples to handle. The result is a range of wines that are often either exclusive to the independent retailer, or imported by only a few other independents.

While I respect the need for supermarkets and the range and offers they present, the independents bring out the wine nerd in me. They are the key to bringing in new, exciting, vibrant wines to the UK.

They don't always offer the most tremendous value – but that's not really the point.

More important is that they are often run by people who are ultra-passionate and ultra-knowledgeable about their wines. A decent independent may charge you a few more pennies for a wine, but you'll stand more chance of walking out with the right bottle.

The problem with independents, however, is that they are often havens for some of the biggest wine snobs. It's an appalling catch-22 situation – and many people have probably fled from an independent wine merchant into their nearest supermarket precisely because they've been made to feel ignorant or unworthy. However, I'd encourage you to shop around and try a few in your area before you abandon them.

WHY SHOULD YOU SHOP AT AN INDEPENDENT?

In a word: service. A good independent will give you all the advice you want and help you find exactly the right bottle of wine to suit whichever situation you find yourself in.

Then there's excitement: the wines you find in a good independent will often be much more interesting than the average list available in a supermarket or high street multiple.

You'll also find knowledge. If you've found a friendly independent it's often a lot nicer to pop in and have a chat about wine for fifteen minutes than spend an hour poring over a thick wine manual.

'Fine wine' is a relatively loose term and in most cases the word 'fine' is a euphemism for 'expensive'. But, if you are thinking of investing in some wine, or buying some decent wines at £10 or above, you really ought to be talking to a decent independent rather than a supermarket shelf stacker in the wine aisle.

They're the specialists – a lot of independents will specialise in a specific area, region or country, as well as offering a broad selection from other countries. So, if you want to find out what the best wines Italy, say, has to offer at a broad price range, then you're best going to an independent that stocks mainly Italian wines.

WHY SHOULDN'T YOU SHOP AT AN INDEPENDENT?

Intimidation. Walk down St James's Street in London, home to some of the UK's oldest wine merchants, and you'll know exactly what I mean. The intimidation factor of a pinstripe suit alone is quite frightening.
Make the most of: their knowledge and expertise.
Don't be duped by: bin ends. Sometimes they can be great – truly

great. And sometimes they can be wines an independent merchant bought, but just can't shift. And logic dictates that often that's because they bought a duff one. Try before you buy, always. Just when you think it's impossible for a Rioja at £2.99 to be bad value, Sod's Law will prove otherwise.

THE INTERNET

We all work longer, harder and more furiously than ever before, so we all tend to have less and less leisure time. It doesn't take long before you wonder whether it isn't worth paying an extra £5 or £10 to buy your weekly groceries on the Internet.

But, aside from sheer laziness, I think the Internet is perhaps the single most effective way of taking snobbishness out of wine. A great example of this is the ancient and esteemed firm of Berry Brothers & Rudd in Saint James's Street, London. It's the city's oldest wine merchant – and don't you just know it when you walk through the doors! Even I feel slightly apprehensive when I enter the shop.

Yet this venerable institution now does almost more business over the Internet, after just a few years, than it does through its shop, which has been going for three hundred years or more. Why? Because there are no pinstripe suits on the website. You can ask all the questions you like, read articles about the wines and spend as long as you like clicking through the various wines listed. In short, the likes of www.virginwines.com, www.bbr.com, www.thewinesociety.com and several others offer you complete unfettered access to as much, or as little, information as you might care to be given about wine. And that has to be good.

WHY SHOULD YOU SHOP ON THE INTERNET?

Lack of intimidation makes it easier to browse through wines and experiment with new wines or find out more information.

Many sites, such as Virgin and Berry's, offer a bespoke service, all of which can be done over the Net or the phone.

You often get the same choice, excitement and interest as you do with a good independent, but without venturing outside your front door.

Then there's service: the wines are delivered to your door, and increasingly sites are offering a 24-hour service as standard.

Look out for offers, too: as the volume of wines being sold over the Internet grows, there are better and better deals being offered, sometimes giving the supermarkets a run for their money.

WHY SHOULDN'T YOU SHOP ON THE INTERNET?

Some people like interaction with human beings. It's that simple.

Modern technology is a great thing, but not all of us have cable or broadband. And trying to shop online with a 52K modem can sometimes be a little bit like trying to suck treacle through a straw.

People are still wary of using credit cards on the Net even though it is far more secure than paying for tickets over the phone or paying your restaurant bill by credit card.

Of course, if you need a wine for tonight's dinner and have run out, you'll need to pop out for something a little more immediate. **Make the most of**: being able to sit in the comfort of your own home, order your wine and then have it arrive at your door the very next day. **Don't be duped by**: the 'get-out clause'. When you sign up with any Internet service or site, there's always some point where, by law, the company must ask you whether or not you want to 'opt in' or 'opt out' of further contact by email about special offers and so forth. Reputable firms will mail you only when they have an offer, but, if you don't even want *this* limited form of contact, make sure you tick the box, and make sure you read what you've ticked for: was it 'opt out' or 'opt in'?

MAIL ORDER

Is it worth the paperwork? Anyone with recent experiences with the Royal Mail will not necessarily be overwhelmed by the prospect of having their wines delivered next door but one, two weeks late and partially damaged. But presumably it doesn't happen all that often, especially when you consider that mail-order wine is still big business in the UK with the likes of the *Sunday Times* Wine Club and the Wine Society doing much of their business in this fashion.

The challenge with mail order these days is that, compared with the Internet or your local retailer, the cost of selling by this method is increasing. That's not because the postal and courier services are putting up their prices, but because of the cost of paper, print and postage.

The result is that, while it is convenient and relatively simple and straightforward, buying wine by mail order doesn't always yield the best value. However, some companies, such as the Wine Society, still manage to offer not only a great selection but some great bargains as well.

WHY SHOULD YOU SHOP BY MAIL ORDER?

It's often reliable and safe and can provide extraordinary good value. Many of the firms operating in this area have been around for a long time – and look as if they'll continue to do so.

If you're a housebound technophobe, it's a good way to get your favourite bottle of Chablis from the merchant's shelf to your table.

WHY SHOULDN'T YOU SHOP BY MAIL ORDER?

Unlike the Internet, or standing in a shop, it's very difficult to get more information about the product. Unless the tasting notes in the catalogue or offer are detailed, you'll end up with only the basics on the wine you're buying.

Like the Internet, it can be seen as a fairly impersonal way of buying your wine.

Many mail-order firms are pushing more and more of their business through the Internet, and have incentives to encourage you to buy there. **Make the most of**: the efficiency of the process. The big firms have been doing this for many years, and they've honed their service pretty well. Invariably, if they say it's going to be with you in 36 hours, you can more or less bet it will be.

Don't be duped by: the introductory offers. They're priced to drag you in, and twelve months later you suddenly find that you've actually been spending a lot more on your average bottle of wine than you planned to. Before you sign up for a great offer, check out what the company's 'regular' wines are priced at on average.

CHANNEL HOPPING

Is crossing the English Channel worth the effort? I am always a little sceptical about people who spend the day zipping over to the other side of the Channel to dip into some duty-free wine. Apart from some horror stories involving customs, I genuinely believe the choice isn't nearly as great as it is over here, that the wines aren't as exciting or even of as good a quality and that the experience is not all that enjoyable.

However, increasingly the likes of Sainsbury's and Majestic (the latter with Wine and Beer World) are investing heavily in the duty-free market, especially in Calais – and even bringing some big brands from the likes of Australia, New Zealand and California into France, where the pricing is definitely more attractive.

And there's no doubting the fact that, if you need to buy a significant amount of wine for a special occasion, then you can make significant savings if you cross the Channel. If you do go for this reason, however, make sure you take sufficient proof that you intend holding an event, so that you can prove that the wine is for personal consumption and not for resale. The ability of the Customs officers to confiscate goods and vehicles should they deem fit is simply frightening.

WHY SHOULD YOU SHOP OVER THE CHANNEL?

It can provide great value if you are buying significant amounts of wine for a big event. It can be a nice day out – though remember: once you chuck in lunch, petrol and even the cheapest away-day ticket, you have to bring in huge volumes in order to make a proper saving.

In particular you'll find some very good French wines that, once duty has been added, wouldn't be nearly as attractive on a wine shelf over here, but can represent very good value if bought in Calais.

Don't be snobbish about it. If you're on your way back from a holiday in France, you'd be foolish not to. Even if you drink bottles of £10 Chablis, the saving on duty alone will be significant.

WHY SHOULDN'T YOU SHOP OVER THE CHANNEL?

The choice simply isn't the same as you get over here. Most will be French-dominated, so, if you're a big Australian fan, you won't find all that much choice.

It may sound like a nice day out, but Calais superstores are hardly the most sophisticated of venues.

If you are buying significant amounts of wine, it's worth having a chat with your local independent merchant or chain about getting a decent discount. It may not be as low in price, but it will save you all the hassle.
Make the most of: the bargains, by taking along a few catalogues from Sainsbury's or Majestic. You can then compare the real prices from the UK, which aren't always specified. Look in your local supermarket before you go, because – you never know – they may have a more attractive deal. And most of the big Calais stores have websites with the prices listed, giving you the opportunity to compare prices before you even book your away-day ticket.
Don't be duped by: cheap, non-branded champagne. Sometimes it's great. Sometimes it's absolutely dismal and you'd be better off with a good Cava from Asda.

AUCTIONS

Auctions are fascinating, wondrous events. No more so than when there is a big sale, and some heavy hitters in the audience. The two biggest auction houses in the UK for wine are Sotheby's and Christie's – but it's not like buying a house at auction, or a second-hand car. The chances of your walking away with a bargain are minimal, and the chances of your walking away without spending a fistful of dollars are equally small.

Invariably wine auctions in the UK are directed towards collectors and enthusiasts with deep pockets. If, on the other hand, you'd like to find out more about buying wine at auctions, perhaps get hold of a few catalogues, or even register an interest in attending a sale, then contact either of the above. More details can be found at their respective websites (www.sothebys.com and www.christies.com).

WHY SHOULD YOU SHOP AT AN AUCTION?

If you're serious about your wine and serious about collecting it, storing and eventually drinking it, then auctions are an option.

But you should know your stuff – it's an expensive place to make amateurish mistakes.

WHY SHOULDN'T YOU SHOP AT AN AUCTION?

If you fall into neither of the above categories – you are neither serious nor know your stuff – well, you'll be heading for trouble.

chapter three
all that glitters . . .
buying by label

Whenever wine companies do research on what factors influence people's choice when buying wine, two things always head the 'choice' league. The first is price – which shouldn't come as a great surprise, really, since most of us walk into any store with a specific price in mind, whether we're buying scuba gear, cheese, replacement tyres or funnily enough, wine.

The second is label. And really, that should be no surprise, either. Most of our society is geared towards having things look pretty. There are countless marketing success stories based in a smart, attractive piece of packaging. Just ask soap-powder manufacturers.

The difference with wine is that, while the marketeers will argue the toss over the 'quality' of soap powder in the various smartly packaged containers, the reality is that it is just soap powder – to a greater or lesser degree it will always get your whites whiter.

With wine it's a whole different ball game. At one end of the spectrum you have appallingly bad wine packaged well, and made to look expensive, for which you pay absurdly large amounts of money. At the other end of the spectrum, you have absurdly good-quality wines that look like trash. Basically, you can make a label look pretty but it doesn't necessarily mean the wine inside is pretty. Ergo, buying by label is something of a lottery. And that is exactly why there are certain things on labels that make it slightly *less* of one. For example, on the front labels the following information tends to be included, often by law.

ALCOHOL CONTENT

Most countries demand that alcohol content be shown. Partly, this is so teenagers can spot which is the most alcoholic wine to blag from dad's wine cupboard, but also so adults can assess the amount of alcohol they're pouring down their gullets. Knowing the amount of alcohol of a wine can be useful from a style point of view, too. A big, broad, ballsy red is likely to be 14 per cent upwards, whereas a more medium-bodied red will be 12–13 per cent. Likewise with whites, an 11 or 12 per cent white is likely to be fairly easy drinking, with a 13 per cent a little more serious.

COUNTRY OF ORIGIN

It's handy to know where a wine comes from, and that tends to be the third-biggest factor in deciding to buy a wine next to price and label. As well as country of origin, regions will often be specified, such as Margaret River in Western Australia, or perhaps Margaux in Bordeaux.

VINTAGE

If a wine is from a specific single vintage, it has to be shown on the bottle

– with basic wines it means very little in terms of indication of quality. Further up the price ladder, however, the vintage can give an indication of whether the wine was from a 'good' year, a 'mediocre' year, or 'get that stuff out of here' year.

PRODUCER

There is always a producer listed, whether it's a co-operative in southern France, a château in Bordeaux or a wine company in Australia, e.g. Penfold's.

BOTTLE SIZE

Most bottles sold in the UK are either full 75 cl bottles or half-bottles, at 37.5 cl. The size is always stated on the label. There are some wines, fortified and dessert wines, however, that come in 50 cl bottles.

GRAPE VARIETY

Grape varieties are rarely given on French wines, where often it is not allowed to give this information on the front of most labels, because the country's *appellation* system (see Page 26) dominates the front label. However, in most New World countries, such as Australia, the USA and New Zealand, the wine label states the major grape varieties used and in many cases producers are legally required to do so.

On the back labels there tends to be more descriptive information, perhaps a tasting note and the name of the importer, as well as geographical notes.

What's all that foreign stuff about?

Each individual country tends to have terms and classifications that appear on labels that are specifically designed to help you get a better idea of what's in the bottle. But if you're looking at a German label, for instance, unless you speak fluent German or are aware of the basic descriptions and what they mean, they're frankly useless.

So the following is a little speed guide to put you in the picture, featuring the main useful terms for the five major non-English-speaking wine-producing countries – which is a bit of a mouthful, somewhat like the terms listed below.

FRANCE

AC or AOC – the Appellation Contrôlée system and Appellation d'Origine Contrôlée system, which govern a large part of French quality wine production. Each *appellation* will have strict rules concerning use of grapes, winemaking techniques and so forth, and they are there to act as a guarantee of a minimum quality and specific style of wine.

Cave – cellar, but it is usually used as a prefix to a co-operative, or collection of winemakers, hence the Caves des Pyrénées, for example.

Château – 'castle' but in legal terms on a bottle it means that the property is registered as a wine producer.

Cru – 'growth' in French, but more loosely translates as 'vineyard site'. It's often prefixed with a classification, as in Bordeaux's 'Premiers Crus' or First Growths, and Burgundy's 'Grands Crus'.

Mis en Bouteille – it's been bottled at the château or estate where it was made. Sometimes wine is shipped in bulk and bottled elsewhere, but this tends to be inferior wine, so look out for this term. It's not much of a hint of quality, but every little helps.

Vin de Pays – one step up the ladder from vin de table in quality terms.

Vin de Table – the most basic classification of wine in France.

ITALY

Cantina and **Cantina Sociale** – the former means literally cellar or winery; the latter is the term used for a co-operative, or collection of wine producers.

DOC – Denominazione di Origine Controllata. It is almost identical to the French AC and AOC systems, but not as effective. It means very little in quality-guarantee terms, even if it does sound very official.

DOCG – Denominazione di Origine Controllata e Garantita – a later addition to the above system and bizarrely a much more effective one. You can actually assume that this means you're drinking something half decent.

Frizzante – slightly sparkling.

Spumante – the full-on fizz factor.

Vendemmia – vintage.

Vino da Tavola – technically the same as France's Vin de Table, but, because of the often silly restrictions of the DOC system, a lot of winemakers have opted out and produce excellent, not inconsiderably expensive, wines but market them under this simple title. It panders very nicely to the Italians' love of sticking two fingers up to authority.

SPAIN

Bodega – winery.

Crianza – the lowest classification for a wine that has been aged in wood, usually for a minimum of one year.

DO – Denominación de Origen. This is the Spanish version of the French Appellation Contrôlée system and is split on a mainly geographical basis. Thanks to strict regulations it is still seen very much as a quality guarantee.

DOCa – Denominación de Origen Calificada. This is a new addition to quality classifications that is one step up in quality terms from a DO.

Joven – the most basic level of wine in Spain. It usually refers to a young wine that has not been aged in wood.

Reserva – a special bottling that has been aged in wooden barrels for a longer period than a crianza, usually for at least two to three years.

Gran Reserva – a step up from Reserva, again based mainly on the length of time the wine is aged in wood. Only the best wines, theoretically, can hold up to such long ageing methods, usually of around five years and above.

Vendemmia – simply means vintage.

Vino de la Tierra – literally 'wine of the land' and equal to the French Vin de Pays.

Vino de Mesa – the most basic quality of table wine.

PORTUGAL

Adega – winery or cellar.

Colheita – simply vintage.

DOC – Denominação de Origen Controlada. Again, same as French AC system, but not overly helpful at pointing the finger at Portugal's best wines, which was its intention when set up.

Garrafeira – term used to describe older, theoretically higher quality wines.

Vinho Regional – again, like the French Vin de Pays classification.

GERMANY

Auslese – in the main, a medium-sweet wine produced from fully ripe grapes. The odd dry version exists, but they are few and far between.

Beerenauslese (BA) – very sweet wines, made in tiny amounts.

Deutscher Tafelwein – the most basic German wine classification.
Eiswein – Ultra-sweet wine made from grapes left to freeze and 'raisin' on the vine over the winter months.
Halbtrocken – half-dry wines.
Kabinett – dryish style, although the fruit flavours are still ripe with a touch of sweetness.
Landwein – German version of Vin de Table.
Qualitätswein bestimmer Anbaugebiete (QbA) – largest and most variable category of German wine. A lot are of poor quality, but some can shine forth.
Qualitätswein mit Pradikat (QmP) – the best-quality classification in Germany.
Sekt – sparkling wine.
Spätlese – means 'late harvest' and the wines can be dry to medium dry.
Trocken – dry.
Trockenbeerenauslese (TBA) – sweetest and richest style within the QmP classification.

chapter four
dining out

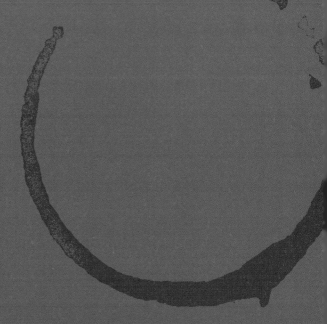

'We want the finest wines known to humanity. And we want them here. And we want them now.' Richard E Grant as Withnail in Bruce Robinson's *Withnail and I*

Ordering a wine in a restaurant is one of the most fearsome tasks known to mankind, for all the obvious reasons:

► you're surrounded by people, listening to your every word;
► reading a wine list can often be like trying to decipher Ancient Hebrew when you got an F in languages at school;
► some restaurants have what's know as a sommelier – or wine waiter – and, ooh, they can be scary; and
► it's often bloomin' expensive.

So how do you get your head round a restaurant wine list? What are the dos and don'ts of buying a bottle of wine when you're out on a romantic dinner or dining in a trendy restaurant? How should you address the sommelier? Is 'Oi, over 'ere!' really acceptable? And can you know very little about wine, but still end up with a decent bottle?

Well here are ten basic tips that should answer all of the above:

TIP 1: FACE FACTS

Restaurants are expensive and, yes, they do overprice their wine a lot of the time. Get over it. Lots of people complain about mark-ups on wine and, while some restaurants really are taking the Pinot, others are simply trying to get by and make a profit.

Think of it this way – 2003 was a record year for restaurant openings, and yet more restaurants closed than actually opened. It's a hard business to survive in. So it's best to look at wine as the restaurant equivalent of a bucket of popcorn in the UCI or a pint of beer on the Champs Elysées – i.e. there's absolutely nothing you can do about it. You're there, you've paid for it, so sit down, stop complaining and start enjoying yourself.

TIP 2: ON THE OTHER HAND, DON'T GET TAKEN FOR A RIDE

Just because you went once, it doesn't mean you have to go again. If you think it's overpriced, steer clear next time.

Also, it's quite easy to tell a restaurant that cares about wine. If it has a good selection of wines by the glass, as well as a relatively wide number of countries on the list, then you're probably on to a winner. If the glasses are clean, large and clear, as opposed to tumblers or Paris goblets, then life's looking up.

TIP 3: TRY TO SPOT A GOOD LIST

There several ways to do this. A decent wines-by-the-glass list is one good indicator, as is a broad spread of countries, both New World and Old World. But one very good way is to look at the champagne list. If there are just two champagnes, the house one and a well-known brand, you could be in trouble. If, on the other hand, there are four or five well-known brands and possibly a couple of lesser-known ones, you've found a restaurant that cares.

Check out the price, too. Most of us know what a bottle of Veuve-Clicquot or Moët & Chandon costs in the shops. If you see a bottle of the latter – normally £22 – for more than £40, you know you're in the lair of a possible rip-off merchant.

TIP 4: DON'T SKIMP

Some 30–40 per cent of the wine sold in restaurants will be the house wine. So figure it out. Which wines do you think the restaurant will be putting the biggest mark-ups on? Spend just a few more pounds per bottle and you should find yourself drinking better for not much more.

TIP 5: IF YOU DON'T KNOW, DO ASK

If the waiter looks blank, then points to the house white, give up. But, if there's a sommelier wine waiter, pull him over and ask.

TIP 6: DON'T SHOW FEAR

Wine waiters thrive on fear. It gives them the upper hand. Seriously, though, a lot of people are scared of sommeliers/wine waiters. They think they'll be made to look the fool, or look ignorant. But a wine waiter is there to answer your questions and find you a wine that suits your tastes and what you're eating. It's what he's paid for, and it's why your service charge will be so large, so stop being a silly scaredy cat!

TIP 7: TRY TO TELL A GOOD WINE WAITER FROM A RUM ONE

This is actually relatively easy. When you call him over, tell him what you like and don't like, and, importantly, give him a price. If you tell him you like white with your steak rather than red, and only want to spend £20, and he comes back with a red costing £35, he's essentially taking the Piesporter.

TIP 8: DO MAKE THE MOST OF WINE BUY THE GLASS

If a restaurant you go to has a decent selection of wines by the glass (half a dozen of each colour is a good start), then don't be afraid to mix and match. It's a darn sight less expensive and unpleasant to work your way through one glass you don't much like than a whole bottle.

TIP 9: ALWAYS TASTE THE WINE

A lot of people feel self-conscious when the waiter stands and pours you a little to taste. Don't. It's a lot more difficult explaining that you think the wine is duff once you've worked through half a bottle of it. Take your time, there's no hurry. Most wines will of course be fine, but there might be a poor one and, if you've any doubts, send it back.

And don't get all worried about offending the restaurant. They just send it back to the supplier and claim the money back off them, so no worries there.

TIP 10: DON'T LET THEM TAKE THE BOTTLE AWAY

If you've ordered a bottle of wine, you've every right to have it by your table. In my opinion any restaurant that takes the bottle away, rather than leaving it in an ice bucket or on your table, is either weird or up to no good – or both.

chapter five
back to basics

How to get a lot more enjoyment, with just a little bit of effort

Let's look at that old political slogan, 'back to basics'. Getting back to the basics is about as good a place as any to start when it comes to learning more about wine, and, more importantly, how to enjoy it more.

Most chapters dealing with the basics start off with lengthy descriptions of how wine is made. In truth, you take a grape, you squeeze the juice out. Then you take a thousand more bunches of grapes and do the same. You collect the juice, ferment it (turn the sugar into alcohol), perhaps age it, then bottle it and hopefully you will eventually serve it to an appreciative audience.

But knowing all that won't necessarily help you to enjoy it more. Knowing the tools of the trade, however – how to get the most out of tasting a wine, and how to work out what you do and don't like in a wine – certainly will.

WHAT KIT DO I NEED?

1 A DECENT GLASS HELPS

If only tumblers are available, don't bitch to the host or hostess. I've never once known someone to go a full dinner refusing to drink out of one, unless they were either teetotal or on antibiotics.

That said, the right glass will make a difference. It can't make a silk purse out a sow's ear of a wine, but it can enhance the enjoyment just enough to make a real difference to whether you decide to buy that bottle again or not.

The best advice when it comes to glasses is to choose one with a reasonably tall stem, and a sizeable bowl – not a fish bowl, you understand, but if it holds a normal-sized glass of wine and is half full towards the top that's about right. If it tapers towards the top, all the better. Most of all it should be clear glass. That's so you can see the wine.

2 A GOOD CORK SCREW IS ESSENTIAL

Corkscrews are ten a penny, but the one you want should be very basic, as long as it has a decent length of screw and is preferably Teflon coated so that it slips into the cork easily and cleanly.

You can spend a fortune on corkscrews, but for a fiver you should be able to equip yourself with one that'll last a good long time and treat the corks it pulls with the respect they deserve.

3 A BOTTLE OF WINE WILL BE ESSENTIAL
You see, it's really not that complicated.

HOW DO I TASTE PROPERLY?

People get hung up about tasting wine. There are many long explanations about how it should be done, and even aroma and taste charts to show what you should be doing. But a lot of it, while grounded in scientific fact, is too complex and pointless for most of us.

The real question should really be, do you taste at all? Most of us don't. We sit down at dinner, open a bottle and chuck the wine down our throats. But, if you spend just two minutes going through the following steps every time you open a bottle (not every time you pour a glass – that would be too embarrassing in public), then you should hopefully get a lot more out of the liquid you just poured into the glass.

1 HAVE A LOOK AT IT
You can tell a lot by a wine's colour. You can get an indication of age and style pretty quickly and accurately. A Chardonnay that is light yellow, almost straw-coloured, is likely to have little oak and be mid- to lightweight and young in style, whereas a darker-yellow, almost gold-coloured Chardonnay is likely to offer big, fat, oaky flavours, possibly with a bit of bottle age. It's not essential, but it prepares you and your mouth for what may be in store.

2 SWIRL AND SNIFF IT
If you've ever read a book by Patrick Suskind called *Perfume* you'll no doubt know that we spend most of our life ignoring the one sense that is our most powerful and evocative. So many people ignore the smell of a wine, which is the equivalent of driving a Skoda with a Ferrari engine in it: you get only half the enjoyment.

So swirl the wine around in your glass and have a good old sniff. Get your nose right in there. Swirling opens up the wine and releases the aromas fully. The most effective way to ensure this is to fill your wineglass a third full only, then grip the base of the glass with your thumb and forefingers and simply move it in a gentle clockwise circle while it's still resting on the table, speeding up as you go. Within a few seconds the wine will have released its primary aromas.

3 SLOSH IT AROUND

Once you've had a good old sniff, take a sip – not a mouthful – and then sloosh it around your mouth a bit. See how it feels on the different parts of your tongue compared with the sides of your mouth and gums. You could spit, but its generally considered impolite, so swallow and let it slip down.

4 THINK ABOUT IT

Using a bit of grey matter never did any harm. Just spend thirty seconds, that's all, thinking what you liked and what you didn't like; what tasted good and what tasted bad. If you want to be a bit of a nerd, then write it down. Next time you taste another wine, you'll be able to compare or contrast.

5 GET ON WITH IT

Once or twice is nice. Any more and you'll probably look like the odd one out at the table, so just get on and drink the stuff. That is what it's made for and there's no point in getting overly serious about the whole thing.

WHAT AM I LOOKING FOR?

When you listen to wine gurus or read tasting notes in magazines or books, this one included, you'll often find the following terms used: *structure*, *body* and *complexity*. However, they rarely mean much to anyone who doesn't have a grasp of the basic makeup, in flavour and taste terms.

The first thing to note is that the last two, while sounding very like the same thing, are very different. We taste through our mouth via sensors in our tongue, gums and cheeks – known as taste buds to us mere mortals. And our taste buds have four main categories in scientific terms: acidity (mainly the upper edges of the tongue), sweetness (the tip of the tongue) bitterness (the back and sides of the tongue) and saltiness (the front edges of the tongue). But we actually *sense* flavour through our nose, in the same way we detect smell. When we taste a wine, particles of wine are forced up the back of the throat into the nasal passages and the same receptors 'decode' the flavour particles for our brain to register. It may sound a bit esoteric, but it's true.

It's a combination of what our taste buds are telling us and what our nose is telling us that makes up our impressions of a wine. But when we talk of structure or body or complexity we're more often than not talking about the physical makeup of the wine itself. Indeed 'body' is perhaps the perfect word to use, because a wine does have an anatomy and it's made up of five principal body parts:

1 SUGAR

Every wine has sugar in it at some stage or another. Apart from anything else, without sugar, there'd be nothing for the fermentation process to turn into alcohol. When all the sugar is turned into alcohol a wine will obviously be dry (and higher in alcohol). If not all of it has been fermented, then the wine may be semisweet or sweet (and usually lower in alcohol). The presence or lack of sugar within a wine therefore makes a massive difference to the style, but it also has an effect on the structure – or rather the balance between the other four factors.

If a wine has been fermented fully dry, it will have a high alcohol content. If the alcohol content is high, but the fruit content is low and the acid content too high, the wine will be out of balance. Structure is about getting all the body parts working together in harmony.

2 FRUIT

The reasons the Aussies are giving the French such a beating in terms of wine sales these days is that they realised a decade or two ago that what people really wanted in wine was fruit. And the French, in the main, had forgotten it. Fruit is the core of a wine – the torso if you like. On its own it's useless, but in a good, balanced wine it's always going to play a larger role in terms of our taste buds than the other four components.

People often confuse sweetness and fruitiness. Essentially, all fruit tastes sweet to some extent, even in a wine, where all the sugar has been fermented out. And some grapes produce fruit flavours that sometimes taste sweeter than others. For example, if a wine has the flavour of raspberries, it may easily taste sweeter than a wine that has a flavour of red cherries – even though the sugar content of both is the same.

Real sweetness in terms of wine, however, is less a flavour sensation and more a textural sensation. Personally, I think it's better to refer to this element as juiciness rather than sweetness. It avoids all-round messiness – and, besides, it makes the wine sound much more drinkable.

3 ACID

In scientific terms acidity is calculated by what is known as the pH content of a wine (the initials pH stand for 'potential of hydrogen', and the pH is a measure of acidity or alkalinity). In taste terms, however, you'd describe it in a variety of ways: 'bite', 'kick', 'zest' and 'raciness' are the ones that spring to mind.

The easiest way to get a true feeling for acid – and the part it plays in a wine – is to take a lemon and cut it in half. Slice the first half and soak it in water for a couple of hours. Once that's done, take the second half and slice that up. Then take a bite out of a slice.

Your face will pucker up, and your tongue curl. That's the extreme of one end of acid. Then take a taste of the soaked lemon. You'll still get a 'bite' probably, but it won't have as much 'kick', though you'll know it's there. Most wines, red or white, need some level of acidity – it just depends on which point on the scale between those two extremes is needed. Reds need acid to balance out the tannin and the fruit flavours. White needs acid to add backbone, body and balance out the fruit flavours.

4 TANNIN

Take a small teapot. Stick two tea bags in it with some hot water and let it stew for half an hour. Then take a gulp (making sure it's cool of course) and swirl around the mouth. Spit or swallow – it's up to you. But the dry, claggy feeling you get down the sides of your mouth and the bitter taste on the back of the tongue are caused by tannin.

In wine, if acid is the backbone of white, then tannin is the backbone of a good red. Too much and a red will become rigid and overbearing; too little and it flops around in the mouth not knowing what to do.

Tannin actually comes from the skin, pips and stalks of a grape and the substance is squeezed and crushed out during the pressing and fermentation process. Not only does it give a wine structure, but it acts as a crutch for the fruit as a wine ages, propping it up as the years take their toll.

You'll often hear tannins described as being 'firm' if they are strong and positive or 'harsh' if they're raw and too overbearing. They get 'softer' and 'silkier' as time goes on, but can be described as 'green' when a wine is very young. As well as in the grape skin, pips and stalks, tannin is also present in wood, especially new wood. So, when a wine is aged in new oak barrels, a certain amount of tannin will be imparted by the wood itself.

5 OAK

Oak is the odd one out here really. It's the only one of the components that give a wine structure that can be added or left out at the winemaker's whim. To make a good red, you have to have tannin; to make a good white, you need a good streak of acidity; in both, fruit and sugar are essential. But oak is an optional ingredient.

So why would a winemaker use oak? Well, first, to add layers of flavour. With whites it's creaminess, sweetness, essence of vanilla and a toastiness. With reds it adds all that plus a distinctive aroma of coffee beans and a smokiness. In other words oak adds complexity.

But it also adds structure. When a wine is aged in oak it is exposed in as controlled a way as possible to small amounts of oxygen via the grain of the oak. The effect is to soften the otherwise harsher edges of wine, and it adds a certain amount of tannin along with an element of 'grip' in the mouth – all of which makes the wine a more pleasant experience.

There are different ways of using wood. With the cheapest wines, oak chips or staves are used. They are thrown in the tanks for a short while and contribute merely a few flavour elements – a touch of wood, perhaps some vanilla. For properly oaked wines, however, wooden barrels are used to store and age the wine. Often they are 'new' oak barrels – untouched by wine before – and these impart very strong flavours. At other times they are barrels that have held wine already, and the result is much subtler. It just depends on how much of an oak character the winemaker wants to give the wine, or how much of an oak character the wine can take. And, ultimately, how much we the drinker can take.

SO WHAT HAPPENS NOW?

Tempting as it is to say open it and drink it now, it's important to take a look at how you serve your wine, because how you serve it can have a big impact on how it tastes.

Temperature is the biggest potential hazard. Too cold with a red or white and it's flavourless; too warm and it will be completely out of balance. It can get very scientific, with lots of recommended degrees of Celsius – but who on earth takes out the baby thermometer and attaches it to a bottle of wine?

Essentially, the following is the simplest way I've ever learned to work out which way a wine should be served. Unless you live in Baltic conditions, or a sauna, room temperature means room temperature and, for 95 per cent of reds, that's absolutely fine. There are some reds you might want to chill for five minutes in the fridge, but not many. Sticking a red by the stove or radiator will bake it.

With whites, if you stick a bottle in a properly working fridge, set medium to high, for an hour to an hour and a half, it's the right temperature. If it's been in overnight, then take it out for half an hour – it'll be too cold to taste any of its more delicate flavours otherwise.

Some wines, particularly older wines, throw a sediment – which is simply the crystallisation of tiny particles within the liquid over time. If that's the case, you might have to decant. But don't get panicky: you don't need a decanter, just a clear jug. Leave the bottle to stand, preferably for a day or two, although three or four hours will do. Then carefully uncork the bottle, place the neck to the lip of the jug or decanter and pour in a continuous action until the sediment *begins* to make its way through. Then stop. If you don't have a decanter, simply rinse the sediment out of the bottle and pour the wine back into it.

Finally, a safety announcement. When opening a bottle of champagne, always keep your hand – or preferably a tea towel – over the head of the cork. Loosen the wire cage with the other hand, then grip the bottle and twist in a clockwise direction. But twist the bottle, not the cork, which should be firmly held by the other hand. Every year countless people in the UK are injured by champagne corks. It's not only dangerous, but it's a silly reason to be stuck in A and E on a Saturday night.

chapter six
storing wine

Imagine the scene. You've invited some people round for a dinner party. The wine needs to be selected. It's Jeeves's day off, so you pick up the antique wine carrier and walk down the long corridor and the steep flight of stairs to the cellar, wondering as you amble whether it will be the Margaux '45 or the Mouton '82 that you'll select for dinner. Perhaps a quick mobile call to the chef in the kitchen to check what's being served for din-dins would be a wise investment of time. Thank goodness for modern technology and the benefits of mobile phones.

Oh, let's get real, for goodness' sake. Cellars are a thing of the past. Even if we are fortunate enough to own three- or four-storey Victorian and Edwardian houses with what technically passes as a cellar down below, it's no doubt undergone a slight change of use over the years. More likely than not, it's been turned into either a spare bedroom or a flat to rent out to pay for the hideously large mortgage you've taken on to afford the whole thing in the first place.

We've changed. People used to cellar wines for two main reasons. First, the best wines were usually produced in a style that required significant ageing before they would be deemed drinkable. Thus wines would be 'laid down' to develop and be plucked out at the appropriate moment – preferably when they were ready to drink, rather than 'over the hill'. Second, wine enthusiasts wanted a broad 'choice' of wines, but didn't have the modern benefits of wine merchants on their doorsteps.

The fact is that most of us couldn't afford to store and cellar our own wines in the traditional way, even if we wanted to. And it's also a fact that 90 per cent of the wines served up in shops these days, whether a supermarket or an independent store, are made to be drunk now – and most are. The average bottle of wine in the UK is drunk within 24 hours of purchase. So the idea of having a cellar to lay wines down in seems slightly preposterous. Also, you can walk to your corner shop and find wine from virtually any country around the world these days.

It doesn't mean, however, that sometimes you may not have to store a wine. Nor does it mean you can't keep a 'cellar'. You just have to give it a modern slant.

WHY AGE A WINE?

Well, as I said, some wines are made in a style that requires a bit of time in bottle. Mostly it tends to be reds, because the tannins in the wine often need time to soften and meld with the fruit characters. Big Chardonnays often need time in the bottle, and high-acid whites such as Riesling can benefit from some time tucked away.

IS IT ONLY FINE WINE THAT BENEFITS?

A lot of the wines that really find themselves improving with age tend to be the higher-quality, or 'fine', wines. But it isn't always the case. Take champagne, for instance. Young champagne can be quite green, raw and overly acidic. It doesn't always mean it's a bad champagne, just a little out of balance. Sometimes six months tucked away in the dark can be enough to balance out the wine and you can end up with a far better bottle of fizz than you may have actually paid for – as long as you can be relatively patient.

WHAT IF I'M GIVEN SOMETHING REALLY NICE?

Well, if you do happen to have extremely generous friends who spoil you with the odd bottle of fine wine that needs a bit of time, the best place to store it is somewhere with a constant, steady temperature – preferably on the cool rather than warm side.

That means you can more or less count out the attic for a start. In summer it will be boiling and in winter it will be freezing. So the precious wine you've been given is going to catch an alcoholic version of pneumonia, thanks to the temperature fluctuations – and we all know that pneumonia can often be fatal, especially in the case of the aged and infirm.

Also, the kitchen is a big no-no. Quite why kitchen designers seem so keen on sticking a wine rack right next to a cooker I'll never know, but, if you want to avoid baked Merlot to match your baked Alaska, then I suggest you look elsewhere.

My best find yet has been the cupboard under the stairs in a hallway. It's usually fairly constant in temperature and, while not ideal, will do the trick with most wines. Just make sure you lay the wine down on its side, preferably in a proper wine rack. They come in all shapes and sizes these days so squeezing one into a cubbyhole under the stairs shouldn't be a massive problem.

HOW DO I KNOW IT'S WORTH SAVING?

I've done various wine shows in my time and at nearly all of them I
am approached by a usually charming elderly gentleman who asks me
whether I can tell him when he should drink his 1993 Bulgarian Cabernet
Sauvignon and will it be any good. Invariably I tell him it's getting on in
years and is probably best put out of its misery.

How can you tell if it's worth keeping? Well you can't, really, but price
and vintage are as good a bet as any. If a wine is maybe two or three years
old at most, but cost more than £10–15, it is pretty likely that it will benefit
from a bit of ageing. That's not to say it may not be delicious now, but a
bit of time shouldn't do it any harm.

If it's under £10, you're not going to get much extra out of it and may
risk spoiling it altogether. And if it's around £5 or £6 it's been made to
drink now – so don't waste any time!

WHAT IF I'D QUITE LIKE
A MINI CELLAR AT HOME?

Well, no problem, really.

It's pretty easy to create what is probably best described as a 'capsule'
cellar – much in the way that the fashion magazines are always encouraging
women to go on holiday with a paired-down 'capsule' wardrobe.

The idea is that you can cover all your wine options within a small
selection of wines, and not have to worry about not having the right
bottle in the fridge or under the stairs at the right time. Just remember
to order more of it every month.

If I were putting a capsule wine wardrobe together I'd definitely opt
for the following mix.

Chardonnay: Most wine experts will roll their eyes at the unambitious
choice of Chardonnay as the main white, but let's be honest: it is one
of the greatest and most versatile grape varieties. Oaked or unoaked,
from Burgundy, New Zealand or Australia – you take your pick and enjoy.

Riesling: Whether it's a semisweet but crisp German Riesling or a bone-
dry version from Down Under, having a couple of bottles of Riesling
around is a must. For starters, it's a great apéritif wine, but it's also a
sterling match with food, especially anything Oriental or Indian.

Rioja: Rioja is a fantastic all-round red, especially if you choose a nice soft
and juicy one (perhaps a young one – look out for the term *crianza*) – one
that's not too heavy. That way it combines as a great red for slinging back

on its own while you're watching *Friends* or *Will and Grace*, but also a wonderful red for pairing with a bowl of pasta or a nice juicy steak.

Fizz: You can limit it to a good old Aussie sparkling, or a nice crisp Cava, or you can splash out on a decent bottle of champagne. Whichever, having something cold and sparkly in your fridge is *de rigeur*.

A huge red: A style rather than a specific variety, it can be from any number of grape options. An Aussie Shiraz, a Rhône Syrah, a Californian Zinfandel, a beefy Cabernet from the Languedoc. The point is it has to be big, bold and brassy. You need a wine that can give a big rib of beef a good roundhouse – a slap between the chops.

The bargain slot: This is almost heresy for many in the wine trade, but let's face facts: we all love a decent bargain. Whether it's a pound off, two for one or a baker's dozen, a wine often tastes that little bit sweeter in the mouth knowing you got it on the cheap. Remember, though, that not all bargains really are bargains, so pick, mix and always move on.

A couple of bottles of each of the above, ordered once a month and placed in the wine rack, and Bob's your uncle – no need for a cavernous underground cellar, no need for huge investment in expensive wines. And you can be as lazy about your wine as it's possible to be: with the Internet these days you don't even need to leave the comfort of your own sitting room. It's not the most adventurous solution to your wine problems, but it is a practical one.

chapter seven
questions, questions, questions

There are so many questions concerning wine, but, as with anything, there are a few that crop up more than most. I've plumped for what I think are the twenty most basic questions people have about wine, how it's made and how it gets to the shelf, and how they should choose it. And I've tried to answer them in a way I hope makes it easier to choose a decent bottle next time you're standing in front of a shelf packed with wine.

1 HOW IMPORTANT IS VINTAGE?

Vintage is pretty important. Although some wines are blends of different years – non-vintage champagne, for example – most tend to be produced from a single harvest in a single year. And, basically, Mother Nature is a little bit schizophrenic. She can be either a right madam or as nice as pie. If it's the former, the winemakers have to work a lot harder; if it's the latter, they can breathe a little sigh of relief.

With a wine around the £5–6 mark, it will be more difficult to spot 'vintage variation', as they describe it. Above £10, however, it can make the difference between getting a good wine and a stunning wine. A good independent wine merchant will keep up and let you know the gen.

2 HOW IS WINE MADE?

Ooh, difficult one, this. We can either get very technical, à la Magnus Pyke, or keep it nice and simple, à la breakfast TV. I'm going for the latter, for the simple reason that I don't really think it matters an enormous amount whether you know the internal workings of a combustion engine to appreciate driving a Maserati, and I think the same goes for enjoying a bottle of wine.

Essentially, grapes are grown in the vineyard, then harvested when they're good and plump and ready for pressing. Once harvested, they are pressed (in olden days with feet, these days with nice, shiny stainless-steel presses). The juice runs off and is then fermented. Fermentation is essentially a chemical reaction in which the sugar in the grape juice reacts with either natural or man-made yeasts (the former exists already in the grape, the latter is added) at the right temperature and basically is converted to alcohol.

Once fermentation has stopped, the wine is bottled and sold. See, it's not that difficult really. Obviously there are other stages (some are aged in oak for example), but, essentially, that's it!

3 WHAT'S THE DIFFERENCE BETWEEN RED AND WHITE?

Heck! You do have to go and get complicated, don't you? Essentially, there is little difference between the two. With red wine, often the juice, once pressed, will be mixed in with the grape skins and left to macerate (that means soften by soaking, and is the term used in the wine industry for this stage in the process). This allows more tannins to seep out – an essential part of red wine.

Depending on the style of wine being made, both white and red may then be aged in wood. However, red wine, with its more robust nature, is much more capable of being aged for a considerable time in wood, whereas white wine needs a softer, more gentle interaction with a good piece of oak.

Oh, and just in case you didn't notice, one ends up red and the other ends up white.

4 SO ROSÉ IS A MIX OF THE TWO?

Er, no. Rosés can be made in several different ways. First there is the method whereby the juice is pressed off from red grapes, but skin contact is kept to a minimum. Hence the colour of the wine is a touch pink, but the juice has run clear, giving the rosé colour. There *are* some rosés in which a touch of red wine is added to the white to give it the pink colour and more of a red-berry taste – but they have a tendency to be cheap and nasty.

Please note: if a wine aficionado tells you that rosé wine is common or passé, tell him exactly where to shove his Mouton. On a hot day, a chilled rosé is one of the most civilised drinks known to humanity.

5 HOW DO THE BUBBLES GET INTO A SPARKLER?

Ah, well, you know that fermentation we referred to earlier? Well one of the byproducts of fermentation is the production of carbon dioxide (CO_2). In still wines, because they are usually fermented in large containers, the CO_2 escapes, or is ventilated out. However, with something like champagne, after the first fermentation occurs, a second fermentation is encouraged (with the aid of a bit of added yeast), but this in the bottle – all sealed up. This way the CO_2 has nowhere to go but into the wine. There are other methods of making sparklers, but, for most quality-led producers, this is the most popular way.

6 WHAT IS A FORTIFIED WINE?

In most cases a fortified wine is one to which neutral spirit, or 'brandy', as it is known, is added to a still wine. Usually the idea is to boost the alcoholic content from around 13 to 14 degrees to something like 18 or 19 degrees.

Port is perhaps the best example of a fortified wine – and it came about through a desire to make the shipping of the wine a little more survivable, hence the 'fortification' of the wine.

7 **HOW DO I TELL A GOOD WINE FROM A BAD ONE?**

Another tricky one. I really don't mean this to be patronising, but a good wine is essentially what you want it to be. I've opened bottles with people who have raved about a particular wine when it's been badly corked – and yet they've been quite happy to drink the lot. Why? Because one person's tastes are different from another's, even if a corked wine happens to be your taste.

However, picking a good wine off the shelf with no prior knowledge of the subject matter is always going to be something of a lottery – which is, I guess, where wine journalists and wine competitions come in handy. As a journalist who has many samples sent for free, I may have only a minimal grasp on the reality of 'good value', but the fact is I do try a lot of wines every week. So it's a fair bet that I stand a half-decent chance of telling the wheat from the chaff. And with competitions it's even better.

8 **SO DOES A MEDAL MEAN IT'S A GOOD WINE?**

Usually it means it isn't a bad wine – but what it doesn't necessarily mean is that it's the right wine for you. However, if you take the International Wine Challenge, the Decanter awards and the International Wine and Spirits Challenge – the three biggest competitions in the UK – you'll find that, between them, they taste more than 15,000 wines. That's a lot of wine. And most of the tasting is by experts. So, if you want to work out which is the best wine on the shelf, looking for a shiny little medal is at least a pointer in the right direction.

On the other hand, don't get carried away. If you know you hate Merlot, but the only Gold Medal winner on the shelf is a Merlot, it'll still end up being a waste of money.

9 **DO LABELS MAKE A DIFFERENCE?**

Yes and no. Knowing what a label means is quite helpful (see Chapter 3) when you are trying to buy wine. You won't get far with a German Riesling or a Spanish Rioja unless you know the basics that appear on the label.

But if you mean 'Can I tell the difference by looking at the label?' then the answer is no. It's as easy to put a lovely-looking label on a bad bottle of wine as it is on a good one. And you wouldn't believe the number of sandal-wearing, beard-sporting winemakers who make the most delicious wines, but send them out to us – the punters – sporting labels that even a four-year-old child wouldn't dare present to the primary-school teacher.

10 HOW DO I SPOT A CORKED WINE?

Well this is a difficult one. Some people are incredibly sensitive to the cause of most corked wines – a chemical called TCA (see Page 56) – and some people could sniff a bucketful of it and not notice it one jot.

The best thing I can think of to describe how to spot a duff wine is really simple. If it tastes of fruit and the fruit tastes fresh, go for it. Fruit is the essence of wine, and cork 'taint' (as they call it) will eat fruit up faster than a ravenous monkey with a bunch of bananas.

11 IS AN OAKED WINE BETTER THAN AN UNOAKED WINE?

Another fudgy-sounding one, but, truthfully, it really does depend. Some wines simply aren't worth putting in oak barrels. Perhaps the fruit is too delicate; perhaps the wine is too fragile. It doesn't mean it is a bad wine, though.

Take, for instance, the Rieslings of Germany. Most never see wood. And yet they are the most fantastic wines. Likewise, the vast majority of champagne has no trace of wood. However, there are some wines, particularly those that have the 'structure' to age well, that benefit from wood-ageing. Not only does the new oak provide extra complexity, but it provides extra body – especially in the case of reds.

What is true, however, is that, in wines under £6, most oak is used for one of two reasons. First, and more acceptably, is that the wine is aimed at people who like an 'oaky' flavour in their wine. Second, and quite *un*acceptably, is that the winemaker is trying to cover up faults and flaws in the wine. Even to the novice, this is usually pretty obvious, so don't panic about not being able to spot it.

12 DO I NEED TO SPEND LOTS TO GET A GOOD BOTTLE?

No. Spend as much as you like or as little as you like. But remember this. If you have a couple of million quid in the bank, spending £120 on a bottle of champagne, is neither here nor there – even if you don't like it. If you've got only £3.99 in your pocket, it seems like the biggest waste of money possible – no matter how good the wine is. Everything is entirely relative.

13 WHAT'S THE DIFFERENCE BETWEEN OLD WORLD AND NEW WORLD?

Fundamentally, Old World consists of France, Italy, Spain – well, all of Europe. New World consists of the entirety of the southern hemisphere and the Americas. It doesn't actually mean that much. Vines, for example, first pitched up on South African shores in the mid-1600s, but the country's winemakers are still referred to as New World.

And so many Bordeaux winemakers are producing more upfront, fruit-led wines in imitation of Australia's best concoctions, that really the terms are becoming a little tired. To be honest, 'modern' and 'traditional' are better terms, but, once something is fixed in the head and the heart, it's difficult to let go, despite logic that proves otherwise.

14 I LIKE BAG-IN-BOX WINES – DOES THAT MAKE ME A CHEAPSKATE?

Not exactly. If you were drinking wine in Sweden, it would make you cutting-edge and reasonably quality-conscious. However, the average wine in the UK sells for just shy of £3.99 a bottle. And yet most bag-in-box wines sell for just over £3 a bottle. So, yes, it does make you just a little bit of a cheapskate. The question really is why most producers don't put more decent stuff in bag-in-box, because it's very convenient.

15 WHICH ARE THE BEST WINE-PRODUCING COUNTRIES?

If only life were that simple. The French will naturally tell you they are, while the Australians are pretty convinced they've got it cracked. The point is that each and every one produces good wine, and some produce great wine. It depends on what style you like, how deep your pockets are and whether you were born there or not.

If there's one thing to learn about the wine world, it's this: the moment you start putting boundaries up is the moment you start cutting out potentially scintillating new discoveries.

16 DOES IT MATTER IF I LIKE SWEET WINES?

No, but be picky. A lot of cheaper wines are sugary sweet – because they simply add sugar (yes, unbelievable but true). Proper sweetness comes from the grape itself. That's probably the sweetness you like and a wine can be almost dry and still possess some of that. If on the other hand you like a nice drop of Liebfraumilch, well at least you've found something you like.

17 WHAT IS TERROIR?

Aah, the big one. You'll hear a lot of experts talking about *terroir*. Essentially, it's referring to the connection between the land, the soil in which the vines are planted, and the character of the grape (indeed, the French word *terre* means soil). The idea is that *terroir* has a direct effect on the wine's flavours and character and that truly great wines come from truly great *terroir*.

As usual, it's the French who have coined the word, and the French who have made it terribly complicated and terribly elitist, but it's not really. A French person speaks French because she is a product of her environment; an Italian speaks Italian because he's a product of his environment; and an American speaks ... well, rubbish most of the time, for exactly the same reason. So it is with *terroir* – it speaks a different language in the wine depending on where the wine is from. Or, as John Edwards, the Aussie behind the fantastic Starvedog Lane winery in the Adelaide Hills, puts it so eloquently, 'Taste the bloody dirt, mate.'

18 WHAT DOES ABC MEAN?
It means Anything But Chardonnay – and it's a little-known catchphrase spread around by wine enthusiasts, wine journalists and wine pedants who usually use it as a way of hinting that they are so erudite that they find Chardonnay ever so boring.

My view is that it is snobbery at its worst – for a more detailed rant please go to Chapter 9, 'Myths and Monsters'. I really let rip there.

19 IS WINE HEALTHY?
If you use the Google search engine on the Internet and type in this exact question, you get about 120,000 results. Most, however, come to a similar conclusion, which isn't particularly groundbreaking. Drunk in moderation, wine can have health benefits, but don't overdo it.

OK, here's the scientific part. Red wine has molecules called polyphenols, and the most potent of polyphenols, resveratrol, is an antioxidant found in red grape skins (among other things). When scientists experimented on yeasts, they found these added some 70 per cent to the life span of the yeast. So there you go – like yeast cells, we could possibly live another 70 per cent longer. Conclusive evidence.

20 WHAT IF I CAN'T REMEMBER ALL THIS?
You don't have to. You just bought a book about it all. Just keep it handy at all times.

chapter eight
lost in translation

The one thing you can guarantee about wine is that over the many centuries its purveyors and devotees have spent an awful lot of time developing terms that will baffle and confuse. Sometimes, it can easily seem as if you were talking a different language. So here's a brief guide to some of the terms that may get rolled out to you in your pursuit of a decent bottle of wine. You could try to remember them all, but actually it's better to remember the following should you be confronted with some of the terms that are listed below: 'Excuse me, I can't understand a word of what you're saying. Can you speak in plain English and pass me another glass of that nice red [or white] stuff.' It's actually quite effective in cutting down on the confusion.

Here are the top fifty words or phrases you're likely to come across, and an idea of what they mean.

1 ACID/ACIDIC
We're not talking battery acid here but rather natural acidity. Bite into a lemon and you'll know exactly what I mean. It's tasted down the sides of the tongue and it's a pretty important component of any wine, red or white. Too much acidity in a wine and you'll be pulling a face (for more details see Chapter 5, 'Back to Basics').

2 AFTERTASTE
This is sometimes known as the 'finish' – and it's very important. When you taste a wine, if within seconds the flavour is all gone, then you're pretty disappointed. If you can still 'feel the fruit' for several minutes afterwards, then that's good – and it's called aftertaste or finish. Mind you, sometimes you can have a nasty aftertaste, especially with overly acidic or tannic wines.

3 AROMA
Posh word for smell. Not too difficult, that one.

4 AUSTERE
The wine isn't overly fruity or 'giving'. It's one of those words that you'll find in the bluffer's guide on Page 72, because frankly it's so general that it's a great one to throw into a conversation to make you sound very knowledgeable. But, to put it in context, a very fruity Aussie wine might be described as 'generous' while a classic claret from Bordeaux, especially when young, can often be 'austere'. Think of the first as your best mate, in a pub, paying for lagers. Think of the second as your miserly Uncle Algy waiting for you to get a round in.

5 BALANCED

Another classic bluffer's word, but this time it has a real meaning, too. Essentially, when a wine is balanced it has all the right qualities – fruit, acidity, tannin, oak – all in the right degrees.

6 BITTER

Not as in 'a pint of . . .', but rather the taste. If a wine is bitter it can be for several reasons. If it's red and has particularly young tannins, sometimes these will leave a bitterness in the mouth, particularly at the back of the tongue. With most wines, you don't want too much of this, but there are some, such as good Italian reds, that have a slightly higher level of bitterness, which makes them much better matches for food.

7 BODY

Essentially body refers to the weight of a wine: is it full-bodied (big and rich), medium-bodied (well, medium, I guess) or light-bodied (thin, less intense)? And, as you can tell already, those three terms are about as practically useful as a chocolate teapot.

8 BOUQUET

Another posh word for smell. You can see a pattern forming here, can't you?

9 BRILLIANT

Often used in several ways, but rarely used in the obvious way. When someone comments that a wine is 'brilliant' they are usually describing the colour rather than the overall quality. So a wine, theoretically, can be 'brilliant' but also rubbish. Confusing, isn't it?

10 BUTTERY

This is often used to describe one of the flavours that are imparted by oak to white wines. If you think of taking a bit of a slice of thick, white, fresh bread, with a layer of butter on, that's what this flavour is like. Oak also imparts a vanilla essence and a creamy edge to both whites and reds.

11 CARBONIC MACERATION

If someone uses this term, it means you're trapped with a wine bore. I mean, really, there's no real need for knowing this term, except that it's the major way of producing Beaujolais. Effectively, the grapes are kept in whole bunches and fermented, so that much of the skin isn't actually very broken. The result is that you get a fruity red wine, but very little tannin.

12 CHAPTALISATION

Ditto for this. Particularly widespread in France, it's the practice of adding sugar to a wine during the fermentation process. It is used to boost alcohol in wines lacking in natural sugar. Can be done sensitively, but invariably is used to hide mistakes in wines.

13 CHEWY

Not chewy like gum, but, rather, 'chewy' often refers to a big, tannic wine, where it literally leaves you chewing.

14 CIGAR BOX

Describes the smell you often get from an oak-aged, high-quality Cabernet or Shiraz. There's really only one way to find out exactly what it smells like and that's to stick your head in a cigar box.

15 CORKED

Term used to describe a bad wine, and often misattributed. See 'Troubleshooting' (Chapter 15). A real corked wine is infected with TCA (trichloroanisole), a naturally occurring chemical that can leak from the cork contaminating the wine and 'spoiling' it. Leaves a wine smelling musty, corky and stale.

16 DECANT

Take a bottle, pour its contents into another bottle or vessel and you've just done exactly that, decanted it. It's done to expose the wine to more oxygen, thereby allowing it to open up or 'breathe', and its aromas and flavours to be fully realised. It also looks very posh and poncy.

17 DRY

You probably think you know what 'dry' means, but there are various interpretations and levels of dry in wine. However, the main area that often confuses is when you get a very rich, fruity wine that is also dry. 'Dry' tends to refer to the finish, whereas often wines can have a 'fruit sweetness' when first swirled around the mouth.

18 FAT

Having been taunted with this word for years at school, I find it rather nice to be able to use it to describe a wine. It's used to describe a rich, well-rounded (i.e. big) wine, but also can refer to texture. So, if a wine is slightly thicker and more viscous with quite a heavy weight to it, you can call it fat. Not to be confused with the modern term 'phat', meaning excellent – although I guess you could have a phat fat wine.

19 **FILTERED**

Most wines are filtered these days. Filtering strips out the impurities and residue and reduces the likelihood of unsightly deposits being thrown in the bottle.

20 **FINISH**

Exactly what it says. The finish is ... well, the finish. But, when people use the word, it's to distinguish the flavours at the end of a mouthful once the wine has been swallowed rather than those that you get during the initial fruit hit when the wine first enters your mouth.

21 **FORTIFIED**

Term describing a wine that has had neutral spirit added to it to 'fortify' it and help preserve the fruit and quality. Port is the most famous fortified drink, but there are others.

22 **GREEN**

The term used to describe a wine that is very young, usually too young. The fruit is not as full as it should be, nor as mature as one would like. So in essence it's a derivation of the old phrase, 'green behind the gills'.

23 **HERBACEOUS**

If you say a wine tastes like a cross between grass and a load of green leaves, you wouldn't sell a lot. Tell someone it's 'herbaceous' and it almost sounds sexy.

24 **LEGS/TEARS**

Ah, one of the most wonderfully pretentious terms in the wine trade. When you swirl a wine around in a decent wineglass, you'll see that it settles back to the base leaving 'legs' of wine running down the side of the glass. It indicates a fairly high level of alcohol or glycerol and is often used as an indication of quality. Which is absolute tosh. A wine can be jam packed with alcohol and still be undrinkable. Same with glycerol content. What it indicates is that the wine isn't thin and weedy – and that's about it.

25 **LENGTH**

As in other areas of life, whatever they tell you, length really does matter. Length is essentially used to describe how long a wine's flavour lasts, from the initial fruit hit as you draw it into your mouth, to the last little drops of flavour after you've swallowed. Sometimes interchangeable with 'finish'. A wine with great legnth is essentially a wine with a long finish.

26 **LUSCIOUS**
Used to describe the plumpness and richness of a wine. Think of Brigitte Bardot's pout circa 1969 and you'll have an approximation of when, where and how this term is used.

27 **MAGNUM**
A bottle size that holds the equivalent of two bottles of wine – so 1.5 litres as opposed to the standard 75 cl. You should always bring magnums to dinner parties, especially mine – it's the height of civility and generosity. A Nebuchadnezzar, however – equivalent to twenty standard bottles – is a bit flash.

28 **MELLOW**
Refers to wines that have often had some element of ageing. Particularly with red wines, ageing tones down tannins, which become softer, silkier and more 'mellow', i.e. they lose their grippy, hard edge.

29 **MÉTHODE CHAMPENOISE**
This is the traditional method of making champagne, where the second fermentation (the bit that gives the wine the bubbles) is done in the bottle.

30 **MÉTHODE TRADITIONNELLE**
This is the method used by many wine producers outside Champagne. It's the same as *méthode champenoise*, but they aren't allowed to use that term, because their sparkling wines don't come from Champagne.

31 **MOUSSE**
Not referring to Angel Delight, but rather the bubbles in a wine. You can have lots of bubbles: a 'harsh' mousse. Or a small number of bubbles: a 'soft' mousse.

32 **OAK**
Essential part of the whole process for ageing fine wines. Oak tends to be the wood of choice for barrels made to store and age wines, although there are the odd regions in the world that use cherry wood. The word 'oak' is bandied around as a tasting note, but, in wine that costs less than £5 a bottle, very little owes its taste to real oak barrels, but rather to oak chips or oak essence. Real oak barrels manifest themselves with flavours of cream, vanilla and butter.

33 OENOLOGY

This is the term used to describe the science of wine. It's a catch-all term for the stuff you *don't* need to know unless you have become a wine nerd. See Chapter 18 to find this out.

34 PALATE

Fancy word for mouth and its taste buds.

35 PROCESSED

Usually used to refer to the flavour of cheap, low-quality wines. If a wine tastes or feels processed in the mouth, then it's probably because it's been made badly or has additives (sugar, perhaps oak flavouring etc.). Another, similar, term is 'confected', when the fruit and flavour of the wine tastes sweet and sickly. Both are fairly derogatory terms.

36 RAISINY

Can be good or bad. Sometimes fruit flavours in a still red or white can be raisiny if a wine has been exposed to excessive heat in some form or another.

37 RESIDUAL SUGAR

This refers to the sugar left after fermentation – the sugar that did not turn into alcohol. This amounts to wasted opportunity in my view. But then I do like my reds around the 15–16 per cent range, so I have a slightly warped view on this.

38 SAIGNÉE

This is the term used to refer to rosé wines that have been made by bleeding off a portion of the red wine before they have had too long a period of contact with the skins of the red grapes, resulting in a pink rather than red wine.

39 SOFT

Opposite of 'hard', which in the case of wine means that it's very easy to drink with no overly acidic spiky flavours when it comes to white, and has a nice, easy, fruity, low-tannin style when it comes to reds.

40 SPICY

When the word 'spicy' is used to describe a wine, it's generally not used in the poppadoms-and-lime-pickle sense, but more in reference to white and black pepper, or a mild chilli spice. Essentially, it means the wine has got a little bit of a kick in flavour terms, usually on the finish. There are some wines that are so spicy it is a bit like shoving your nose in a pepper grinder. Shiraz in particular is like this, and on the white side Gewürztraminer is the same, but more white-peppery.

41 STELVIN

This is actually a trademark for a particular type of screw-cap closure. However, because it is the most widely distributed of screw caps, it tends to be used 'generically' to describe screw caps.

42 STEMMY

This means a wine has been vinified with a proportion of the stems included. It gives it a bit of an overly tannic, quite stalky feel to it. The best way of describing it is for you to eat a seeded grape. Spit the grape out and have a chew on the pip. It'll be a mixture of tannic (that's the dryness) and stemmy (that's the green woody element).

43 TANNIN

One of the cornerstones of a red wine's structure, tannin comes from the skins of the grape, mainly, but also from the new oak barrels in which red wine is often aged. It provides that dry, mouth-puckering sensation at the sides and on the roof of the mouth, akin to drinking very strong cold tea.

44 THIN

Exactly as it sounds, 'thin' means a wine lacks body and substance. It is usually used in a derogatory rather than complimentary manner.

45 ULLAGE

This refers to the level of wine in a sealed bottle and is measured at the neck. As wine ages over a long period of time, some is lost via evaporation through the cork. The result is that the level of wine drops slightly, and level of ullage can have a significant effect on the value (and the potential quality) of a very old wine.

46 **VARIETAL**

Essentially, this is another word for grape variety. So, when someone describes a wine as a single varietal, it means a wine made from a single grape variety, which is also often the main information on the front of the bottle. The term is not used with something like Chablis, which, although made from a single grape variety (Chardonnay), is named after a region and the grape's name is not used in the marketing or labelling of the wine.

47 **VINEGARY**

Wine vinegar is actually made when a specific bacterium spoils a wine – and, while it may be nice in a salad, it isn't so hot in your wineglass. A vinegary wine is one that has been slightly affected by this bacterium. It's pretty easy to spot even for novice wine drinkers. Although, rather than describe it as 'vinegary', you will probably just say 'Yuck!' It's not as technical, but it works.

48 **VOLATILE ACIDITY**

In the way a person can be volatile, so can a wine, and usually it is the result of excessive levels of acetic acid within it, often exacerbated by the fermentation process. All sounds very technical, but at the end of the day it makes the aromas on a wine quite 'high' and not all that pleasant, and it loses balance and concentration in the mouth.

49 **WINEY**

Sounds ridiculously obvious, but actually winey is often used to describe pretty cheap wines. The idea is that the wine is so basic that really there's only one description for it, and that's that it tastes like wine. So it's winey.

50 **YIELD**

Used in reference to vineyards. The yield is the number of grapes produced per vine, and it has a dramatic effect on the quality of the wine. If the yields are high, often the wines will lack concentration. Low yields tend to produce very intense, fruity grapes and therefore more intense, better wines.

chapter nine
myths and monsters

It's part of the world's culture to nurture myths and monsters. Whether it's the more erudite tall stories of Greek mythology or the more common, less sophisticated tales of bogeymen to keep the kids in bed at night, myths are a part of our very fabric. They inspire awe and wonderment and fire the imagination. And that's probably what makes the myths that surround wine something of an anomaly, because they don't inspire awe, but actually sap confidence and sow misconceptions in people's minds. They strip away the fun of wine, and replace it with stuffiness – *unnecessary* stuffiness – and bunkum. In the world of wine, myths are the very bedrock of the intimidation that people feel when they approach the subject. It's the origin of many people's fear of 'doing the wrong thing'.

The myths you're more than likely familiar with range from the well-known 'You should never drink red with fish' and 'Ooh, it's got a crumb of cork in it so it must be corked' to the increasingly topical 'Screw caps are only ever used on cheap wines'. Whichever myth it is, however, it has the possibility to steer you off course once it's become embedded in your subconscious. That means it's time for a bit of myth busting. What follow are the twelve most damaging myths – myths that make my blood boil and pull the wool over people's eyes.

MYTH NO. 1: THE MORE YOU PAY, THE BETTER THE QUALITY

That you get what you pay for is simply not true in the wine world any more than it is in many other sectors where personal taste, quality and cost all intermingle in a complex relationship. Paying more doesn't act as a guarantee that you'll get great quality – it ups the odds, sure, but the risk factor is that, if it doesn't deliver, you've wasted even more money. And that is why so many people are nervous about spending more on a bottle of wine.

Chablis is the perfect example of that. You won't find much Chablis on sale for less than £7–8 a bottle. Some will be considerably more, and some of those are well worth the investment, if it's a style of wine you like. But unfortunately it's also one of those areas where you can easily shell out Ferrari-style prices but end up with a Skoda.

If you think this contradicts my previous advice to pay a few pounds more for a bottle if you can possibly afford it, then think again. There's a big difference between paying a pound more by splashing out on a £5.99 or £6.99 bottle – where you get demonstrably more bang for your buck with a small increase in price – and spending double or triple your usual budget. As you go further up the price scale, you're increasingly paying larger amounts of extra cash for incrementally small improvements in the wine, or increases in complexity – increases that often take experienced and enthusiastic palates to spot and appreciate. Unless you are really getting into your wine in a big way, then my advice is to limit yourself to £10 and below – you won't be short of choice and you'll still find top-quality wines.

MYTH NO. 2: WINE GETS BETTER WITH AGE

The only other more annoying phrase than the one above that I hear regularly is, 'My daughter/son is only three months old but she/he sleeps right through the night.' And both are equally false, as anyone with kids knows, and anyone who's opened a bottle of Bulgarian Cabernet after it's been sitting for two years in a dusty corner under the stairs knows – to their cost.

Very few wines are made for ageing. Reds generally age better over time, because of their tannin and acidity combination. But most reds and whites are designed to be drunk within two to three years, first, because they are relatively inexpensive, and, second, because who has a cellar these days? Also, when you consider that most bottles of wine purchased within a supermarket are consumed within 24 hours – and the majority are actually opened within six hours of being bought – it would be fairly stupid for most winemakers to make their wines anything other than early drinkers.

Those wines that are capable of ageing do tend to command a premium in price terms. Top-growth claret from Bordeaux, first-class burgundy, vintage champagne, vintage port, top-of-the-range Aussie reds, New Zealand, Australian and German top-flight Rieslings – these are all often traded on the basis that they are being bought while in their infancy, but have a certain future ahead of them. The secret to ageing potential in wine is structure – that is the right combination of fruit, tannin and acidity that will give balance, harmony and longevity to a wine. The problem is structure costs.

Equally important, however, is how you store a wine. Stick it in the attic next to a whole load of pipes from the hot-water tank and you may as well pour your Château Latour into the Christmas punch bowl – which, at more than £150 a bottle for the latest vintage, seems a tad excessive for punch. Put it in a temperature-controlled cellar, in decent racking, however, and – provided you've bought wisely and paid accordingly – you should get a few good years out of your purchase.

MYTH NO. 3: 'RESERVE' MEANS TOP QUALITY

Sadly, nothing could be further from the truth. There used to be a time when it did, but, thanks to the march of modern marketing, it can mean more or less anything an adman wants it to these days.

The definition of the verb 'reserve' is, according to the *Oxford English Dictionary*, 'to put aside for future or special use; order or set aside for a particular person; retain; postpone'; and the noun is something 'reserved for future or special use ...' There are still wine-producing countries – Italy and Spain are two – in which this definition of the word 'reserve' is still valid and indeed upheld by law. When you look at a Rioja from Spain, you may find the words 'Gran Reserva' on a bottle – it will literally mean 'great reserve' and will refer to a wine specifically set aside and aged for a longer period than the standard wines. Unfortunately – and this will be one of the few criticisms you'll hear from me of the New World – the Australians and South Africans play fairly fast and loose with the term, resulting in wines that appear on the shelf at £3.99 with the word 'reserve' emblazoned on them. In reality, they are just bog-standard wines and there's nothing remotely 'special' about them. What can you do about it? Remain sceptical, I guess, and practise a little bit of good old British cynicism.

MYTH NO. 4: RED WINE NEEDS TO BREATHE

It's not so much that red wine needs to breathe that's the myth, but rather the method that is most frequently used to achieve this. The idea that you need only pull the cork on a bottle of red and then let the air do its trick is fairly ridiculous. Once the cork is pulled you are displaying only a very small flat surface area of the wine to air – so roughly 1–2 ml of actual wine. That's roughly $1/700$ to $1/350$ of the total volume of the wine in a standard bottle. It's like getting someone to drop you from a helicopter three feet from the top of Everest, and then claim you've climbed the entire mountain. In reality, you've achieved nothing.

Breathing a red wine is simply allowing it exposure to the air, or, more precisely, oxygen, which helps aerate the wine and enables its full potential to be released. Most red wines benefit from it, and even the odd white, but, in particular, it is tight, young, full-bodied red wines that do best. To let a red breathe properly you have to expose it totally to the air, i.e. decant the bottle in full, or, alternatively, pour a glass of it, swirl it around and let nature take its course as you learn new levels of patience when it comes to drinking.

MYTH NO. 5: BEWARE OF SCREW CAPS

If you remember the 70s, you'll remember that screw-cap wines were all the rage. Like flares and Kevin Keegan perms, however, they then spent the next three decades in a state of purgatory.

Thirty years on, though, and in a new millennium, screw caps are, believe it or not, coming back! I know, I know. It's like being told that pink jumpsuits are coming back into fashion. You just can't believe it. It doesn't make sense. The world has clearly gone crazy. I mean, look at the screw cap's heritage: Liebfraumilch, Black Tower, Babycham – it's impossible to find a piece of technology that has been so associated with naff drinks of the 70s. Oh, and don't forget Advocaat, too. I rest my case.

Pink jumpsuits never came back into fashion, but screw caps have. Many wine producers are swapping from cork to screw cap, particularly with whites, because they claim the advances in screw-cap technology over the last five to ten years has made them virtually foolproof.

Without getting all scientific on you, the theory briefly goes like this. One of the major causes of faulty, or corked, wines is TCA (or trichloroanisole), a compound that is often found in varying levels in natural cork stoppers. This can react with oxygen and cause the damp, musty, corky smell and taste that denotes a 'corked' wine. Rough estimates put the number of wines that suffer from this at between 2 and 6 per cent, with the culprit more often than not the cork itself. Hence the hunt for alternative stoppers.

For a while it looked as if synthetic corks might be the answer – those tight, multicoloured seals that forced you to use copious amounts of padding, a bench vice and a block and tackle to pull the cork out. Well, they're still there, but not so common as they used to be. Instead, the good old screw cap came back – modified, with lots of new-fangled technology, admittedly, but essentially still a screw cap.

There are two chief questions for anyone buying a wine with a screw cap. First, is it really all that 'pikey'? Second, does it work? Well, first, yes. It is very 'pikey'. I don't care what people say, it still looks as if you've picked the wine equivalent of a bottle of Nokyorrsocksoff vodka off the wine shelf in your local corner shop. I mean, for goodness' sake, Hirondelle came in a screw cap. Let's get real here.

However, in answer to number two, yes, it does work. Very well indeed. The cork manufacturers claim otherwise, but according to producers using the screw caps they get none of the complaints they used to when they used corks and they claim that, particularly with aromatic wines, such as Sauvignon Blanc and Riesling, you actually get a better, fresher product. The jury is still out on this, but I have tasted the same product with cork and screw cap over several different wines, mainly white, and I think it probably does allow for a fresher, more vibrant wine – especially with those wines that are made for early drinking, that is within the first couple of years of their life.

The bottom line is that screw caps are here to stay, they are more sophisticated than they were in the 70's, and it's fair to say that most winemakers use them because they're the best solution, rather than the cheapest. Indeed, in most cases it's just as expensive. So feel at ease buying a wine with a screw cap and count yourself lucky you don't have to spend time hunting around for the corkscrew so much.

MYTH NO. 6: THERE ARE CRUMBS OF CORK IN MY WINE SO IT MUST BE CORKED

Er, excuse my French, but that's utter bull. Nine times out of ten, cork in your wine means only that whoever opened the wine used a dodgy corkscrew and it's punched through the bottom of the cork and deposited a bit of it in the wine. As we saw earlier, the main cause of a corked wine is TCA. That chemical reaction with the cork has happened long before you open a bottle. If someone at your table in a restaurant thinks otherwise or tries to lecture you in your own home about it, put them right. You'll save them a lot of embarrassment in the future – and can feel quietly smug about it.

MYTH NO. 7: SMELLING A CORK WILL TELL YOU IF A WINE IS BAD

Smelling a cork will tell you one thing and one thing only: that the cork smells of cork. I've had corked wines where the cork doesn't smell any different at all, but the wine is still bad. I've had wines where the cork stinks to high heaven, but the wine has been perfectly fine.

But, worst of all, I have been in restaurants – respectable restaurants in which you have to mortgage your house just to get a booking – where the wine waiter has opened a bottle and sniffed the cork before pouring the wine to taste. If I could actually be bothered to find out, I'd call the school of sommeliers and ask them whether it's in their training manual and why, but I can't be bothered because I have better things to do with my time.

However, it doesn't help dispel the myth when wine waiters, theoretically in the vanguard of wine education for us poor punters, reinforce this ridiculous concept. I sometimes wonder whether it's a psychological thing. They smell the cork, giving the unsuspecting customer the impression that all is well with the wine, and making it all the more difficult for him or her to voice any doubts they might have. It's a very blatant, visual form of harassment and there's no reason for it. If you see it happen, start panicking a little.

MYTH NO. 8: A WINE WRITER HAS ANY CONCEPT OF GOOD VALUE

Personally, I would no more believe a wine writer who told me a wine was good value than I would a parking warden who says I can leave my car on the double yellow line without getting a ticket. The difference between the two is that, while the latter is obviously lying and can't wait to slap a ticket on your windscreen once you've turned your back, the former is at least well intentioned, but sadly misguided.

Why misguided? Well, most wine journalists get their wine sent to them for free. They rarely, if ever, pay for a bottle of wine, and, when they do, it's usually to indulge themselves in a bit of luxury because – well, because they can. I'm no different. On the odd occasion that I have to buy a bottle of wine to take round to friends I usually find myself standing in front of the local merchant's shelf, thinking, Flaming heck! That's an awful lot for a Chablis.

So, again, the advice is simple: be sceptical and make up your own mind about what is and isn't good value for you according to what's in your pocket at the time.

MYTH NO. 9: CHARDONNAY/ CABERNET IS YESTERDAY'S GRAPE

The wine world is like the fashion world: it has its prima donnas, it has its *enfants terribles*, its *grande dames*, and its flashy supermodels. There are those who stay the course and those who go by the wayside. And that applies to winemakers, wine companies and, most of all, wine grape varieties. The two most drunk grape varieties in the world are Cabernet and Chardonnay, and, at one point or another, for at least as long as I have been writing about wine, one or other of these two noble grape varieties has either been old hat, or the new black. The truth is, Chardonnay and Cabernet are like the Hardy Amies of the wine world: timeless, in and out of fashion, but always on the scene. And it won't change.

Oh, you'll hear a lot of people go on about the 'Anything But Chardonnay/Cabernet' movement, about how wine lovers across the world are turning their backs on the grapes in favour of new, more exciting and interesting varieties. But that's wishful thinking – usually promulgated by bored wine writers, unable to face up to the deluge of letters in their postbag asking them to recommend a 'decent Chardonnay' or 'wonderful Cabernet' rather than something more exotic and testing.

In the case of Chardonnay a lot of people like it because it's a lovely grape variety – full stop. Whether it's oaked or unoaked, big and fat, or lean and mean, New World or Old World, when it's treated with respect in the vineyard and winery, it makes great wine. And, compared with other grapes, it is infinitely more diverse in variety and style from all parts of the world. Likewise, Cabernet is the stalwart of some of the greatest wines produced across the globe and always will be.

Of course, I think anyone who likes Chardonnay or Cabernet should always try other grape varieties, even if it's just to prove that Chardonnay or Cabernet is the one they like. Let me put it this way. I love cars, but I also know that I'm likely to drive Audis for the rest of my life because I like them best. I might trade up, as I grow fatter and wealthier (the latter, I hope!), but I will probably always stick to the same marque. And so it is with some people when it comes to Chardonnay or Cabernet. They just bloomin' well like it, and want to stick with it – and nowhere in this world is there a single statute book that says that's a crime. So be proud and loud if you belong to that group.

MYTH NO. 10: FRENCH WINES ARE THE BEST

The only people who have ever told me this are French winemakers, which gives the game away a bit. However, because French wines are a strong part of the UK wine trade's offering, there is a tendency to rely on France as the purveyor of only quality wines. If we recognise no other names on the shelf, we'll always recognise Chablis, or Burgundy, or Claret.

Yet there are many better wines sitting just a few feet away, often for less money, that are no more risky to buy and try than taking part in the French wine lottery. True, France makes some of the world's best wines, but in consistency terms it often lets itself down. I could buy ten Aussie Chardonnays in a row and they might all taste mighty similar, but most would be of the same reliable quality. I certainly couldn't say that about Chablis.

MYTH NO. 11: ORGANIC IS GOOD

No, it is not. In the wine world at least, it is usually diabolical and overpriced. There are very few decent organic wines around. Some of those that are decent aren't allowed to call themselves organic, because the world and many individual countries have yet to come up with a universally agreed definition. Frankly, it's my opinion that this area of the wine world is a complete mess, and an absolute minefield for the average member of the wine buying public.

I don't think it shouldn't be talked about by wine journalists, or pressures brought to bear to resolve the mess. But, as far as the average punter goes, encouraging them to drink organic wines is a little like asking them to play Russian roulette with five bullets rather than one in the chamber. And that's because, for every decent bottle of well-made organic wine that's reasonably priced, there are another two or three that are overpriced and of poor quality – but clearly happy to trade solely on the point that they are organic. I wouldn't recommend you *not* to drink organic wines, but at the moment I couldn't recommend that you actively seek them out.

MYTH NO. 12: RED WINE WITH MEAT, WHITE WINE WITH FISH

We all have preferences, and I can honestly say that, if you like red wine mainly, and find white wine difficult to get your head round, well, go ahead and have a juicy Pinot with your bit of Dover sole. Likewise, if you find reds just too over the top and too tannic, and prefer the subtleties of white, have a nice bottle of Riesling with your Châteaubriand.

The reason I've included this 'rule' among the myths is that, while there is something to be said for it, it's also responsible for making too many people too conscious about what they drink with what they eat, rather than just having a laugh and enjoying themselves.

I often drink white wine with my steak. The problem is that I am often too scared to admit it, especially when it comes to being in a public venue, in front of my peers, sitting down to a nice rare filet mignon. Invariably, I fold and end up drinking red wine so that I don't look like a pleb.

I don't actually disagree with the fact that usually the red wine makes for a better combination – more often than not it does. But I prefer drinking white wine – and it's as simple as that. However, I have been to dinner parties – and this happens frequently – where, the moment the main course is served, the white disappears and I find myself stuck in a sea of red, red that the host has meticulously paired with the butterfly roasted lamb or venison steaks.

Chapter 14 recommends food combinations. At the risk of sounding hypocritical, I still think there are some classic combinations and I do think in most cases red wines are better with meat, and white wines are – on the whole – better with fish. There are some wonderful exceptions, but, as a rule, it does have some common sense to it.

chapter ten
bluffing it

How to bluff your way with winespeak

Basically, there's a cheat in all of us. It's our lazy side, the side that couldn't be bothered to read the entirety of *Wuthering Heights* for A level, so read the first and last pages and hoped for the best. The problem with wine is that there are so many parts to it, so many variables, that it can be quite complicated to convince someone that you know your onions – or grapes, to be precise – when in reality you don't.

That is why I've written this chapter. It's designed to appeal to those who haven't grown out of the above phase (and that includes me: I *still* haven't read *Wuthering Heights*!).

It's meant to be a short cut to bluffing it, with an emphasis on making sure that, whatever the occasion – dinner party, wine tasting, funeral, wedding – you can make a sensible but suitably vague comment on the wine and give all those around you the impression that you actually do know what you're talking about. So I've put together twenty key words or phrases that you can use to make sure everyone knows you're an expert – of sorts. But first ...

THE RULES

Rule 1: This works only if you say and use these words and phrases with the utmost confidence. Any sign of weakness will be pounced on by real wine aficionados.

Rule 2: If you encounter another bluffer, never, *never*, ever call his or her bluff: there is honour even among bluffers.

Rule 3: If someone calls your bluff, just smile, look at the ceiling in a resigned, 'I'm dealing with a child' type look and say, 'Goodness gracious, let's not fall out over a glass of [insert appropriate grape variety or style here]. After all, wine is a totally subjective thing.' Then run – you've been rumbled.

Rule 4: Don't try this at home – it's your home and if you can't behave in an ignorant manner in your own home, where can you – unless of course you've stupidly asked your boss round for dinner? Which leads me to ...

Rule 5: Don't ever ask your boss round for dinner.

THE TERMINOLOGY

And so to the key phrases that you have to learn if you're going to get by on the minimal knowledge. And those key phrases, or in many cases words, are generally designed to be completely noncommittal and as vague as possible, yet imbued with certain authority that – if delivered in a forthright and confident voice – will be convincing.

AGGRESSIVE

Fantastic catch-all. A wine can be aggressive if it's too tannic or too acidic, or lacks fruit. But, fundamentally, it can also mean it's rubbish. Spotting an aggressive wine is relatively easy. If it's too tannic, then you will feel the sides of your gums drying up, and you'll want a glass of water. If it's too acidic, then you'll look as if you'd just shoved a lime in your mouth and chewed hard. If it's too fruity it will feel as if you were drinking fresh jam from the jar. Often its 'aggressiveness' will be exaggerated if the wine is very young.

So how would that go? 'My oh my, this is a touch aggressive, dontcha feel?'

Likely response: 'Do you really think so?'

Double bluff: 'Perhaps I'm being a little aggressive, nay, harsh on it myself' (said with a slightly camp olde worlde weariness).

Advanced use of phrase: 'My, but the tannins/acidity are particularly aggressive on this young whippersnapper.'

What not to say: 'Put 'em up, put 'em up, I'll fight you with one hand tied behind my back' (apologies to the Cowardly Lion).

ATYPICAL

This is perfect for when you come across a grape variety that you've never known or tasted before. You can peruse the glass for a few seconds. Sniff. Slurp. Swirl. Slurp again. Then roll this little number off the tongue like a smoking grenade, ready to cause friction among the rest of the dinner party. Always a good one to use for traditional varieties that have been made in the New World, e.g. Pinot Noir, Cabernet Sauvignon, Chardonnay, Sauvignon Blanc.

So how would that go? 'I'm not sure, but seems quite atypical for …' [insert appropriate grape variety here].

Likely response: 'But I think it's classic.'

Double bluff: 'Do you really how fascinating?' (said with raised eyebrow and followed by musing silence).

Advanced use of phrase: 'Incredibly atypical, so much so that I actually thought it was …' [fill in alternative grape variety here].

What not to say: 'This Chardonnay is so atypical it tastes just like Pinot Noir.'

AUSTERE

I love this one. Again, it's suitable for many different occasions, but fundamentally is used to describe wines that are less intense, say, than an in-your-face-Aussie Cab or Chardonnay, i.e. somewhat reserved. It can also mean that the fruit is a little 'green' or young. If you're not sure, look at the label. If you see a very young vintage – up to two years before you're drinking it, say – and it's from the Old World (France, Spain, Italy) rather than the New (Australia, South Africa, California), then it's perfectly possible that it will be on the austere side.

So how would that go? 'Mmm. A little austere on first glance. Perhaps it will open out as time goes by.'

Likely response: 'Do you really think so?'

Double bluff: 'Well, difficult to tell these days.' (Again, a very good all-round get-out clause should someone try to call your bluff.)

Advanced use of phrase: 'For a 2003 it's awfully austere, but then I guess that's the French [or Italian/Spanish] for you.'

What not to say: 'I find the 1945 is still a little austere and needs a little more time in the bottle.'

CLASSIC

Like 'atypical', this can go either way. But, if you're talking about an Old World wine, you're perfectly likely to get away with an explanation that this is a 'classic'. It has multiple, almost endless, applications, but overuse at the same dinner party can give away your amateur status very quickly indeed.

So how would that go? 'My goodness! Absolutely classic Chablis.'

Likely response: 'You're so right.'

Double bluff: 'Well thank you. What do think of it?' (I'm a great believer in quitting while you're ahead.)

Advanced use of phrase: 'Classic use of barrel fermentation techniques.'

What not to say: 'I don't like that classical music much and the same goes *pour mon vino, mon brave*. Know wadda mean?'

DUMB

A word more often used to describe the various members of the royal family, this is a very useful word when you're trying to disguise the fact that you're not sure what you're smelling. In fact it's multifunctional. It can be used for smell, for taste and for the finish (that is the last, lingering dregs of taste after you've swallowed it). Spotting a 'dumb' wine couldn't be easier. If you can't smell anything, if you can't taste much fruit or there's little lingering flavour you can use the word dumb with gay abandon. The only problem is that sometimes wines can be good, but dumb – and need some time in the glass. If you leave it for five minutes and it starts to taste better and more fruity, then it's 'opened up'.

So how would that go? 'I'm trying really hard to get more on the nose/palate but I think this is coming a cross a little dumb at the moment.'

Likely response: 'What on earth are you talking about?'

Double bluff: 'I was talking about the wine, not you – although I'm having second thoughts.'

Advanced use of phrase: 'It's very dumb on the nose but I think it's coming round slowly on the palate. Perhaps it's suffering from bottle shock.' (Don't ask!)

What not to say: 'That label's a bit dumb, don't you think?'

FAT

The nice thing about the word 'fat' is that it is the sort of word that allows you to imbue it with a hundred and one different meanings – all of which are right. A wine can be fat because it's full-bodied; it can be fat because it has lots of big, round oak flavours; it can be fat in the negative sense. You name it, fat can *be* it. But it has to apply to big wines – heavily oaked Chardonnays, blockbuster Shiraz, good old earthy Pinot Noirs from the New World.

So how would that go? 'This Chardonnay is very fat.'

Likely response: 'Really, I thought it was a little on the lean side.'

Double bluff: 'I meant the nose rather than the palate – which is why it's such an interesting wine.'

Advanced use of phrase: 'Very fat wine – reminds of the '69, which did of course last for decades.'

What not to say: 'This is fatter than your Aunt Hilda – and that's saying something.'

FEMININE

Yes, I know it's terribly sexist, but it is a phrase that's used a lot and frankly, if you want to sound like a wine bore, it's very, very effective. Essentially, it refers to a wine that is elegant, lighter in body and structure and perhaps quite dainty. So if it doesn't knock your socks off in taste terms, and smacks of any subtlety, then you can get away with describing it as feminine. Mind you, you might get a good kicking from any females present at the table when you explain your reasoning.

So how would that go? 'Wonderfully feminine, gamine, little number.'
Likely response: 'Would you like to explain that disgraceful remark?'
Double bluff: 'Er ... not really. I mean, it's beautiful, well proportioned, it doesn't look too fat in that glass ...'
Advanced use of phrase: I wouldn't bother: any further attempt at explanation will only land you in trouble.
What not to say: 'Very feminine wine – one moment I'm enjoying it to the full, the next I've got a nagging headache that just won't stop.'

GRAPEY

It's the classic catch-all and completely, utterly, undeniably kosher. Apart from anything else, all wine is grapey. But grapey is actually a term that's used to refer specifically to a wine that is very basic, with a very pungent, freshly fermented aroma. However, it's pretty widespread in terms of application and always works when you can't think of anything else.
So how would that go? 'Mmm, wonderfully grapey aromas.'
Likely response: 'I thought it wasn't bad.'
Double bluff: 'Well, naturally, I meant in the positive, fresh and vibrant sense.'
Advanced use of phrase: 'Very grapey.' (Sorry, that's about as advanced as it gets.)
What not to say: 'This diet Coke is somewhat grapey on the nose.'

GREEN

This sounds very authoritative, and indeed it is, as long as you follow a few guidelines. Essentially, green means that the wine is quite young. So a champagne, for instance, can be described as very green if it's young and acidic. Likewise, a Cabernet Sauvignon can be quite green if it's young, and perhaps a little too tannic. Again, look at the vintage and then taste the wine – if it tastes a little bitter or sharp, you can probably get away with the term, especially if you check out the vintage as well.
So how would that go? 'Very green in the mouth. The fruit's not very forward.'
Likely response: 'I thought it was quite generous.'
Double bluff: 'I meant in comparison with the last vintage I tasted of this.'
Advanced use of phrase: 'This champagne is very green. They really ought not to have released it on the market so early.'
What not to say: 'I like my reds as green as freshly cut grass.'

HOT

A wine is described as hot if the alcohol is either a little too much or slightly unstable. The higher the alcohol in a wine, the more chance there is of its being either a little hot or slightly unstable. Stick your nose in the glass. If you get almost a watering of the eyes, a little as you do with a spirit, then you can probably bandy this term around. Tends to refer to reds more than to whites.

So how would that go? 'Ooh, there's a little bit of heat on this wine, isn't there?'

Likely response: 'Mmm, quite punchy.'

Double bluff: 'Aggressive, I think you'll find.' (You score extra points for the use of *two* key bluff words.)

Advanced use of phrase: 'In general, it's quite well balanced, but it's just hot enough on the finish to throw the whole wine out of kilter.'

What not to say: 'Wow, that's hot as Hades and I like it.'

LEGS

The beauty about this description is that it's simple to spot: when you swirl the wine around in the glass as it settles, there should be little lines or 'legs' of wine falling down the sides. It's usually when there's a fairly high content of alcohol or glycerol – and basically means there's a fair whack of body to the wine. It's purely observational, means very little, but sounds wonderfully impressive.

So how would that go? 'Mmm, nice legs on this little baby.'

Likely response: 'It's a wine, not a baby.'

Double bluff: 'All my wines are babies that I care for and nurture.' (Pass the sick bag!)

Advanced use of phrase: 'These legs would indicate that the alcohol content is on the high side. But I'll just check the label to be sure.'

What not to say: 'Legs eleven, I'm in heaven.'

INTERESTING

Very useful word when dealing with friends and family, but should never be used when dealing with winemakers. A rough interpretation of 'interesting' can range from 'it's not bad' to 'bloody hell, this is the worst wine I think I've ever had the misfortune to taste'. Winemakers will always, always assume that you are using it in reference to the latter.

So how would that go? 'Very interesting, cheeky little number, this.'

Likely response: 'What do you mean by interesting?'

Double bluff: 'Well, it's very interesting. What the hell else do you think I mean?'

Advanced use of phrase: 'It's very, very interesting.' (Again, limited application when it comes to advanced use.)
What not to say: 'So you made this wine, then. Very interesting.'

MASCULINE

Obviously, it's generally used to refer to the opposite styles of wines from those described as feminine, and means big, mature, full-on, fruit-driven wines with plenty of structure and complexity. Or, rather, that's what we men would quite like it to represent. Females usually use the term to refer to a wine that is brutish, dull and very one-dimensional. Take your pick.
So how would that go? 'Very masculine wine with lots of body.'
Likely response: 'What?'
Double bluff: 'You know, it's got quite a lot of muscle to it.'
Advanced use of phrase: 'It's masculinity hides a plethora of unfortunate faults.'
What not to say: 'Quite manly, this wine. Which means it promises the world, but seems to deliver very little indeed.'

pH

This refers to the acid levels in a wine. The term pH is the chemical measurement in hydrogen ions for the relative acidity or alkaline contents of a liquid. In the case of wine, this is relatively easy to con your way through. If a wine tastes very sharp, tart and therefore acidic, it probably has a relatively high pH. The opposite means a relatively low pH. Getting the balance is all part of the skill of winemaking. In fact, you can't actually spot pH – it's a chemical measurement. But a highly acidic tasting wine is likely to have a relatively high pH.
So how would that go? 'Mmm, I'm thinking the relative pH on this quite high.'
Likely response: 'How do you know that?'
Double bluff: 'Well, obviously, I don't have my lab equipment here, so I'm winging it a bit, but for chrissakes give me a break here.'
Advanced use of phrase: 'In my experience the high pH on this wine has contributed to its slightly less bright and less dazzling colour.' (High pH can affect the colour of a wine.)
What not to say: 'I quite like a nice high pH on my wines – helps strip the dentures out from time to time.'

RESIDUAL SUGAR

Again, one that's easy to use, even for pure dunces, but has quite an impressive effect around the tasting room or dinner table. Essentially, residual sugar is the sugar that's left after fermentation – so that is the sugar that hasn't been turned into alcohol. If a wine tastes slightly sweet, or very sweet, it's perfectly reasonable to expect it to have a high residual-sugar content. But remember, the real sweetness tends to be on the finish of a wine, whereas fruit sweetness is that initial burst of sweet flavour you get when you first taste a wine, which then dries out.

So how would that go? 'Wow, quite a high residual sugar on this little tyke.'

Likely response: 'You mean it tastes sweet.'

Double bluff: 'If you want to put it in such a pedestrian way, then yes.'

Advanced use of phrase: 'High on the residual sugar, but I feel that it has the acidity to carry it, don't you?'

What not to say: 'It's too sweet, it's too sweet. *Yeauch!*'

RESTRAINED

It's a bit like using 'dumb', but a little more refined. Essentially the idea is that the wine is holding back, not giving as much of its wonderful potential as it could. Usually, it's used only in reference to fine wines, and the easiest way of deciding whether you'll throw this one into the conversation is to gauge the price of the bottle and whether you think the wine is very fruity or not. If it's over a tenner and quite 'restrained', then you've got nice friends and you can use this little gem.

So how would that go? 'Lovely claret, but it's a little restrained on the nose and palate.'

Likely response: 'Oh, I think it's quite nice actually.'

Double bluff: 'Yes, but give it a few years and it'll really come into its own.'

Advanced use of phrase: 'Quite restrained now, but, given the vintage, I'd say it had a good five years in it before it reaches its peak of drinking.'

What not to say: 'Can someone take the restraints of this wine?'

SHORT

This is simple pimple really. When a wine is 'short' it means its flavours don't last in the mouth for very long. So if you find you're getting an instant buzz of fruit, and then nothing else, you can say the wine is 'short'. Make sure you sneer a little, too, when you say it – adds to the general air of disapproval.

So how would that go? 'It's a little on the short side.'

Likely response: 'Oh, it's not that bad.'

Double bluff: 'If it was any shorter it'd be in kindergarten.'

Advanced use of phrase: 'This is extremely short.' (In all honesty a wine is usually short or not, so it's difficult to get too fancy with this term.)

What not to say: 'It's a bit of a midget, this one.'

TEXTURE

This is perhaps the vaguest word around – which does of course make it the ideal word to use when you're trying to bluff your way through a wine conversation. Essentially, it refers to the feel of a wine in the mouth. If it's a lightweight wine it will have quite a thin, silky 'texture'; if it's more fruity, with more body, it'll be more viscous, or thicker, in texture. But every wine has *some* sort of texture, so, as long as you're not too specific, you should be fine.

So how would that go? 'Lovely texture – wonderfully rich [or thick, creamy, soft, silky, subtle].' (Delete as applicable.)

Likely response: 'You really think so?'

Double bluff: 'Well, so few wines have texture these days, you kind of jump on one when it has. Don't you think so?'

Advanced use of phrase: 'Wonderful interplay between the multiple textures on this delicious Cabernet.'

What not to say: 'I love the Artex on this fruity little number.'

TOASTY

This is quite specific and usually used on whites and fizzes. Certainly with the latter, when the champagne has some bottle age, it develops a toasty aroma – like the smell of freshly toasting, thick white bread. Or it can sometimes smell like fresh bread dough. Likewise with Chardonnays that have been in bottle for a little while and aged in new oak (which has been literally 'toasted' on the inside). It's a delicious smell, and when you sniff it you'll realise it immediately, which makes this one quite an easy bluff to use.

So how would that go? 'Ooh, lovely bubbles, and it's a bit toasty on the nose, too.'

Likely response: 'Toasty?'

Double bluff: 'Exactly. Or is it more like freshly baked bread. Mmm?'

Advanced use of phrase: 'They must have used a heavy toast on the nose for this Chardonnay.' (NB: this one's not to be used with champagne or Chablis, neither of which sees a jot of oak.)

What not to say: 'This wine's toast' or 'Where's the Marmite?'

VOLATILE

Another technical term, which theoretically should be 'volatile acidity'. But it can be used generally. If the wine's not rocking and it smells quite alcoholic and almost spirity, it's probably suffering from some imbalance, and describing it as 'volatile' is only going to earn brownie points. Use it when you're pretty convinced a wine is bad – not just a bit boring.

So how would that go? 'Very volatile, this one. All over the place.'
Likely response: 'So you think it's bad.'
Double bluff: 'Dunno. Who bought it?' (Difficult to move on from this one, I'll admit.)
Advanced use of phrase: 'The volatility of this wine is doing the aromas no favours, but it doesn't seem too bad on the palate.'
What not to say: 'Ooh it's got a vicious temper, this wine.'

chapter eleven
wine by style

Which style are you?

Are you soft and juicy, or are you clean and crisp? It's all very well knowing which grape comes from where, but most of us think in terms of taste. The following is meant as a quick introduction to this chapter, which addresses each style in detail. The question is, which style do you think you are? And remember, variety is the spice of life, so don't think you have to be just one!

OAKY CHARDONNAY
Do you like your whites, in particular Chardonnay, to have a good whack of oak? Do you fancy having your taste buds wrapped in a lovely creamy, vanilla-flavoured cloak of oak? Then look no further.

FRAGRANT BUT DRY WHITES
You like the decadence, you love the smell, you crave the fruit. These are wines for those who are just that little bit bored with Sauvignon and perhaps oh so tired of Chardonnay and want something that will give their taste buds – and nose – a whole new sensation.

SWEET GERMAN STYLE
Some of the world's best wines are sweet or semi-sweet, and there's no shame in liking them that way. The question is, are you prepared to pay for it?

CLASSIC CHARDONNAY
Clearly you're a sophisticated drinker. You like your whites to be bone dry and lightly oaked, or even oak free. Classic regions, classic flavours and you're willing to pay for it.

KIWI SAUVIGNON BLANC
You like Sauvignon, but it's got to have fruit, fruit, fruit. You're looking for that all essential zap that will get the mouth watering and have you shouting for a decent plate of shellfish before you can make it to the second mouthful.

CLEAN AND CRISP WHITES
Throw out the oak, bring in the zip and the zing. You like your whites to be refreshing, tongue tingling and tooty fruity.

CLASSIC SAUVIGNON BLANC
All that kiwi stuff gets a little bit fruity. You're a traditionalist when it comes to your Sauvignon, but that doesn't mean you're boring …

CLASSIC REDS
You like your red in the purely traditional style. A nice drop of Burgundy, a good bit of Claret, classic Rhône. And that's fine. You're even willing to entertain the odd New World red that has pretensions to be otherwise. More than anything, though, you don't like your reds to be 'in your face'.

FULL AND FRUITY REDS

It's fruit that gets you all excited when it comes to your reds, backed up with a good bit of oak. If Ribena with an alcoholic punch sounds good to you, then this is the style you should go for.

CLASSIC FIZZ

It's Champagne all the way … almost. You like classic, well-made fizz which has plenty of fruit, lots of character and an elegance and richness that only come from splashing a bit of cash around.

SWEET AS PIE

A little bit of sweetness goes a long way, but you like a lot of sweetness, which is why you like dessert-style wines. As long as it's sticky, not icky.

HUGE REDS

Turbo-charged reds that put the pedal to the metal when it comes to fruit, tannin and oak. These are larger than life reds that will give your taste buds a good slap around the chops and leave a side of beef quivering with anticipation.

SOFT AND JUICY REDS

If you could wallow in a bowl of crushed cherries, you would. Instead, you'll settle for something that does exactly what it says on the tin i.e. provide lots of juicy red fruit and soft, silky, smooth flavours.

MODERN FIZZ

Fresh, light and oh so bright, you like your fizz to be simple, clean and zippy. Nothing too complicated, nothing too expensive, nothing too grand … just good clean, bubbly fun.

LUNCHTIME REDS

You like reds that aren't going to knock your socks off, or leave you snoozing rudely at the table by the time the second course turns up. Light, peppy, with bright fruit flavours, these are reds you could drink, and drink, and drink …

RIOJA-STYLE REDS

You like your fruit – preferably strawberries or ripe red cherries – but it needs to have a lovely injection of creamy vanilla oak to bring it to life. Rioja is the perfect example, but there are plenty of others from around the globe to get your taste buds tingling.

POWER ASSISTED

You like your wine fortified and fruity. So we're talking ports and Madeiras – traditional but not as crusty and fusty as you might think.

When I started working for Virgin Wines several years ago, I was told that they were going to divide the wines by taste rather than grape variety or geography. People were going to be able to search the website by country and grape variety, but 'virtual' wine aisles were going to be divided by taste, so there'd be the soft and juicy section, the clean and crisp section and so on.

You're mad, I thought. But then I did a little research. Not particularly qualified stuff, but rather asking friends around the dinner table. And I discovered something: that most of them found this a far more useful way of classifying wine than by variety or geography.

What it comes down to is that, like life, wine isn't a black or white affair. A Chardonnay from Chablis is completely different from a Puligny-Montrachet – and yet they both fall under the title of Burgundy. Likewise, a person might like a Shiraz from Australia because it's big, bold and ballsy – but will also like a good Châteauneuf-du-Pape that's made in a similar fashion. So why shouldn't they be side by side on the wine shelf?

And that's why the following style guide is included in this book – and why I'd encourage you to have a good read and try to work out which you like. I've included a decent chapter on grapes after this (Chapter 12), along with what I hope is a whirlwind but useful guide to the world's major wine regions and the wines they make (Chapter 13). But, if I didn't know that much about wine but wanted to discover something different, I'd be far more likely to ask for something 'soft and juicy' in the red department than a Chilean Merlot or southern French Grenache. And when you consider that you can get, say, an oaky Chardonnay from more than ten different countries, which will deliver you essentially the same flavour hit you're looking for, that approach begins to make sense.

On the white side …

OAKY CHARDONNAY

What grapes are we looking at? Chardonnay in the main, with a little bit of support from the likes of Sémillon and Grüner Veltliner.
From where, exactly? All over: Argentina, Australia, Chile, France (Burgundy, southern France), US (California), South Africa, New Zealand, Spain, Hungary, Bulgaria.
What do they taste like? Lemon, lime, pineapple, mango and lots of creamy oak.
Any other styles I might like? If you like oak and red wine, then Rioja is likely to be one of your favourites.
Most important thing to note? You like oak, so don't be ashamed of it.
And the cost? Oak isn't cheap, especially good oak. But, thanks to the likes of the Aussies, you should get good choice between £5 and £8, although places like California are more above the £10 mark for something decent.

If you like Chardonnay, then it means you probably like a variety of fruit flavours running from pure, classic lemon and lime from the likes of France and Italy, through to the more tropical pineapple and mango flavours you find in areas such as Australia, Argentina, New Zealand and California. But most importantly you like these fruit flavours wrapped in a velvety cloak of oak, all fresh cream, vanilla and butter.

Oak is what helps a good Chardonnay become a great Chardonnay, but it can make you love it or loathe it. Not so long ago, a lot of Chardonnays from the New World used to be all oak and no fruit – a factor that made them appealing to begin with, but one that has lost them fans. In recent years, however, winemakers have gone to great efforts to 'integrate' the oak better and make it a little more subtle, particularly in the New World.

Other grapes you might encounter in this style section would be the likes of Semillon, from Australia (not really Bordeaux) along with the little-known Grüner Veltliner from Austria, which can compare to the best of Burgundies, though it isn't always oaked, so be careful.

CLASSIC CHARDONNAY

What grapes are we looking at? Chardonnay, Grüner Veltliner, Sémillon.
From where, exactly? Australia, France (Chablis, Burgundy, Southern France, Bordeaux), Italy.
What do they taste like? Pure lemon and lime fruit, twinned with steel, mineral and stone.
Any other styles I might like? If you like this style, you're very likely to go for quite a few numbers in the clean and crisp category
Most important thing to note? If you prefer this to the above category, you're not big into oak, and you like your wines balanced, even and in no way in your face.
And the cost? Not much at around the £5–6 mark, much more in the £7–10 mark, and some excellent examples above.

The classic Chardonnay style is essentially the polar opposite of the oaky Chardonnay. If you like oaky Chardonnay you like a bit of flashiness, a bit of bravura. If you like classic Chardonnay style then you like subtlety, you like balance and you possibly like those flavours in Chardonnay that often get masked when oak is thrown into the equation. Chablis, for example, has what is generally referred to as a mineral or steely quality. It's what gives the wine its edge, its definition.

The problem with this style is that, without oak to cover up failings, a poor version is pretty obvious and perhaps a little more frequent, too. So it's the sort of style that invariably you have to end up paying a bit more for. As for the country range, obviously Chablis and certain pockets of Burgundy are on the cards, as is Austria (with Grüner Veltliner) and Sémillon from Bordeaux. You'll find some of this style in Australia, and it's increasing. And Italy currently produces some lovely Chardonnays that evoke that lovely minerally quality of good Chablis.

CLEAN AND CRISP WHITES

What grapes are we looking at? A wide range, from Sémillon and Chardonnay through Chenin Blanc to a host of Italian varieties, including Orvieto, Pinot Grigio, Verdicchio and Cortese. There are also the likes of Pinot Blanc and, of course, Muscadet.
From where, exactly? Again all over: Australia, Italy, Chile, South Africa, New Zealand, Southern France, Alsace.
What do they taste like? Wide range of fruit flavours, from lemon and lime, through tropical to crisp Granny Smith apples or fresh, juicy pears.

Any other styles I might like? Classic Chardonnay is one and, because of the racy, zippy nature many of these have, you may want to dip your toe into a kiwi Sauvignon Blanc.

Most important thing to note? You like plenty of zing in your wine and not a drop of oak in sight.

And the cost? You can pay £5 and get a great wine (no oak can equal great value) or you can spend well over a tenner. It's a wide-ranging style.

This style is summed up in three easy phrases: fruit flavour, fruit flavour and fruit flavour. You can chuck in a racy amount of acidity that give the wines a zing, and that's the total package – with oak definitely not invited to the party.

Of course, the beauty of the clean and crisp style is that there's a wide variety of grapes included and a pretty universal smattering of producers. So, for example, Italy makes the grade in a big way. Pinot Grigio, Orvieto, Gavi di Gavi (which is made from Cortese), Verdicchio – all of these make it in to the style category by leaps and bounds. Likewise Chenin Blanc from South Africa, with its crisp, crunchy, fresh apple fruit flavours, is a stalwart, as are unoaked New Zealand and Australian Chardonnays, not to mention the new wave of more delicate styles of white working their way out of the likes of Chile. Alsace gets in on the act with Pinot Blanc, a grape that teeters on the brink of fragrant but dry, yet manages to hold back on the aromatics to make it the perfect wine for this section with its fresh pear and peach fruit flavours, and zippy tartness.

Even with the more expensive wines in this style, what you're often getting are good, simple, well-made whites that stand on their own as the ideal aperitif wine, but are equally good when it comes to mixing with a bit of food.

KIWI SAUVIGNON BLANC STYLE

What grapes are we looking at? This is mainly Sauvignon Blanc with a touch of South African Chenin Blanc thrown in where appropriate, along with some Verdelho from Spain.

From where, exactly? Australia, New Zealand, South Africa, Chile, Loire (only the more modern styles) and Spain.

What do they taste like? Grass, asparagus, gooseberry aromas, combined with gooseberry and slightly tropical fruit flavours in the mouth, and lots of zing.

Any other styles I might like? This is pretty rare, although clean and crisp is a likely alternative, as is fragrant but dry.

Most important thing to note? If you like this style, you like two things. First that racy, zippy tartness that is otherwise known as acidity. Second, you like the fact that it has *lots* of gooseberry, so you like the fruit flavours. **And the cost?** For good New Zealand Sauvignon Blanc you won't get away with much less than £8–10, although if it's from South Africa and Australia you'll find prices a little more reasonable, even if quality isn't quite up to their Kiwi counterparts.

Compared with the traditional, classic style of Sauvignon, the Kiwi Sauvignon Blanc style is a relative whippersnapper. Perhaps the most famous example of this fruit-forward and zing-tastic style is the original Cloudy Bay, which burst onto the wine scene in the 1990s and took the people's taste buds hostage with its lovely gooseberry and fresh apple fruit flavours, wonderful length and powerful, ever-present zip.

And since then it's a style that's been widely imitated. South Africa is one prime example, where the Sauvignons are a little more grassy but no less intense or racy – and the Kiwi style has even inspired the country's winemakers to give the otherwise poor relation, Chenin Blanc, a new lease of life. Likewise, Australian Sauvignon Blancs used to be fairly flabby and unexciting, but, inspired by the Kiwis and with a bit more attention to where they've actually been growing the stuff, they're now producing some Sauvignons that give the likes of Cloudy Bay a run for their money.

The problem is that when they started, almost two decades ago, the prices for these wines were fairly reasonable. Now, it's often hard to get a really decent Sauvignon Blanc from the likes of New Zealand or Australia that doesn't actually cost something like its Old World counterpart, Sancerre from the Loire. South Africa and Chile provide a little better value – but it's still going to cost more than your average bottle of £4.99.

FRAGRANT BUT DRY WHITES

What grapes are we looking at? A whole bundle, really. There's Riesling, Gewürztraminer, Albariño, Pinot Blanc, Pinot Gris, Viognier, Roussanne, Marsanne, Malvasia, Verdelho and a whole lot more besides.
From where, exactly? All over including Germany, Australia, France (Alsace, Condrieu, Rhône), Spain, New Zealand, Portugal – the lot.
What do they taste like? All of them are extremely aromatic. Some smell of flowers, others peaches, some of apricots. They have very rich, intense fruits, from lemons in the case of Rieslings to apricots and white peaches in the case of Viognier. But, despite this richness of fruit, they all finish dry.

Any other styles I might like? The odd clean and crisp, plus Kiwi Sauvignon Blanc – another very aromatic category.

Most important thing to note? Sweet, luscious fruit flavours don't necessarily mean a sweet finish.

And the cost? A fiver will buy you something pretty basic, but just a couple of pounds more will take you to heaven and back.

This is one of the best examples of why choosing by style can introduce you to an incredibly wide choice of grape varieties, and a wonderfully diverse range of wine-producing countries. It can also encourage you to think differently about a category. Most people tend to shun German Rieslings, for instance, because they think they will all be sweet. And yet walk into a decent wine merchant's and ask for a fragrant but dry style of wine, and it wouldn't surprise me if a German Riesling turns out to be one of the suggestions.

For some people these wines will still be too intense, too perfumed, too exotic, but they offer a nice alternative to the big two, Chardonnay and Sauvignon Blanc.

CLASSIC SAUVIGNON BLANC

What grapes are we looking at? Essentially Sauvignon Blanc, with perhaps a little Chenin Blanc thrown in.

From where, exactly? Well, the most obvious is Sancerre and Pouilly Fumé, but there are other whites from the Loire, as well as the South of France, and even some New Zealand Sauvignons have turned their coats towards a more classic style.

What do they taste like? You've got heady, grassy, herbal notes on the nose, with a little of that 'classic' cat's-pee aroma (nice!). On the palate it's a mix of gooseberry, asparagus and fresh cucumber.

Any other styles I might like? You could always cross over to the dark side as far as the French are concerned and pick a Kiwi Sauvignon Blanc style of white off the shelf.

Most important thing to note? The style is dry but it's not fruit-led.

And the cost? Classic Sancerre and Pouilly Fumé usually start at around £10 and above. But you can get more reasonably priced versions from the South of France and South Africa.

It's a fairly narrow style category, this, but it's essentially for people who like their Sauvignon Blanc, or derivatives thereof, relatively understated and less in your face than the Kiwi style. Sancerre and Pouilly Fumé are the best known of this category. But there are some Chenin Blancs from South Africa that have similarly gone for this more classical style.

SWEET GERMAN STYLE

What grapes are we looking at? Rieslings, mainly, but also the odd
Gewürztraminer and perhaps a drop of Vouvray demi-sec.
From where, exactly? Germany (Mosel, Nahe, Pfalz), Austria, France
(Alsace, Loire).
What do they taste like? The typical wine in this style will have a Germanic
flavour profile, so crisp lemons possibly with some white peaches and the
odd apricot thrown in, all of which will be sweet and luscious and kept
perfectly in check by a lovely, racy zip and zing in the mouth.
Any other styles I might like? Little else matches, but it doesn't mean
to say you can't appreciate the odd dry style, too.
Most important thing to note? Sweet in this category does not mean
sickly. Nor does it mean dessert wine. Many of these are drunk as aéritifs
before dinner.
And the cost? The decent ones certainly aren't cheap. You're looking
at around £10 or more.

For those who think this is some nod to the 70s, think again. The
German style of sweet apéritif wines has been around for centuries,
and the problem is that most people get them mixed up with two things.
First, Liebfraumilch, which, while German and sweet, is not the same
thing. Second, dessert wines, which are not stickies but are wines that
have not had all the alcohol fermented out of them, although, thanks
to their acidity, they don't appear nearly as sweet as they really are.

In the case of the German Rieslings, most of the good-quality ones
can be very refreshing when drunk on a hot summer's day.

And now for the reds …

CLASSIC REDS

What grapes are we looking at? Cabernet Sauvignon, Merlot, Cabernet Franc, Pinot Noir, Syrah, and some Barbera thrown in for good measure.
From where, exactly? Mainly the likes of France (Bordeaux, Burgundy, Rhône, Loire) but also from Italy, and there are some New World Australians, Californians and even some from Washington State.
What do they taste like? It's less the specific flavours or aromas with this category, but rather the overall impression. These wines are traditional wines, perhaps a little tight, a little reserved, holding on to their full potential for years to come. Also, they are the perfect evocation of their surroundings or *terroir* and probably require significant ageing.
Any other styles I might like? Virtually all the others, but you might have to let your taste buds break through a few barriers to enjoy them fully.
Most important thing to note? That there could be a whole load of new wines out their that you're missing out on.
And the cost? Not cheap, usually. Around £8 and above for something decent, expressive and worth waiting for.

The classic red style is less defined than most others here, mainly because it's more of a fallout for the wines that don't hit any of the other categories. That sounds awful, but it's not meant to be. Think of it this way. If you took a bottle of Château Latour from Bordeaux, or perhaps an excellent Côte-Rôtie from the Rhône, you'd find it difficult to place them in the other categories. Somebody is hardly going to pop their head into the local wine merchant asking for something full and fruity, and expect to be offered a bottle of Latour priced at £100 or more. But they might expect to be offered a decent claret for around £8–10, or perhaps a good basic Côtes du Rhône. That's why you'd classify some New World contenders in this category – the top-of-the-pile Australian Shirazes and Cabernets for a starter; California's Cabernets are another, along with some Pinot Noirs from somewhere like Oregon. All have those classic, long-ageing, big-potential characteristics that tend to suggest that, rather than be categorised as 'classic reds', they should perhaps be reclassified as 'Not to be drunk tonight or any other night for a decade or so'.

FULL AND FRUITY

What grapes are we looking at? Barbera, Cabernet Sauvignon, Carmenère, Garnacha, Malbec, Merlot, Nebbiolo, Shiraz, Syrah, Tempranillo.
From where, exactly? Australia, Chile, Argentina, Eastern Europe, South of France, Spain, California, Italy, South Africa.
What do they taste like? There are various degrees of taste, but importantly the fruit flavours tend to be a mix of red and black – so fresh blackcurrants, redcurrants, plums, damsons, the odd mulberry and blueberry. Most will have been hit with oak, so you can expect some cream and vanilla characteristics as well.
Any other styles I might like? If you like full and fruity, you're just one step away from huge, so go on and take the plunge.
Most important thing to note? That these wines have a decent balance of alcohol, fruit and oak. They're big, but they're not monsters and they lead from the front with fruit.
And the cost? Real mixture, so you should be able to find one at your price, however low or high that is, but most decent ones will weigh in between £6.99 and £9.99.

The full and fruity style is essentially for people who want big, ripe, chewy fruit flavours to gnaw on during their crucial drinking time. They don't want overpowering tannins, yet weakness is not an option. They want their taste buds beguiled rather than assaulted. That's why you tend to find the newer wave of Australian winemakers in here with their Cabernets, Merlots and Pinot Noirs; most of the traditionalists are firmly in the 'huge' camp, rooting their blockbuster Shiraz on to victory with its big tannins and powerful oak character.

'Full and fruity' also tends to include those top-level Chianti, Vino da Tavola (Italy) and even the odd Riojas that have gone for a more international style.

Another way of describing this style is to say that it provides instant gratification in the mouth.

HUGE REDS

What grapes are we looking at? Cabernet Sauvignon, Malbec, Montepulciano, Nebbiolo, Pinotage, Primitivo, Shiraz, Syrah, Touriga Nacional.
From where, exactly? Australia, Argentina, Chile, Eastern Europe, France, California, Italy, Portugal, South Africa.

What do they taste like? Very dark, intense berry-fruit flavours. All blackcurrants, black cherries, damsons, plums, stewed figs and the odd prune-like quality. 'Broody' is a good description.

Any other styles I might like? Full and fruity is as good a compromise as any.

Most important thing to note? They're huge and that means the tannins, too. In fact *especially* the tannins, so prepare the mouthwash now.

And the cost? How long is a piece of string? You can get a decent drop for a fiver, but easily spend £50 on a decent Côte-Rôtie.

If you check whether your red is above 13% ABV, it suggests that you're a huge-red sort of a person.

While it's a category that's open to a wide mix of different grape varieties, it's principally dedicated to three: Shiraz, often from Australia and occasionally from South Africa; Syrah, from the Rhône; and Cabernet from a host of regions, including California, Australia, Chile and Argentina. Bringing up the rear, however, are grapes such as Zinfandel, Nebbiolo and Barbera – all of which have the capacity to administer an almighty punch to mouth. Likewise, Malbec from Argentina is increasingly giving as good as it gets in this style category and emerging as one of the key choices when you take the decision to 'go huge'. And then there's something like Primitivo, reportedly the father of California's Zinfandel, or Portugal's Touriga Nacional, both of which make stunningly intense and certainly huge wines at times.

But what defines a huge wine? Well, the fruits tend to veer towards the dark and intense and are backed up by fearsome tannins that have come from a long soak on the grape skins, followed by a significant time in barrels – giving them extra structure, pepper and a very rich, spicy kick. It's a style that needs big hunks of freshly roasted meat to do it justice. It's not a sipper.

SOFT AND JUICY REDS

What grapes are we looking at? Barbera, Cabernet Franc, Corvina, Gamay, Grenache, Merlot, Pinot Noir, Sangiovese, Tempranillo.

From where, exactly? Australia, Argentina, California, Chile, France (South of France, Loire, Burgundy), Italy, New Zealand, South Africa.

What do they taste like? These reds have quite a cherry-and-raspberry-scented nose, which often follows through on to the palate. The fruit flavours are relatively red-dominated, so redcurrants, red cherries, raspberries etc., all with one thing in common: a lovely soft, rich, juicy style of fruit.

Any other styles I might like? Full and fruity at a push, lunchtime reds definitely.

Most important thing to note? They ain't heavy – in flavour terms at least.

And the cost? Pretty widespread range of prices. You can get a lot of satisfaction with a fiver – but spend more than a tenner and you have to seriously consider your perspective on money.

Soft and juicy doesn't mean light. But it does mean this style is essentially there to be drunk and there to be enjoyed to the full. Usually the flavours are dominated by red fruits, and there are medium tannins, but there's also a pretty good shot of racy acidity, making these reds not only pleasant to drink on their own but also great with a wide variety of food dishes.

Some countries and regions are better than others at this style. California can be a little lame above the £6 mark, for instance, while New Zealand tends to do the soft very well, but is less good at the juicy. Chile is more or less perfect with the traditional varieties, making some excellent soft and juicy Merlots and Cabernets, but Italy is the one that excels. From mid-weight Barbera in the Piedmont to the lighter Sangioveses from Tuscany, through the 'rossos' from the Marches and down to the delicious reds from Sicily and Sardinia, it offers almost a job lot of soft and juicy. Also the reds from La Mancha, Spain's largest but least well-known wine-producing region, are sometimes really stunning, though hunting them down can be a little difficult. Naturally, though, the big daddy of them all is Australia, especially around the £5 mark, where the country has carved out a niche, including soft and juicy wines, with an emphasis on fruit-forward flavours.

One handy way of finding out whether the bottle in your hand may be truly soft and juicy is to have a quick look at the alcohol content. If it's around 12 to 13% ABV, it stands a good chance of being that way.

LUNCHTIME REDS

What grapes are we looking at? Barbera d'Asti, Cabernet Sauvignon, Dolcetto, Gamay, Grignolino (Piedmont), Merlot, Pinot Noir, Sangiovese, Tempranillo

From where, exactly? Argentina, Australia, Chile, France (Beaujolais, Burgundy), Italy, New Zealand.

What do they taste like? The emphasis is on relatively low-alcohol wines but with peppy, bright and light fruit flavours – again redcurrants, cherries and strawberries.

Any other styles I might like? Soft and juicy will work just as well.
Most important thing to note? Just because it's light in style, it doesn't mean it has to be of poor quality. If it is, take it back to the merchant or send it back in the restaurant.
And the cost? Not too much, really. A decent bottle should cost between £5 and £7. Much more than £10 and you're probably beginning to miss the point and waste your money.

There used to be terms used in English gentlemen's clubs around the land several years ago, including the likes of a 'luncheon claret', and a 'luncheon cognac'. The idea was that these were slightly lighter than the normal tipples that were reserved for evening encounters.

These days most of us lead hectic lives, and sipping a couple of glasses of red at lunch without falling face first onto our computer keyboard in the afternoon is usually quite welcomed by all but hacks and journos. That's why this category is essentially the same as the soft and juicy, but with a little less edge and a little less poke.

A prime example is something like Beaujolais, with its sweet, luscious but relatively lightweight Gamay fruit, guaranteed to give you an up without the usual inevitable down. Pinot Noir is another – if made in a mid-weight style, so something like a Burgundy Villages is absolutely ideal. Likewise Italian Merlots, very young Chianti and basic '*joven*' (young) Riojas all make the grade for this style, as do relatively inexpensive New World Pinot Noirs.

RIOJA-STYLE REDS

What grapes are we looking at? In this case, just Tempranillo.
From where, exactly? Rioja, although similar things are done in Ribera del Duero and other parts of Spain, and you can get Tempranillo in California and Australia.
What do they taste like? Classic Rioja tastes of fresh strawberries and raspberries that have been wrapped up in oak and given a creamy, vanilla-scented and -flavoured bath. As they age for longer, the oak component gets more intense and dominant.
Any other styles I might like? Anything oaky – full and fruity and huge reds will probably have something suitable.
Most important thing to note? Rioja may be a region, but it's also a state of mind and mouth.
And the cost? You can get an excellent basic Rioja or Rioja-style wine for as little as £4.99, but can easily spend well over £20 on some of finest exponents of the style.

Why, I hear you ask, is there a specific regional category after all my hectoring about freeing the mind and exploring by style rather than geography? Well, put simply, Rioja is in many cases in a class of its own. It has a unique flavour profile, thanks to the tradition of ageing the wines in oak for a significant period of time. The funny thing is that many wines that appear in the Rioja section will also appear in other style categories, and yet it doesn't happen the other way round, because few other grape varieties and regions combine to offer the same or even a similar product to Rioja. Ribera del Duero is one, as are a number of sites outside Spain, such as California and Australia. By no means are these Tempranillos better than Rioja, but they are different and bring something else to the party. Rioja's greatest strength is that it tends to have the most fantastic racy acidity, which makes it the perfect food wine.

Something Fizzy …

CLASSIC FIZZ

What grapes are we looking at? Chardonnay, Pinot Noir, Pinot Meunier.
From where, exactly? Champagne, but also Australia and New Zealand.
What do they taste like? This one's difficult, but champagne tends to have slightly more structure, complexity and, with age, richness than a more modern style of fizz. So after a couple of years, as well as the fresh lemon and apple fruit flavours, you're also getting a toasty aroma, with quite rich, freshly baked dough and yeast flavours.
Any other styles I might like? Give modern fizz a try.
Most important thing to note? Classic is coming out across the world, not just in champagne.
And the cost? Not cheap!

When I use the term 'classic fizz', I do of course mean, 99 per cent of the time, what comes from Champagne – the French region whence the eponymous and original fizz hails. However, if we just classified this as a champagne sector that would be misleading. These days if you asked for a classic fizz, and explained exactly what you meant, you could as easily be handed a vintage New World fizz as you could something from Champagne. And that's because the winemakers in the New World are adopting and adapting more techniques from their Champagne counterparts, and turning out very good fizz with it as well.

MODERN FIZZ

What grapes are we looking at? In some cases the classic Chardonnay, Pinot Noir, Pinot Meunier mix, but there's also Chenin Blanc, Xarel-Lo and Parellada, not to mention Shiraz.

From where, exactly? Australia, California, France (Loire), Italy, Spain (Cava), New Zealand.

What do they taste like? It varies, but they tend to be much more fruit-driven than champagne, with less emphasis on structure and more emphasis on creating an instant impression in the mouth.

Any other styles I might like? Try classic fizz if you have the money.

Most important thing to note? You're not buying champagne, so it's wise not to pretend otherwise to all and sundry.

And the cost? Anything from a £5 up to £15 – once you're past £15, you may as well start going for the classic style of fizz.

The great thing about fizz these days is that it really has become an everyday drink, and the New World, in particular Australia, has been a big part of that – though not as big a part as somewhere like Spain, where for a long time Cava has undercut virtually every other fizz on the market. The point is, though, that you can get great bubbles these days for a fraction of the price of champagne, making it something you can afford to experiment with.

The perfect example is sparkling Shiraz from down under. Not something most people have had a crack at, but, with the right hot day, a barbecue blazing and the bottle slightly chilled, it's something a lot of people fall instantly in love with. The beauty of modern fizz is that it's not pretentious. It's just a mouth of lovely, luscious fruit, from crunchy apple or fresh lemons through to pineapple and mango, that happens to have bubbles in it as an added, refreshing bonus.

Last but not least …

There are stickies and fortified wines. Now there's not much point in separating them out into styles for one obvious reason: unlike Cabernet, which is made across the globe, drinks such as port or Madeira or sherry are exceptionally region-specific. Likewise, when it comes to something like Sauternes, you can't really get away with pretending that there's a similar sticky the other side of the world that could add up to a new style category.

However, for both these sets of wines, the same theory goes as what we've seen above in terms of experimentation. Take the time to try something different, because you need to give the variety of styles a go. Port may be your favourite fortified tipple, but, unless you've had a crack at a good Madeira, you haven't really lived. Likewise, you may love a nice Barsac from Bordeaux or a Beerenauslese from Germany to finish off a meal, but, if you haven't tried a decent late-harvest Riesling from down under, then you don't know what you're missing.

chapter twelve
wine by grape

Grapes are wine; wine is grapes. It's really that simple. Without grapes there wouldn't be any wine. But how much of a wine's character does a grape contribute? How key is it to the flavour, style and quality of a wine? Well, the easiest way I can think of to explain the overriding importance of the grape in the wine is to consider that the grape is to a bottle of wine what DNA is to the human body and character. True, a winemaker can shape a wine in much the same way as we are shaped by – among other things – our surroundings and our family as we grow up. He can use oak, stainless steel and any number of methods to subtly alter the grapes' character, to mature it, to turn it into the model wine, but at the heart of it will always be the distinctive and singular DNA of the grape. Only when things have gone horribly wrong will that DNA be eradicated – and that's probably a wine you don't want to drink too much of.

And, if there is one area that will help you most in working out which wines you love and which wines you loathe, it will be understanding grapes. Grasp the essential differences between the dozen or so major white and red wine grape varieties and you can more or less shop with confidence, whether it's in your local supermarket or the most upper-class of wine merchants. Here I've gone into detail about the main star attractions of the grape world, and given a brief rundown of their fellow supporting actors. I haven't even covered the tip of the iceberg in terms of the hundreds if not thousands of clones and variations that exist. For instance, it is to my great regret that I have no room to talk about the highly amusing Portuguese variety known as Bastardo – oh how I've longed for the opportunity to offer a glass of that across the table to someone I'm not overly keen on. But space is limited, and you'll find everything you need here to really kick-start your passion for the grape world, including a handy hint on how to pronounce them all – even the most difficult tongue-twisters among them.

Great whites

THE MAIN ATTRACTIONS

CHARDONNAY

Despite the best efforts of the TV drama *Footballers' Wives*, Chardonnay is not the name of a waif-thin bit of fluff on a footballer's cuff, but rather the name of the big daddy of white grape varieties. There is virtually nowhere on this planet that it isn't planted – certainly nowhere that has grapes as one of its major crops – and it's the variety at the source of some of the world's greatest wines. The majority of great white Burgundy is made from Chardonnay; Chablis is exclusively Chardonnay; champagne uses Chardonnay as one of its principal varieties; Chile made its name with Chardonnay; some of California's most expensive and sought-after wines are made from Chardonnay; Italy, especially in the north, makes superb wines with Chardonnay; England plants it with some success; even the normally neutral Swiss are big fans of the grape – and the list goes on and on.

Why is it so dominant? Well, probably its versatility has something to do with it. It takes to most climates, produces a half-decent wine in most regions and gives even the laziest of winemakers a relatively easy time, if they want it. More importantly, though, its homeland, Burgundy, has forged its reputation as the grape behind one of the finest wines in the world – so it's no surprise that many other winemakers across the globe want to get in on the act and emulate such greatness.

What's also wonderful about the grape is that, because it has such a diversity of sources, there is an infinite variety of styles. It can be wooded or unwooded, depending on the winemaker's preference of the quality being produced, Chablis being the perfect example of an unwooded Chardonnay. If it comes from the New World (Australia, New Zealand, South Africa etc.), it could be more tropical in terms of fruit flavours – lots of pineapple and mango. If it comes from the Old World (e.g. Burgundy, Italy, Spain), it tends to display the more classic citrus fruit flavours of lemon and lime. And that means you could litereally spend the majority of your years working your way through Chardonnay and still keep on turning up new and exciting versions. The downside of that, of course, is that you'll also have to work your way through quite a few duff ones while you're at it.

How does it go again? Shar-dun-ay.
Where do I find it? Everywhere.

What does it taste like? Chardonnay can run the gamut from lemon and lime citrus fruit through to a full range of tropical flavours, from pineapple through mango and guava, depending on where it's from. Old World tends towards the former, New World towards the latter.
Tell me something I didn't know: For a long time Chardonnay was mistaken for a white bastardisation of Pinot Noir. Also, it's so far spread in wine-growing terms that you can even find examples from both the Lebanon and Israel. Not that you necessarily want to, but if the mood takes you ...

RIESLING
Riesling is a classic German grape variety that has spread itself across the globe with the same enthusiasm as Chardonnay but not necessarily the same success. If Chardonnay is the Big Daddy, however – loved by everyone outside the ring – Riesling is the Giant Haystacks. It may not always triumph, but in stature and potential it's always been the professional's favourite.

Germany is of course the major source for Riesling – though a lot of the Riesling that has made its way over here in the past has been in the form of Liebfraumilch or Piesporter, so the impression given has never been the most positive one. However there are both dry and sweet versions produced in Germany and in neighbouring Alsace in France that would surprise the average wine drinker with their power, finesse and downright deliciousness. Elsewhere in the world, Riesling is being picked up as the newest next big thing – with Australia, New Zealand and even California and Chile getting in on the act, and producing some mouthwatering versions.

One of the delights of Riesling is that again, like Chardonnay, because it is planted in so many different places, the range of flavours and characteristics is wide. From Germany you can expect dry Rieslings with a slightly mineral (a bit like biting on slate) or oily texture to them, while the sweeter versions develop more honeyed, nutty tones. From the likes of Australia or New Zealand you get very limey, citrus-fruit-driven styles. In all, though, the sign of a good Riesling, dry or sweet, is a good chunk of bite or zing – otherwise known as acidity, but easier to understand as that zip at the finish of a white wine that lets you know there's life in it. It's also, incidentally, what makes Riesling a very versatile food wine.
How does it go again? Rees-ling.
Where do I find it? Germany, Austria, Alsace, Australia, New Zealand, California, Hungary.
What does it taste like? Firmly citrus-based, so that's freshly cut lemon

and lime fruit flavours, though some can have a more green-apple quality to them and in the New World you can even get the odd hint of pineapple creeping in. It is almost never oaked because it is such an aromatic variety, so it's great if you like unoaked whites.

Tell me something I didn't know: Two decades ago in Australia lots of winemakers ripped up Riesling vines and replanted them with Chardonnay. Twenty years on they're doing exactly the reverse. It's a funny old world.

SAUVIGNON BLANC

As with Chardonnay, Sauvignon Blanc's historical homeland is in France, where it made the names Sancerre and Pouilly-Fumé famous. In these two instances, Sauvignon forged itself a reputation as the source of two of the world's finest dry white wine styles. And then the New Zealanders got hold of it, Cloudy Bay came along and Sancerre and Pouilly-Fumé have been playing catch-up ever since in the popularity stakes.

Sauvignon Blanc is one of the most distinctive grapes around, both in aroma and in flavour. It's almost instantly recognisable, even for the newest of wine buffs, with its freshly cut grass and gooseberry nose. In classic Sancerre you even get what they call a whiff of cat's pee – a slightly ammonia-like, powerful scent. It's not really a description that I would use for such a lovely grape, but, hey, whatever floats your boat.

What Cloudy Bay Sauvignon Blanc, and a host of others from New Zealand during the 90s, did was prove that the New World could take a grape variety that had been grown for centuries in the Old World, and give it a new lease of life. They emphasised the fruity, forward nature of the grape and illustrated how the New World could give structure (i.e. balanced zip, or acidity) as well as flavour to a wine.

Like Riesling, Sauvignon is rarely oaked, but there are one or two versions in California, known as Fumé Blanc, where this occurs. Generally, it doesn't work all that well. Sauvignon is a grape variety that is designed to be drunk young, very young – with most versions being consumed within a year of their 'birth', and few designed to age.

How does it go again? So-veen-yohn-blohn (the last syllable should be pronounced as French, with that twang of nasality).

Where do I find it? The Loire (Sancerre, Quincy, Pouilly-Fumé), Bordeaux, Southern France, Northeastern Italy, Australia, Chile, New Zealand, California and South Africa.

What does it taste like? You'll find all sorts here, but gooseberries dominate, along with some asparagus flavours, elderflower and often a nice limey edge.

Tell me something I didn't know: Sauvignon is often blended with Sémillon, especially in Australia, where the two are combined to make dry wines. In Bordeaux, however, Sauvignon and Sémillon combine to make one of the world's best dessert wines: sauternes.

SÉMILLON

Most people won't know Sémillon from semantics, but this rather humble grape variety, which is often hidden in blends, is responsible for some of the best wines in the world. It's the main ingredient in the deliciously sweet dessert wine, sauternes, but produces fantastically dry whites next door in the Graves region of Bordeaux. In Australia it combines with Chardonnay to make some fantastically fruity, easy-drinking wines, but is also at the heart of some its longest-living whites from the famous Hunter Valley region. And in Chile it comes into its own as the main variety behind the bulk of the country's basic white wines. However, most people wouldn't have it on their list of grape 'stars'.

The reason it is so popular as a blending grape is that it is a relatively high-acid wine. As we've seen, acidity is what gives a white its pep, its zip and zing. It's what makes it tingle slightly in the mouth. It's also essential in balancing out fruit flavours, and a must when it comes to either propping up grape varieties such as Chardonnay (which can often have lots of great fruit, but not enough acidity). Also, when producing sweet wines, you need that zing to cleanse the palate of any stickiness. In many ways it acts as the 'first grip' or 'chief gaffer' in the credits of a film. You'll see it on the label, but never really know it's there or fully give it credit. But you should.

How does it go again? Sem-ee-yohn (that French nasal sound again).

Where do I find it? Bordeaux (Sauternes, Graves, Pessac-Léognan), southern France, Australia, South Africa.

What does it taste like? When it's very young, you get a pure lime flavour, almost like drinking neat Rose's Lime Juice, but this turns into a lemon and honey concoction as it ages. And with the sweeter versions it takes on an almost pure, runny, honey, nature – the sort that used to get Pooh very, very excited.

Tell me something I didn't know: In the early 1800s only 7 per cent of South Africa's vineyard area *wasn't* Sémillon.

GEWÜRZTRAMINER

It's difficult to pronounce, sounds vaguely like a German term for your rear axle and has an umlaut over the 'u', all of which makes Gewürztraminer one of the most difficult grapes to fall in love with. And, to be honest, it's a great variety but one that splits opinion right down the middle. Some people love its fragrant, floral smell – all white jasmine, rose petal and lychees – but others quite comfortably loathe it. Some adore its pungent oily white peach and apricot flavours while others won't even think of giving it the time of day.

'Gewürz' means 'spice' in German and that's exactly what you get: a nice kick of white pepper and a clean-cut zing on the finish of a decent version of the grape.

It's homeland is Germany, though it is actually planted far more in the French region of Alsace, which specialises in its cultivation. But, unlike Riesling, it isn't quite as well travelled as fans of it would like. Australia and New Zealand are currently experimenting with the odd version and I've tasted some great ones from Washington state in vineyards just above Seattle, but generally it's best sourced from Germany or Alsace, with the odd one from Austria thrown in for good measure.

How does it go again? Guh-vurtz-tram-in-ner.

Where do I find it? Alsace, Germany, Austria, Australia, New Zealand, Washington state and California.

What does it taste like? A mixed bag. In the main, white peach, lychees, with a touch of honey, though sometimes it can be more pineapple. Good racy zip to it and a spiciness as the last drop from each mouthful slips down the gullet.

Tell me something I didn't know: While it makes excellent white wine, the grape itself has a slightly pinkish tinge to its skin.

CHENIN BLANC

Sémillon may often be ignored and underappreciated but, compared with Chenin Blanc, it is practically the high school prom queen. Chenin Blanc's history, as with so many of these classic varieties, lies in France, specifically in the Loire, where it makes some of the most underrated wines to emerge from that great wine-producing country, eclipsed as they are by the flashiness of Burgundy and the gravity of Bordeaux. However, Chenin is the ultimate in versatility when it comes to winemaking.

It makes the most amazingly long-lived sweet wines – for example, Vouvray can be turned into delicious sparkling wine such as Crémant de Loire – and is used to produce everything from cheap and cheerful jug wine to top-class whites in its second home from home, South Africa. It was originally brought to that country as long ago as 1655 and has thrived ever since.

How does it go again? Shun-nahn blohn (remember the French nasal sound).

Where do I find it? The Loire (France), South Africa, New Zealand, California.

What does it taste like? Lemon mixed with soft, succulent peach fruit flavours, laced with a honeyed edge in the dessert versions, and in older wines a slightly nutty quality. Always quite high in acid, giving it great ageing potential, but often a little too zesty.

Tell me something I didn't know: There's a dark-berried version called Chenin Noir – but finding it is the equivalent of finding the crock of gold at the end of the rainbow.

MUSCAT

This is the scarlet pimpernel of the grape world. It has so many variations, so many pseudonyms and spin-offs that it's often difficult to tell what particular strain of Muscat a grape actually is – one is permanently seeking Muscat here, there and everywhere.

What's not difficult to spot, however, is the unique musky, grapey, pungent smell that emanates from a wine made with Muscat or the honeyed flavours that are usually translated to the mouth, in either sweet or dry versions. Mostly, though, Muscat is used to make semisweet or dessert wines, partly because of its good acid properties, but mainly because it just produces the most deliciously sweet juice when pressed and turned into wine.

The most common and most ancient variety of Muscat is Muscat Blanc à Petits Grains, which bizarrely has three different-coloured variations, producing pink, red and even black berries, most of which are used in the production of white wines (the skins are removed to prevent coloration of the juice). There are three other major varieties: Muscat Hamburg, Muscat of Alexandria and straight Muscat, which actually produces table grapes, rather than wine. In most cases, however, when you pick a bottle off the supermarket shelf, it will simply read Muscat.

How does it go again? Mus-cat.

Where do I find it? All over France, Greece, Australia, California, Italy, South Africa, North Africa.

What does it taste like? It's one of the few grapes that actually *taste* of grapes; throw in some honey, apricots and nuts and you're there.

Tell me something I didn't know: It's one of the only specific grape varieties that were referred to in written text in ancient Greece. Pliny the Elder had a bit of a penchant for Muscat.

VIOGNIER

This has been around for some considerable time, but only really started picking up fans in the mid- to late 1990s. It's traditional home is the northern Rhône, where it's used to produce some superb wines in Condrieu, Château-Grillet and Côte-Rôtie. In the Côte-Rôtie it's actually used as a pep-up for Syrah, adding perfume and giving a slightly softer edge to the overall nature – so in essence it's a white grape used to bolster a red.

As with everything else, the Australians have taken up the cause and are now producing some great affordable Viogniers. Their wines make the most of the grape's mind-blowing perfume and its very sexy peach and apricot fruit flavours, nearly always rounded off with a nice touch of honey. South Africa is also tipping a nod to the grape as a potentially interesting variety to make its mark with.

How does it go again? Vee-yon-yay.

Where do I find it? France (northern Rhône and Languedoc-Roussillon), Australia, South Africa.

What does it taste like? Take a splodge of apricot jam, add a hint of honey, a touch of cream and big chunk of alcohol and, bang, you've got magic.

Tell me something I didn't know: You can find it in Brazil – not a nation known for its avid wine production but rather an obsession with wearing ridiculously short bikinis.

THE BEST SUPPORTING ACTS

ALBARIÑO

How does it go again? Al-ba-reen-yo.

In brief: Found in Northern Spain, mainly, in Galicia and in particular around the Rías Baixas zone. Makes deliciously fruity, quite zesty whites that are great food partners, especially when paired with a wide variety of delicious tapas from boquerones through to a nice spicy chorizo. If you think fresh apples combined with a squeeze of lime sounds lovely, then this is the chap for you.

ALVARINHO

How does it go again? Al-va-reen-yo.

In brief: The Portuguese version of Albariño, grown in mainly in the north of the country. Has a very similar flavour profile, though it's often a little more tart and higher in alcohol. Is used most widely in production of that great Portuguese white table wine Vinho Verde, which is most often compared – rather unfairly, I think – to drinking car battery acid. It's got a lot better in recent years, though.

ALIGOTÉ
How does it go again? Alee-got-y.
In brief: Among white grapes this is the second-in-command to
Chardonnay in Burgundy, where it makes quite spicy, nervy, zippy whites
with a more apple and even grapefruit zing rather than Chardonnay's
lemon tang. A nice, overlooked and underrated wine.

MANSENG
How does it go again? Man-seng.
In brief: No, not a Chinese variety despite its very oriental-sounding name,
but rather a grape of Basque origins that is grown principally in the Jurançon
region of the French Alps. There are too versions, Gros and Petit Manseng. The
flavours are quite close to Viognier, with peach, apricot and citrus fruits all
abounding. It is very tangy – which means it makes great food-friendly wines.

MARSANNE
How does it go again? Mar-sann.
In brief: Lovely variety, this – usually used in the south of France,
principally in Languedoc-Roussillon, where it is blended with Roussanne
and occasionally Viognier. If you're looking for something that tastes
of pure peach juice, with a slightly oily, fat texture thrown in for good
measure, this is the grape to go for.

PINOT BLANC
How does it go again? Pee-no blohn.
In brief: Used to be big in Burgundy, but now is used to make a small amount
of zippy, creamy, apple-rich aperitif whites in Alsace – no oak, no messing,
just good, clean fun. You can find it in some far-flung places: Northern Italy,
Pacific northwest of the USA and quite a lot of central Europe.

PINOT BIANCO
How does it go again? Pee-no bee-an-ko.
In brief: The Italian variety of Pinot Blanc, but usually made in a more
acidic and not always attractive manner. A lot is made in the Trentino area
of northeast Italy, where some is even given a slight spritz. Lots of lovely
fresh green apple flavours when well made.

PINOT GRIGIO

How does it go again? Pee-no gridge-eeo.
In brief: This is the Italian version of the next grape on the list, Pinot Gris, from France. It's also possibly the best known of all the white Pinot varieties. When on form, Pinot Grigio can range from pure lemon and lime through apples, to a little bit of peachiness, depending on how the winemakers handled it – but essentially it's always dry, and always has a fair zip to it.

PINOT GRIS

How does it go again? Pee-no gree.
In brief: The French variety that is the daddy grape to many of the white Pinots. Gris is a very perfumed variety, with lots of white lily and honey blossom tweaks. In fruit terms it's a mixture of apricots and peach with a touch of lime juice added at the last minute. At its best, it's very inviting.

ROUSSANNE

How does it go again? Roo-sann.
In brief: A bosom buddy of Marsanne in the Languedoc-Rousillon region, Roussanne is prized in principle for its aromatic qualities. Lovely apricot flavours make it a good match for Viognier but you'll rarely see the grape on its own because it doesn't tend to have enough body or richness, and is notoriously difficult to manage in poor weather conditions.

TOKAY-PINOT GRIS

How does it go again? Tock-eye pee-no gree.
In brief: Traditional name is Tokay d'Alsace, but, thanks to a bit of good old inter-regional rivalry with the likes of Hungary (which cultivates Hungarian Tokay), it was renamed Tokay-Pinot Gris – on account of its being part of the Pinot Gris family. This is very honeyed, very perfumed and has a nice racy style.

Cool reds

THE MAIN ATTRACTIONS

CABERNET SAUVIGNON

With the exception of Burgundy, there's hardly a wine region in the globe that has neither got Cabernet planted nor has had it planted in the past. Like Chardonnay, it's actually an incredibly adaptable grape. It won't always produce the best wine a region could, but it'll usually produce something decent and drinkable as long as it's been cared for correctly.

Previously, the best-known evocation of Cabernet was in the form of traditional claret from Bordeaux – and for decades the definition of a good claret was tannin, a bit more tannin, perhaps some acidity and a bit more tannin. Ageability was what they were after, not fruit.

The Australians took Cabernet and made its fruit shine forth, at a fraction of the price. Many of Bordeaux's winemakers have now followed suit, which means a good Cabernet, whether from the Old or New World, has proper pure, concentrated blackcurrant fruit flavours and lovely intense deep colouring and, depending on how much you've splashed out, a whole lot more besides. There's no doubt about it, Cabernet has a great ability to age if handled correctly. That means it should have a good tannic structure, a decent balance of acidity and lots of sweet, rich, luscious fruit flavours – all in perfect harmony. The problem with a lot of Cabernet from both Old and New Worlds is that it can be quite 'green', or 'leafy', which usually denotes that it's been picked and pressed too young.

Above all, though, Cabernet is a team player – at its best when mixed with a drop of Merlot, or Cabernet Franc, the two other main varieties traditionally grown in Bordeaux. This classic mix has also been exported globally, and, while you'll find some 'pure' Cabernet, the vast majority usually has these two characters as a 'support network'.

How does it go again? Cab-er-nay so-veen-yohn.

Where do I find it? Almost everywhere, though Bordeaux still produces more Cabernet Sauvignon in the form of classic claret than any other region in the world.

What does it taste like? Blackcurrant, blackcurrant and more blackcurrant. With more complex versions you'll get some minty edges, a touch of smokiness, possibly hints of cedarwood (the stuff that cigars in tubes are wrapped in) and often a streak of dark chocolate.

Tell me something I didn't know: In the early seventeenth century it used to be called Vidure. Not exactly the sexiest name in the world.

MERLOT

This is one of the three classic Bordeaux partners in crime that include the aforementioned Cabernet Sauvignon and the lesser-known Cabernet Franc. There's currently a Merlot mania sweeping the globe, and part of the reason is that it is the principal grape variety used in two of Bordeaux's most famous communes, St-Emilion and Pomerol. Nearly everywhere else in Bordeaux, Cabernet Sauvignon is usually the dominant grape variety in any blend. In St-Emilion and Pomerol, Merlot's the daddy. And the softer, more luscious, immediately appealing wines from these two communes have shown the world that Merlot has as much character as its partner, Cabernet.

The problem with Merlot is that it is a little more fragile than Cabernet, and not as suited to such a wide variety of climates. This means that, while the world has attempted to re-create its success in St-Emilion and Pomerol, the results have not always been quite what they should have been.

But, when it's on form, it's a winner, which is why it's also beginning to find popularity in places such as Italy and Spain – two countries that have traditionally shunned France's grape base in favour of their own. Again, however, it can be prone to the same 'greenness' that Cabernet can suffer if picked too early. And, like Cabernet, it's usually at its best with a little help from its friends. Even the tiniest drop of Cabernet Sauvignon or Cabernet Franc can add that extra bit of life to a good Merlot.

How does it go again? Mer-low.

Where do I find it? Bordeaux is the homeland, but it's grown across France. South Africa, Australia, California, the Pacific Northwest, Chile, Italy, Spain.

What does it taste like? We're talking delicious blackberry and dark cherry fruit flavours, which often have a lovely vein of milk chocolate underpinning them, making a good juicy Merlot a rather naughty indulgence. More often than not it is wood-aged, like Cabernet, so you get quite a smoky, oaky, savoury edge to it.

Tell me something I didn't know: Château Pétrus, reputedly the most expensive top-class Bordeaux red, is made with mainly Merlot – which is nice.

PINOT NOIR

Opinions differ widely about this grape. It is a notoriously difficult one to handle, even in the heartland of Burgundy, from where the greatest expressions of this grape emerge. It's temperamental, difficult, talented, wonderfully expressive, yet prone to sulking.

But when Pinot Noir is on form, either in its Burgundy guise or as one of the principal grapes used in making champagne (yes, a red wine grape used to make a sparkling white), then it is sublime. To champagne it adds richness, body and style. As a red from Burgundy, it produces some of the most complex and exciting flavours that you're likely to find in a wine. Which is why so many countries outside France continue to experiment with it, in the hope of emulating great Burgundy. The Australians have had a stab at it, as have the New Zealand wine fraternity, making some of the best Pinots outside Burgundy. The Californians play hit and miss with it; South Africa makes some good, basic, fruit-driven versions; and there's a small enclave of winemakers in Oregon who get pretty close to perfection. But, at the end of the day, it really is Burgundy where the best Pinot Noir comes from. The problem is, it's disgracefully expensive, and, even in a great vintage, with a great producer behind it, it can occasionally come across as simply average.

How does it go again? Pee-no nw-ar.

Where do I find it? Burgundy, Champagne, the Loire and Alsace in France, Australia (particularly Tasmania), New Zealand, South Africa, California and Oregon in the US, Germany, Spain, Italy.

What does it taste like? It's a mix of sweet black cherry and bitter red cherry fruits, a little along the lines of a Chupa-Chup, but in the more complex versions this can be laced with bits of liquorice, milk chocolate and sweet vanilla (from the oak ageing). People often say that Pinot Noir has 'earthy' or 'farmyardy', 'gamy' flavours, but I think it's easier to compare this element to opening and eating a packet of bacon fries – you get the same slatey, meaty, smoky aromas and flavours with Pinot Noir.

Tell me something I didn't know: There are 46 different versions, or clones, of Pinot Noir in France alone – so it's a big family, many of which are Class A troublemakers.

PINOT MEUNIER

Meunier is one of France's most planted black grape varieties, not that you would know it. It's the 'sleeper' in a wide host of wines, the most famous of which is champagne, where, alongside Pinot Noir and Chardonnay, it makes up a classic, naughty threesome. As reds go it's a very tart, acerbic grape, but that makes it ideally suited to champagne (when it's pressed, like Pinot Noir, for champagne, the juice is run off and the skins discarded, so no coloration occurs). Principally, it's used as a solid support base to the more attractive and overt qualities of Pinot Noir and Chardonnay, and its acid nature helps give the champagnes it forms part of a certain ageing potential.

New World producers of fizz looking to compete with champagne are beginning to use this more and more, and so it is finding increasing popularity in areas of Australia and New Zealand.

How does it go again? Pee-no muur-nee-ay.

Where do I find it? Champagne, Mosel, Switzerland, Australia and New Zealand.

What does it taste like? In its pure form it has an almost raspberry fruit flavour, though it can be quite tough, tannic and overly acidic. But you'll find it more often than not in champagne, where it provides the bite and a slightly sweet, red-berry fruit touch.

Tell me something I didn't know: As grape names go, it doesn't sound the sexiest, but, compared with the German name for it, Schwarzriesling, it doesn't sound too shabby.

SANGIOVESE

In the 70s, Chianti came in raffia bottles that were to be kept and used as candle holders by trattorias across the land. The wine in the bottle was invariably poor.

Nowadays, Sangiovese is still the base for Chianti, but the product has come a long way and we are no longer sent the weak and diluted versions that abounded back then. As well as producing a deliciously fruity sensation in the mouth, Sangiovese is blessed with a good degree of acidity, making it one of the few red grapes that can truly boast a racy, tart edge. Sometimes that can be overblown and out of balance. But in a good version it simply helps accentuate the fresh, red-berry, sweet-fruit nature of the wine and blends well with the creamy, vanilla flavours that emerge from oak-ageing, which the grape, like many of the classic red varieties, is well suited to. While Tuscany is the main address for the grape in Italy, it can be found across the central and southern regions of the country, and has – mainly through immigrant Italian communities – made its way to foreign fields. California has a lot of experimentation going on with Sangiovese, as does Australia.

How does it go again? San-geeo-vay-zee.

Where do I find it? Italy, California, Australia.

What does it taste like? Think of a bowl of freshly mashed raspberry compote, with a few mulberries and some macerated cranberries added to boot, topped off with a big dollop of cream. And bingo!

Tell me something I didn't know: It's excellent when blended with other varieties, particularly in the case of Cabernet, though by law that's not technically allowed in Tuscany without special dispensation.

SYRAH

I've split Syrah and Shiraz because they *can* be split, despite being essentially the same grape but just called different things in different hemispheres. And in the different hemispheres they produce radically different wines, so, to all intents and purposes, they *are* different grapes.

Syrah is the northern hemisphere's version, most famously grown and lovingly cared for in the northern and southern Rhône – perhaps the most undervalued and underrated wine region within France, and indeed the world. For some reason, top-class Châteauneuf-du-Pape from the southern Rhône or Côte-Rôtie and Hermitage from the northern Rhône don't seem to garner the same awards as, say, top-flight Bordeaux. This is odd, given the fact that, several centuries ago, Hermitage was so highly valued that the Bordeaux châteaux used to label their wines as Hermitage in order to get a higher price and greater kudos.

In the southern Rhône it is often blended with the likes of Viognier, Grenache, Mourvèdre and Cinsaut, but it is always still resolutely Syrah, and the deep, inky black, wonderfully structured wines that are produced are a delight. Even a basic Côtes du Rhône at around £6 or £7 can trounce a similarly priced Pinot from Burgundy or Claret from Bordeaux.

A lot of Syrah is grown in the South of France wine regions, around the Languedoc, where the wines are slightly less serious, but packed to the gunnels with fruit and reassuringly rustic in style. You can also find one or two great examples from Sicily. And Washington state is probably making some of the finest Rhône-inspired Syrah around at the moment, though its southern cousin California has been successfully working with Syrah for several decades now.

How does it go again? Sirr-ah.

Where do I find it? Rhône, South of France, Sicily, Washington state, California.

What does it taste like? There are many different fruit elements to decent Syrah, fresh blackberry, brambles and damsons being the most obvious. But, thanks to the use of new oak in most versions from the Rhône, you get a nice, creamy oak character with edges of thick-cut smoky bacon in the older versions.

Tell me something I didn't know: There are actually two versions of Syrah, Petite and Grosse. The Petite, however, is no relation to Petite Sirah, which is grown in South America.

SHIRAZ

While Syrah is principally defined by power and finesse, most Shiraz, which is mainly made in Australia, is defined by fruit, spice and power.

Because of the hotter climate, the wines take on a much jammier, sweeter nature in fruit terms, which is not a negative but is a marked difference in style. The sheer volume of Shiraz being produced in Australia, and increasingly in South Africa, means that you can drink very reasonable, if not overly exciting, versions of the grape for a fiver or so. But if you really want to get a flavour of what Australia can do with Shiraz you

need to spend up to £10 or more – the difference in quality and interest
is amazing at that price level.

How does it go again? Shirr-az.

Where do I find it? Australia, South Africa.

What does it taste like? Much more plum, mulberries and black cherries
than Syrah, with a nice jammy, fruit compote feel to them. Tannins are
usually a lot bigger than with Rhône Syrah, meaning you'll find the sides
of your mouth drying up quite quickly with a big, full-on Aussie version.

Tell me something I didn't know: Never interfere with an Australian's
barbecue and never, ever criticise an Australian winemaker's Shiraz.
It's just not worth it.

TEMPRANILLO

Rioja is perhaps the world's most recognised red wine style. Everyone
knows what it tastes like: sweet, strawberry fruit flavours, lots of oak
and a creamy, vanilla ice-cream finish, thanks to the aforementioned oak.

Tempranillo is the grape that forms the bedrock of this famous wine.
Indeed, it's the base grape for nearly all of Spain's best-known reds.

In truth, Tempranillo doesn't do overly well alone, needing additions
of Cabernet, Garnacha or Mazuelo to help it to come into its own. But
it does have the advantage of standing up quite well to long ageing
in wood, one of the key principles of the production of Rioja.

It's grown outside Spain, but in such tiny amounts that it's almost
negligible, with neighbouring Portugal being the only other real fan
of the grape. There it is known as Tinta Roriz and is one of the five
principal varieties used to produce Port.

How does it go again? Temp-ra-nee-yo.

Where do I find it? Spain, Portugal, California.

What does it taste like? Pure, pure strawberry fruit flavours. A young
Tempranillo given a little bit of wood ageing is like dipping into a bowl
of strawberries and cream. As it ages, you get some slightly leathery
liquorice flavours working their way in.

Tell me something I didn't know: The name comes from the Spanish
term 'temprana', meaning early – which is ironic when you consider that
most of the Spanish I know are wonderfully, but chronically, late.

BEST SUPPORTING ACTS

CABERNET FRANC
How does it go again? Cab-er-nay fronk.
In brief: This is the third of the classic triumvirate of Bordeaux varieties but perhaps the weakest and most temperamental. In Bordeaux it is nearly always harvested too early. It provides great colour but little else. However, in Spain, or Washington State, where it is allowed to ripen fully, it can make some of the most delicious, rounded, blackberry and cherry fruit-filled wines with great power and class.

GAMAY
How does it go again? Ga-may.
In brief: Gamay equals Beaujolais, Beaujolais equals Gamay. The two have not been separated since birth. Recent history has seen a flood of thin, weedy wines come out of Beaujolais, which does Gamay no credit. At its best can be purple-hued, black-cherry-filled and chocolate-laced with no pretensions other than just to be a lovely mouthful of wine.

GRENACHE
How does it go again? Gre-nash.
In brief: Grenache is used in Spain (under the guise Garnacha – see below) but also has prevalence in the Rhône and extensively across France. It is, however, best as a support to the likes of Syrah, unless it's being used for Rosé, in which case its sprightly, light, raspberry and strawberry fruit flavours are just right.

GARNACHA
How does it go again? Gar-natch-ah.
In brief: The Spanish version of Grenache, it makes its presence felt in Rioja as the support grape to Tempranillo, but is grown across Spain and used to best effect as a single variety in the Priorato region, where it makes surprisingly robust, full-on wines. Also a big component of many Spanish *rosados*.

MALBEC
How does it go again? Mal-beck.
In brief: Malbec is the workhorse variety of Argentina, where it's been adopted virtually as a national variety, despite the fact that it has a longer history as a blending variety in Bordeaux. It produces thick, black, tannic, spicy wines, with lots of plum and black cherry fruit flavours.

MOURVÈDRE

How does it go again? More-veh-dr.

In brief: Known as this in the South of France, but also grown in Spain, where it is known as Monastrell, and Australia, where it is called Mataro. Again, a grape principally used for blending but is chiefly prized for its intense aromas, high alcohol kick and rather meaty, gamy flavours.

NEBBIOLO

How does it go again? Neb-ee-olo.

In brief: Sangiovese may be the grape that dominates in Italy, but it's Nebbiolo that produces some of the country's most sought-after and highly priced wines, most notably Barolo in Piedmont. It has wonderfully plummy, spicy fruit flavours with notes of tar as it ages – and it takes a long time to age, needing anywhere between three and five years in the classic versions before it begins to soften up.

PETIT VERDOT

How does it go again? Pe-tee verr-doh.

In brief: Another classic Bordeaux variety that tends to get thrown into blends, but is principally suited to slightly hotter climates. So, when found in the likes of Spain or California and treated with respect, it yields the most intense, blackcurrant and damson fruit flavours, with a delightfully chewy texture and spicy kick.

PINOTAGE

How does it go again? Pee-no-tahge.

In brief: A Frankenstein creation that arose from South Africa's desperation to have a national grape variety unique to itself. When it's well handled it can produce wonderfully sweet and savoury fruit and spice combinations, all plum, blackberry and black pepper.

ZINFANDEL

How does it go again? Zin-fan-dell.

In brief: California's most significant contribution to the worldwide grape family tree, although it is actually European in origin. It's probably best described as the Californian version of Shiraz. Big globules of dark, blackberry fruit pour forth from a decent drop of the stuff, alongside a hefty whack of alcohol and a mini-selection of your average kitchen spice rack.

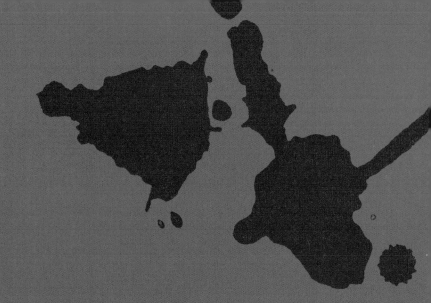

chapter thirteen
wine by country

You've been presented with two distinct ways of choosing your wine so far – by style and by grape variety. Now for the most traditional: by region. In olden days (well, before the 70s), there were regions that were known for quality, and those that weren't. These days, most major regions make a certain amount of top-quality wine, and a certain amount of poor-quality wine – it's just the proportions that vary. This can make it more difficult to use regions as a basis for choosing your wine.

As an example, Chablis used to be famed for its dry, white, unoaked Chardonnays – these days it's more reliable, and certainly more cost-effective, to buy a pseudo-Chablis from the New World, so variable is Chablis' reliability.

However, it's still useful, and sometimes fascinating, to know where your bottle of wine comes from. And, given the rather boring insistence that most supermarkets and major retailers have of relying on setting out their shelves by country rather than price, style or grape variety, it's probably an essential part of decoding what's on your merchant's shelf, and whether you like it or not.

In what follows, some countries have only brief entries, for obvious reasons. Others are considerably longer, such as Italy, France, Australia and Spain. And yet even these longer passages don't do justice to the relevant country. It's a bit like trying to shoehorn the England rugby team into a Mini Cooper: an admirable feat to attempt, but you know that somewhere along the way someone, or in this case somewhere, is going to get left out. I don't think Liechtenstein produces any wine, but if it does I apologise unreservedly in advance.

Argentina

You have only to fly low over the Andes into Argentina to realise that this country is simply stunning, visually – and the hope is always that its wines can be similarly stunning. The challenge with Argentinian wine is that, while it can represent great value, there are only a few producers that are really shining over the £5.99 mark. Under that, however, and they can give everyone a run for their money.

Mendoza is the workhouse of the country's vineyards and one in every two Argentine wines found in the UK has come from this region. And Mendoza is one of the best places from which to sample the hallmark grape variety of the Argentine wine community, Malbec. This Bordeaux variety may come across as green and distinctly dull in its French homeland, but in the hands of the best Argentine winemakers it produces luscious, full, ripe and powerful reds. And a good Malbec is the perfect match for the country's wonderfully succulent beef – a product it exports throughout the world, probably more successfully than its wines. You'll also find some very good-value Chardonnays and some nicely turned-out Cabernet Sauvignon, alongside a plethora of weird and wonderful other, minor, varieties such as Pinot Gris and Tocai Friulano.

 Major white grape varieties:
Chardonnay, Pinot Gris/Grigio.

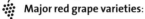 **Major red grape varieties**:
Malbec, Cabernet Sauvignon, Tempranillo, Syrah.

 Key areas to watch:
Mendoza, San Juan, Rio Negro, Salta.

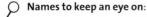 **Names to keep an eye on**:
Catena Zapata, Finca El Retiro, Norton,
Santa Julia, Terrazas, Familia Zuccardi.

Australia

Two decades ago Australia only just registered on the wine Richter scale in the UK. Now, one in four bottles sold is Australian. They introduced the UK to the concept of a decent wine that tasted of something and cost less than a fiver – and they haven't looked back since. It's probably true to say that Australia put everyone else on warning, forcing Old World giants such as France, Spain and Italy to re-evaluate the way they made their wine, and the way they communicated with the consumer.

And they are still going strong. Having cornered the market in good-value, fruit-driven wines around the £5 mark, they are now planning to make us realise how well they can do above that price line, which means some fantastic wines between £6 and £10 making their way onto our shelves. These are wines that give classic regions such as Chablis, Sancerre, Bordeaux and Burgundy a real run for their money. And above £10? Well, Australia has always produced top-flight, top-of-the-range wines; it just hasn't shouted about them as much as it should do. Until now, that is.

Interestingly, what's also emerging from Australia is the concept of *regionality*, whereby each region has a particular style and character of its own. So, instead of looking for an Australian Chardonnay on the shelf, we're all being encouraged to work out whether we prefer a Margaret River

Chardonnay, say, or a Hunter Valley Chardonnay. The idea is essentially the same as the regional divisions in France. We don't ask for a French Chardonnay: we ask for a Chablis or a white Burgundy or Provence Chardonnay. And so, it seems, we may do the same in future with Australian wines.

For the average consumer who has only just managed to get their heads round the difference between basic grape varieties, this might seem an added complexity they could do without. However, for anyone getting into their wine, it opens up a whole new world of interest and discovery. I've concentrated on the four largest wine-producing areas in Australia, to give you a head-start.

SOUTH AUSTRALIA

South Australia is the heart of the Australian wine industry. It makes more than of half the country's total production and contains some of its most famous names in regional terms. If, for example, you want to get a feel for what Australia really does in terms of Shiraz, then the Barossa Valley will show you wines that could easily knock your socks off and blow your taste buds out of the water. But then, at the same time, it houses the likes of the Adelaide Hills, where some world-class Chardonnay is grown, but also Rieslings that are already doing for the grape what centuries of German Riesling production has never quite managed: make it popular with the average consumer. Likewise, the Coonawarra area is producing Cabernet Sauvignons that make some of Bordeaux's most famous châteaux look a little on the puny side. It really is an absolute wealth of wine gems, and covers every single feasible price level.

 Major white grape varieties:
You name it, South Australia has it: Chardonnay, Riesling, Sémillon.

 Major red grape varieties:
Merlot, Cabernet Sauvignon, Shiraz.

 Key areas to watch:
Barossa, Clare Valley, Limestone Coast (Coonawarra), Eden Valley, Adelaide Hills, McLaren Vale.

 Names to keep an on:
Barossa: Grant Burge, Glaetzer, Peter Lehmann, Charles Melton, Penfolds, St Hallett, Yalumba; *Adelaide Hills*: Knappstein Lenswood, Starve Dog Lane, Petaluma, Shaw & Smith; *McLaren Vale*: d'Arenberg, Chapel Hill, Hardys, Maglieri, Geoff Merrill, Rosemount, Tatachilla, Wirra Wirra; *Coonawarra*: Hollick, Katnook, Lindemans, Parker, Penley, Wynns; *Clare Valley*: Tim Adams, Grosset, Knappstein, Leasingham, Wendouree.

WESTERN AUSTRALIA

Although Western Australia is actually quite a vast swathe of the country's land mass, wine is produced only at the southernmost tip. In percentage terms, this area accounts for a tiny amount of the country's total wine production, but is home to some of the biggest heavyweights in terms of quality wine. Apart from anything else it is home to the Margaret River, which, while handling a wide variety of grape varieties, is best known for producing Cabernets. It also happens to be home to one of the most interestingly monikered wineries, Suckfizzle Augusta. It might sound like a porn queen's stage name, but in fact makes some very good wines.

 Major white grape varieties:
Chardonnay, Chenin Blanc, Sauvignon Blanc.

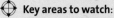 **Major red grape varieties**:
Cabernet Sauvignon, Pinot Noir, Shiraz.

Key areas to watch:
Margaret River, Swan Valley.

Names to keep an eye on:
Alkoomi, Cape Mentelle, Cullen, Devil's Lair,
Houghton, Leeuwin Estate, Moss Wood,
Suckfizzle Augusta (Stella Bella), Vasse Felix.

NEW SOUTH WALES

Not overly massive in volume terms, but home to one of Australia's most famous regions, the Hunter Valley, where some world-class Sémillon is grown – Sémillon that knocks the spots off much of that bottled as Bordeaux Blanc in France. It makes some cracking Chardonnays and good Cabernets, alongside some quite bullish, long-lived Shiraz, but Sémillon is most certainly the jewel in its crown.

 Major white grape varieties:
Sémillon, Riesling, Chardonnay.

 Major red grape varieties:
Cabernet, Shiraz.

 Key areas to watch:
Hunter Valley, Orange, Cowra, Mudgee, Riverina.

Names to keep an eye on:
De Bortoli, Brokenwood, Clonakilla,
Simon Gilbert, Lindemans, McWilliam's,
Rosemount, Rothbury Estate, Tyrrell's.

VICTORIA

This area used to be a far bigger, more important part of the wine scene
in Australia, but over the last century, since wine growing first began in
the state, it's taken something of a back seat. It still produces some of the
country's most interesting wines, but it doesn't have the volume clout that
it once had. However, there are some real gems in Victoria. For a start, it
seems to be able to do things with Pinot Noir that other regions in Australia
simply can't, particularly in the Yarra Valley, and it has a nice little line in
sparkling wines. It also produces some of the best top-class Cabernet in Oz,
and in Rutherglen you can pick up some sticky dessert wines to die for.

 Major white grape varieties:
Chardonnay, Pinot Gris, Riesling, Sémillon.

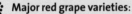 **Major red grape varieties**:
Cabernet Sauvignon, Pinot Noir, Shiraz.

Key areas to watch:
Yarra Valley, Geelong, Mornington Peninsula,
Goulburn Valley, King Valley, Rutherglen.

 Names to keep an eye on:
Bannockburn, De Bortoli, Brown Brothers, Dalwhinnie, Diamond Valley
Vineyards, Domaine Chandon (fizz), Giaconda, Mount Langi Ghiran,
Mount Mary, Seppelt Great Western (fizz), Yarra Yering, Yeringberg.

TASMANIA

It may be an island, but it makes up for remoteness and relatively
tiny output by making sure what little wine it does produce garners
worldwide acclaim and attention. Thanks to its cool climate, it does
particularly well with Pinot Noir, as well as Riesling and Chardonnay,
and has a nice line in particularly well-made Cabernets. There are also
a couple of very good sparklers. Not that many make their way over
to these shores, but those that do tend not to disappoint.

Major white grape varieties:
Chardonnay, Riesling.

Major red grape varieties:
Cabernet, Pinot Noir.

Key areas to watch:
Er ... Tasmania.

Names to keep an eye on:
Clover Hill, Jansz, Stefano Lubiana, Piper's Brook (Ninth Island), Touchwood.

Austria

Austrian wines don't have an enormous presence in the British wine market, partly because most of the production is geared at the top end of the price scale, but also because two of the varieties it goes big on, Riesling and Chardonnay, are among the most competitive in the market. However, Austria has one secret weapon up its sleeve: its native grape variety, Grüner Veltliner. It doesn't sound very sexy, but it does make some fantastic dry whites that can compete with some of the best that Burgundy has to offer, and at the same time offer something different. Again, they're not always particularly cheap, but they are worth having a look at if you spot one on a shelf near you.

In terms of red there is a small production, mainly of Pinot Noir and the snappily named Blaufränkisch, but little if any makes it far out of the country, and it is usually gobbled up by the Austrians themselves. Austria does, however, make some fabulous sweet wine, which, though expensive, is worth every penny, if you can manage to lay your hands on some and have deep enough pockets.

 Major white grape varieties:
Chardonnay, Riesling, Grüner Veltliner.

 Major red grape varieties:
Blaufränkisch, Pinot Noir.

 Key areas to watch:
Wachau, Burgenland, Styria (or Steiermark).

 Names to keep an eye on:
Bründlmayer, Freie Weingärtner Wachau, Franz Hirtzberger, Emmerich Knoll, Alois Kracher, FX Pichler, Willi Opitz.

Canada

If you asked most people to name the drink Canada is most famous for they'd probably cite either whiskey or beer. They would probably need a lot of prodding if you wanted to elicit wine as an answer. But, given the enormous French heritage that is part of Canada, it is really no surprise that it has a very successful and thriving wine market and some wonderful wineries. In size terms, it doesn't match counterparts south of the border in the USA, and is dwarfed by the likes of California, but is large nevertheless.

As for style, it is very mixed, as you would expect from a country that has more than a thousand miles of land separating its two furthermost wineries. Ontario has the largest number of wineries, most of which work with Riesling, a rather interesting variety named Vidal (which is a cross between Ugni Blanc and Seyval Blanc), alongside the likes of Cabernet Sauvignon, Chardonnay and even a smattering of Cabernet Franc. There is also some very good Pinot Noir, as you would expect given the rather cool climate in the north of the country. However, its most famous export is probably its icewine. That is a wine made from grapes that have frozen on the vine during the winter months. The amount of juice extracted from these grapes is absolutely tiny, but extremely concentrated and sweet – as is the wine that results. It's highly prized and – you guessed it – highly priced, too.

 Major white grape varieties:
Chardonnay, Vidal, Riesling.

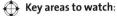 **Major red grape varieties**:
Pinot Noir, Cabernet Sauvignon.

Key areas to watch:
Niagara Peninsula (Ontario), Finger Lakes (Atlantic Northeast), Okanagan Valley (British Columbia).

Names to keep an eye on:
Burrowing Owl, Cave Spring, Château des Charmes, Henry of Pelham, Inniskillin, Mission Hill, Sumac Ridge, Tinhorn Creek.

Chile

During the mid-nineties Chile began to export to the UK in earnest, following the success of Australian wines in the market. For a while they did well, for all the usual reasons. Great wines, good value, smart marketing and a little luck. For a while they were the next big thing. Everyone held their breath and – nothing. They just seemed to fade into the background a bit.

This was a shame, because the country makes some really delicious, fruit-forward, punchy wines that actually do compete very well with the benchmark for good value, Australia.

Recently, however, they've managed to gain some of the lustre they had back in the 90s and are beginning to be talked of as the next big thing – again. Hopefully, they'll actually make it this time, because the country's winemakers are really very dedicated, if not entirely switched on, to the needs of the UK wine drinker.

The country itself has a collection of very different and distinct wine-producing regions running from hot through to relatively cool, most of which stretch along and down the country's biggest area, the Central Valley. Among the most interesting are the Aconcagua Valley, Maipo and Rapel, Curicó and Maule. The last of these has an interestingly named subregion known as Bío-Bío. Unfortunately, the wines it produces are not nearly as interesting as its name.

What may explain why Chile lost some of its focus in the 90s is the number of 'super-premium' wines it seems to have churned out of late – wines over £10 that aim to ape the top wines of Bordeaux. Some are good. The vast majority, however, are unimpressive and don't offer nearly as much bang for their rather considerable buck as the competition from Australia. You have been warned.

 Major white grape varieties:
Chardonnay, Sémillon, Sauvignon Blanc.

 Major red grape varieties:
Cabernet Sauvignon, Merlot, Pinot Noir.

 Key areas to watch:
Casablanca, Maipo, Rapel, Curicó, Maule.

 Names to keep an eye on:
Alvaro Espinoza, Casa Lapostolle, Concha y Toro, Cousiño Macul, Errazuriz, Montes, MontGras, San Pedro, Miguel Torres, Valdivieso, Veramonte.

Eastern Europe

Where does one start with Eastern Europe. Perhaps Bulgaria is the best place – because it is symptomatic of the malaise that has hit this relatively large, disjointed wine-producing collective of Eastern Europe.

It used to be a fantastic source of great-value, easy-drinking wines, particularly the reds. Lovely ripe fruit flavours, a little bit of body, not a lot of money. More or less the perfect combination for the consumer. So how did they manage to screw it up? Well, in a nutshell, capitalism. When the Soviet bloc fell in 1989, it may have meant the ultimate creation of a belt of billionaires across the former Soviet Union's various states, but it meant disaster for the likes of Bulgaria. The wine industry may have been run by the state monopoly, but it was fairly efficient in distribution terms and

had some key markets, one of which was Russia. That imploded with
the fall of the Soviet bloc, and the hiatus between the loss of major
export markets and private investment arriving on the scene meant poor
investment in vineyards and lack of direction. The results were that the
wine got worse, and getting hold of it became difficult. Disaster ensued.
And the story isn't that much different for Romania and Hungary,
the other two big hitters in the region. So, if you ever wondered what
happened to that lovely little Bulgarian Cabernet Sauvignon you
used to knock back a decade ago, now you know.

BULGARIA

Bulgaria produces mainly red, though there is a fair amount of white
consumed domestically – but it's not highly recommended. On the red
side, Cabernet Sauvignon is the grape that dominates and the style that
is made is usually soft, easy-drinking, heavy on the raspberry and plum
side of the taste scale rather than blackcurrant.

 Major white grape varieties:
Aligoté, Chardonnay Rkatsiteli.

 Major red grape varieties:
Cabernet Sauvignon, Merlot,
Mavrud, Melnik.

HUNGARY

This is probably the most successful of the major three and the one that
has done most to drag itself back from the brink of collapse as far as the
wine industry is concerned. It helps that it produces one of the world's
most highly prized dessert wines, Tokaji, which has undergone something
of a revival in the UK over the last decade. At least that keeps its profile
relatively high. As well as some decent red, Hungary does produce some
pretty good dry whites, mainly from the local variety, Furmint. These
tend to be dry and aromatic in style, along the lines of Gewürztraminer
and Riesling.

 Major white grape varieties:
Chardonnay, Furmint, Hárslevelü, Leányka,
Sauvignon Blanc, Riesling, Gewürztraminer.

 Major red grape varieties:
Cabernet Sauvignon, Merlot, Pinot Noir, Kadarka.

Key areas to watch:
Lake Balaton, Szekszard, Villany Siklos, Eger, Tokaj.

ROMANIA

Crippled by lack of investment, Romania actually has more vineyard planted than any other Eastern European country. It also has the greatest unrealised potential. Most of its production is consumed in the homeland, thanks to the Romanians' love of wine, but the stuff that does make it over here tends to be the least exciting and the most uninspired. Still, give it a decade or two, and you never know.

 Major white grape varieties:
Aligoté, Sauvignon Blanc, Feteasca, Welschriesling.

 Major red grape varieties:
Cabernet Sauvignon, Merlot.

 Key areas to watch:
Tirnave, Murfatlar, Dealul Mare.

France

France is one of the most complex wine-growing countries, as well as perhaps the most famous. It claims to be the home of the world's finest wines and in truth it is. Much of the country's wine regions have been carved out over the course of several centuries and have developed a reputation for producing quality wines, Chablis, Burgundy, Bordeaux etc. Because of this, the French have been fanatical about ensuring that this quality reputation is protected, hence the country's Appellation Contrôlée system (sometimes called Appellation d'Origine Contrôlée, or AOC).

This system has divided France into a series of '*appellations*', each of which is governed by strict controls over grapes planted, methods used to grow them, yields, even alcohol strengths. The aim is to protect legitimate producers from poor imitations and ensure that the consumer receives the best there is within a specific *appellation*.

It sounds confusing – and sometimes it is – but once you get a handle on it it's relatively straightforward. The confusing part comes in knowing how *appellations* apply in quality terms. The basic classification for Bordeaux, for example, is AC Bordeaux. To qualify for AC Médoc (an *appellation* within Bordeaux) the quality level and restrictions are higher – and likewise with the *appellation* of Margaux, within Médoc. If you like, it's a simple stepladder to the highest quality. Knowing which is the bottom and which is the top step is the complicated bit.

I'm not going to be able to do justice to France in a few paragraphs – besides, others have done it in far more detail over many more paragraphs than this. But, if this gives you a taster for the country's wines, you can always buy a book specifically on the wines of France – indeed, that goes for most of the countries covered here.

BORDEAUX

Bordeaux is the powerhouse of French wine. Its famous châteaux are talked about all around the globe and its traditional red wine, sometimes known as claret, has become synonymous with fine wine.

But where do you start with an area that has more than 13,000 different producers?

The simplest way to look at Bordeaux – or at least red Bordeaux – is to consider the Gironde, the river that runs through it, as a dividing line. On the one side is the Left Bank, comprising the Médoc – home to some of the *appellation*'s most famous names – and the Graves.

The Médoc includes the '*communes*' of Margaux, St-Julien, Pauillac, St Estephe and Haut Médoc, as well as the *appellations* of Listrac and Moulis. The Graves is the principal home of whites from Bordeaux, and Sauternes and Barsac, further to the south, produce Bordeaux's world-famous dessert wines.

The right bank is formed principally of the *appellations* and sub-*appellations* of St-Emilion and Pomerol, along with Bourg, Blaye and the Libournais District. In between the Right Bank and the Left Bank is a section of land known as Entre-deux-Mers, which makes increasing amounts of white and a fair bit of red.

So far so good – although perhaps you're already getting a feeling for how complicated it can get. Fortunately the French did come up with a pretty good system of ensuring you could tell which château from St-Emilion was worth a punt and which from Margaux was topping the charts. It was a series of classifications. The first took place in 1855 and covered most of the *appellations* around the Gironde river, in particular those with the Médoc and Haut Médoc and Graves. It divided the wines into a series of '*crus*', or growths, from First down to Fifth, with another classification for wines below this, known as 'Crus Bourgeois'. There are only five First Growths, whereas there are seventeen Fifth Growths, and several hundred Crus Bourgeois.

Since 1855 there have been other, later, classifications, such as that of St-Emilion in the 1950s; but, even so, all combined, this covers a fraction of the total number of producers arrayed across Bordeaux's vineyards. And the 1855 classification hasn't even been updated since, so in many cases its 'quality' assurance isn't what it once was.

What does this all amount to? Well, it means that, if you're buying a red from Bordeaux, you either have to get your nose into a more detailed book, or ask someone for help. If I was going to buy anything other than a basic Bordeaux at £6 or £7, I'd be heading for an independent wine merchant and asking for advice – and I've been in wine for more than thirteen years.

 Major white grape varieties:
Sauvignon Blanc, Sémillon.

 Major red grape varieties:
Cabernet Sauvignon, Cabernet Franc, Merlot.

 Key areas to watch:
The wines of the Graves, especially the whites, went through a shaky patch but are coming back on track. From the Médoc, Margaux is often variable, Pauillac and St-Estephe far more reliable. Bourg and Blaye are underrated, and hence can provide good bargains. Entre-deux-Mers is good for basic white and the odd decent red. If you like Merlot, then Pomerol and St-Emilion are the *communes* you should be looking out for. Barsac produces dessert wines as good as Sauternes, but for a more reasonable outlay.

 Names to keep an eye on:
How long is piece of string? Nowhere is it more important to know what you're spending, and where you like, so the variations are infinite. Any names thrown at you now could confuse as much as help. If you're spending between £5 and £7, perhaps up to £8, your supermarket is likely to have done a good job purchasing the best there is.

Above this, you want a specialist or independent merchant, preferably one that specialises in Bordeaux or French wines (see the Merchant Guide on Page 202). Alternatively, look out for the names of some of the region's best '*negociants*' (essentially traders who buy from multiple châteaux and producers). Dourthe and Mau are two good names to look for.

BURGUNDY

Burgundy produces wines from principally Chardonnay and Pinot Noir, that are the envy of the world. Every winemaker I know would probably give their right arm for a couple of rows of vines in a decent strip of one of the few hallowed Grand Crus (the best classification in the region). Why? Well, because when Burgundy is good it is very, very good. The problem is that when it's bad it's awful. And there's not a lot in between. Also, because of its rarity value (particularly the best vineyards, where only a few hundred cases are made), it tends to be highly priced.

There are five principal districts in Burgundy: the Côte d'Or (red and white), the Côte Chalonnaise (red and white), Chablis (white), the Mâconnais (mainly white) and Beaujolais (red – see the more detailed section below). All of these have producers of varying degrees of quality charging prices from the acceptable to the ridiculous. The problem, as in Bordeaux, is being able to tell which Burgundy is worth its hefty price tag and which isn't – and there are a lot that aren't.

Like the rest of France, Burgundy has a classification system. Basic Burgundy is classed as AC Bourgogne. Then there are ACs that take the name of a more specific district (or group of villages), hence AC Côtes de Nuits-Villages (red) and AC Côte de Beaune (red and white). The next classification is where a Burgundy takes a specific name of a village or '*commune*', so we get perhaps Chambolle-Musigny or Pommard.

Then there are the Premiers Crus (good village sites) and Grands Crus (the best sites), comprising the cream of the crop. Again, it's the stepladder to quality, becoming more and more specific as you move up the rungs.

 Major white grape varieties:
Chardonnay.

 Major red grape varieties:
Pinot Noir.

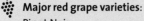 **Key areas to watch**:
Again, like Bordeaux, it is heavily producer-oriented.
The Côte d'Or and the Côte Chalonnaise have the widest
variety of sites and styles, so are a good place to start.
If you like unoaked Chardonnay, however, then Chablis
is your best bet.

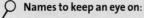 **Names to keep an eye on**:
Again, there are a vast number of growers, but there are also
negoçiants in Burgundy that span most of the different 'villages'
and classifications. Names to go for include Louis Jadot, Laboure-Roi,
Faiveley, Drouhin, Bouchard Père et Fils, William Lefevre, Louis Latour
and Olivier Leflaive.

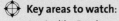

BEAUJOLAIS

Oh, poor old Beaujolais. It used to be such a popular drink in the UK. The Gamay grape variety that makes up the majority of Beaujolais can produce wonderfully rich, black-cherry-dominated reds. Over the last two decades, however, the trend has been for lighter, inferior and sometimes embarrassingly poor wines that do the area and *appellation* little credit indeed. Most of these tend to be Beaujolais Noveau, that is Beaujolais bottled almost immediately after fermentation and sold straightaway.

There are, however, a few producers who are doing their best to bring Beaujolais back to the level it once was – most notably Louis Jadot, a company strong across most of Burgundy.

A decent Beaujolais, to my mind at least, should have a rich, sweet and intense fruit combination of ripe black cherries with a hint of fresh raspberry, combined with lots of tang in the mouth (thanks to that thing called acidity). Few do, but, if you find one on your merchant's shelf that does, seize as many bottles as you can.

 Major red grape varieties:
Gamay.

 Key areas to watch:
In classification terms, there's basic Beaujolais, then Beaujolais Villages (which is often relatively decent). Then there are ten *crus* in Beaujolais, of which I would tend to opt for Moulin à Vent, Morgon, Fleurie and Juliénas if I was going to be picky. Each produces wines very different from Beaujolais Nouveau – which generally I wouldn't touch with a bargepole.

 Names to keep an eye on:
George Duboeuf is about the biggest name there is, but Louis Jadot, Château Thivin, Jean Marc Burgaud and Château des Jacques are all more than worth a punt.

CHAMPAGNE

In the way that a lot of people spend their life drinking Chablis without realising that it's made from Chardonnay, a lot of people drink champagne without realising it is made from both red and white grape varieties. The Champagne region, located to the east of Paris, is perhaps the most famous of all French regions. It's about as close as you get to being a universally known brand in the wine world and has the same recognition value as Coca-Cola. However, while they may both be very fizzy, I know which I'd prefer to have before dinner every evening.

Mostly champagne is made from a blend of Chardonnay, Pinot Noir and sometimes Pinot Meunier. The last two red varieties are pressed without damaging the skins, hence the lack of red colouring. Champagne is the most northerly wine *appellation* in France, and the grapes struggle to ripen fully. This means they tend to have a high acid content, which is ideal for the long ageing process they go through in the cellars – a minimum of fifteen months for nonvintage, but often longer depending on the producer.

There are some very famous producers of champagne, and some completely unknown producers. In the main, the former are among the best quality, and the latter among the most hit or miss. But, as with everything, there are always exceptions to the rule.

 Major white grape varieties:
Chardonnay.

 Major red grape varieties:
Pinot Noir, Pinot Meunier.

 Key areas to watch:
Champagne, really, but remember that the word 'champagne' can be used legally only by producers in Champagne. You will sometimes see it on the odd bottle in the US, thanks to some antiquated law that gives them a get-out clause, but this is not real champagne. The biggest thing to look out for is the style: there's nonvintage (a blend of different years), vintage (a single year), blanc de blancs (Chardonnay only) and *prestige cuvée* (top of the range).

 Names to keep an eye on:
There are many good producers of champagne, so it's easy just to name my top ten: Bollinger, Henriot, Veuve Clicquot, Joseph Perrier, Pol Roger, Taittinger, Gosset, Billecart-Salmon, Laurent Perrier and Ruinart.

ALSACE

The Germans liked it so much they invaded more than twice. And it's perfectly possible that the wines of Alsace were part of the reason – alongside the various centuries' worth of historical dispute over whom it actually belonged to.

It's no surprise, then, that a lot of the grape varieties grown in Alsace and the wines made are German in style and grape origins. The majority of wines produced are white, although there are some very fine reds produced in tiny amounts, often from Pinot Noir. But it's Riesling and Gewürztraminer that dominate on the white front, along with some

Pinot Blanc. The wines produced are very aromatic (in other words smelly, but in a nice way) and also have a spiciness to them and a lot of zing from their relatively high acidity. This makes them great wines for food, especially spicy, Asian food such as Thai, Indian or, in the case of Gewürztraminer, Chinese.

 Major white grape varieties:

Riesling, Pinot Blanc, Gewürztraminer.

 Key areas to watch: What you need to be looking out for is not so much areas but rather Grands Crus, a term that's given to only the best vineyard sites. The wines from these aren't cheap, but they're usually very good.

 Names to keep an eye on:

Léon Beyer, Josmeyer, Keuntz-Bas, A Mann, Rolly Gassmann, Schlumberger, Trimbach, the Turckheim Co-op, Zind-Humbrecht.

LOIRE VALLEY

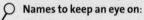

Most people know the Loire as a holiday destination rather than the home of some great wine. And most people would be able to tell you they liked Sancerre, but not where it came from. However, the Loire is home not only to Sancerre, but also Pouilly Fumé, Reuilly, Quincy and Menetou Salon, all of which lie in the upper Loire and are famous for their ability to turn Sauvignon Blanc into delicious dry whites.

In the middle Loire there's Anjou (famed for its rosés), Coteaux du Layon, Chaume (both hot on dessert wines made from Chenin Blanc), Savennières (great dry Chenin Blanc), Saumur (great sparklers and decent Cabernet Francs) and Touraine (which houses Chinon and Bourgeil, home of the region's finest reds, and Vouvray, where wonderful Chenin Blanc is produced).

Then of course there's the famous, or is that infamous, Muscadet. This was once one of the biggest whites to appear on the British market, but has found itself a little lost in recent years. However, a revival is occurring, thanks to a boost in quality, and the eponymous Muscadet grape is now being used to produce some lovely dry whites.

Major white grape varieties:

Sauvignon Blanc, Chenin Blanc, Muscadet.

Major red grape varieties:

Cabernet Franc.

Key areas to watch:

Again, there are many, but my favourites are Sancerre and Vouvray for whites, and Chinon and Bourgeil for reds.

Names to keep an eye on:
Gaston Huet (Vouvray), Pierre Druet, de La Lande (both Bourgeil),
Desbourdes (Chinon), Henri Bourgeois, Vacheron, André Vatan
(all Sancerre), Didier Dagueneau, Château de Tracy (both Pouilly
Fumé) and Bouvet-Ladubay (sparkling Saumur).

THE RHÔNE

The Rhône Valley splits into two halves, one north, one south. Each
produces quite different styles of wine from very similar varieties. In the
north, the vast majority of wine is made of Syrah, alongside some very fine
whites (made from Viognier). The biggest *appellation* for wine production
is Crozes-Hermitage, and its sub-*appellation* of Hermitage, where intense,
thick, well-structured Syrahs are forged. But there's also the famous Côte
Rôtie, where the most fantastic Syrahs emerge: St Joseph (both red and
white wines), Cornas and Condrieu (where fabulously peachy, rich
Viogniers are produced).

The southern Rhône is, however, what you would describe as the
powerhouse of the Rhône region, producing spicy, alcoholic reds, fine
dry whites and some very drinkable rosés. Most will recognise the Côtes
du Rhônes *appellation*, and the more tightly defined *appellation* of
Côtes du Rhône Villages, as both are responsible for majority of southern
Rhône's wine production. But there's also the famous Châteauneuf-du-
Pape, and the relatively recently created Gigondas and Vacqueyras.

In the case of all of these, from the most basic Côte du Rhônes to
top-flight Châteauneuf-du-Pape, the principal red grape is the juicy,
sweet, rich Grenache, with Syrah and Mourvèdre being used as powerful
backup in the blend. A much smaller amount of white produced from
Grenache Blanc, Clairette, Bourboulenc and Roussanne. Also in the
Southern Rhône, you'll find the *appellations* of Tavel and Lirac, home
to some of the country's most popular rosé, Muscat de Beaumes-de-
Venise (dessert wines) and the Côtes du Ventoux, which tends to
produce slightly lighter, more refreshingly summery reds than the
Côtes du Rhônes.

Major white grape varieties:
Northern Rhône: Viognier; *southern Rhône*: Grenache Blanc,
Roussanne.

Major red grape varieties:
Northern Rhône: Syrah; *southern Rhône*: Grenache, Syrah,
Mourvèdre, Cinsaut.

Key areas to watch:
In the north, Crozes Hermitage and St Joseph tend to provide the best value with Côte-Rôtie hitting the height of the quality scale. In the Southern Rhône, Côtes du Rhônes provides great drinking for under, say, £7, but Gigondas and Vacqueyras and certain Châteauneuf-du-Pape producers provide the best-quality peaks.

Names to keep an eye on:
Northern Rhône: Yves Cuilleron, E Guigal, Jean Louis Chave, Chapoutier, Paul Jaboulet Aîné; *southern Rhône*: Brusset, E Guigal, Rayas, Château du Trignon, Château de Beaucastel, Chapoutier, Charvin, Clos des Papes, Paul Jaboulet Aîné.

SOUTHWEST FRANCE

Basically if you take the bottom left-hand corner of France as you look at it on a map, and cut out Bordeaux at the top and Cognac to the east, that's the wine region we're talking about here. And it's a pretty disparate ragbag of vineyards and grape varieties. However, all tend to have a very Mediterranean style to the wines they produce, namely light to mid-bodied, with fruit to the fore and complexity kept to the French terms on the label, rather than the juice in the bottle.

In all, there are around twenty different *appellations* but among the best are Bergerac and Cahors, both of which produce reds that are relatively close in style to some of the lighter clarets from Bordeaux, and both of which use similar grape varieties, namely Cabernet Sauvignon, Cabernet Franc and Merlot. Then there's Gaillac to the east, which makes great spicy reds from Gamay and Syrah, and a local variety called Duras; and Madiran, which uses the relatively unknown variety of Tannat to make big, ballsy, spicy, mouth-puckering reds. Further, there's Jurançon, which takes a mix of weird-sounding local varieties, including Gros Manseng and Petit Manseng to make wonderful dry, biting whites, and very honeyed sweet wines. They're an acquired taste but worth giving a go.

 Major white grape varieties:
Sauvignon Blanc, Sémillon, Gros and Petit Manseng.

Major red grape varieties:
Cabernet Franc, Cabernet Sauvignon, Syrah, Gamay, Merlot, Tannat.

Key areas to watch:
Bergerac, Cahors and Jurancon provide the most interest and value.

Names to keep an eye on:
Moulin des Dames (Bergerac), Clos Triguedina, Lagrezette (both Cahors), Cauhapé, Clos Lapeyre, de Lahargue (Jurançon), Domaine Pichard (Madiran).

LANGUEDOC-ROUSSILLON

The two regions of Languedoc and Roussillon are usually appended together but they both represent very different styles of winemaking, very different terrains.

In the Languedoc, there has always been far more potential than there is in Roussillon, but over the years it has been wasted chasing volume as opposed to quality.

The grapes used are very similar to the Rhône, with the likes of Carignan, Syrah, Grenache and Mourvèdre making regular appearances among the reds, and Grenache Blanc and Bourboulenc vying with increasing plantings of Chardonnay among the whites. Fitou in the south is one of the best-known *appellations*, making strong earthy reds out of mainly Carignan, with Corbières, a little to the north, doing a similar job.

Minervois produces reds, too, but they lack the guts and glory of the Corbières and Fitou. Limoux, on the other hand, a little further inland, produces some lovely whites using Chardonnay. The Coteaux du Languedoc, however, is possibly the most far-reaching *appellation* within the Languedoc, and includes St-Chinian and Faugères, both of which can produce some lovely, balanced, fruity reds. However, the Coteaux du Languedoc is particularly known for producing a large amount of Vin de Pays (this is essentially a 'country wine', and, rather than the name of the town or *appellation* dominating the label, it's the grape variety). Some are great and well priced, some are rather disappointing, but if you've got just a fiver to spend they can regularly deliver you a decent drop of red or white.

Rousillon is much smaller than the neighbouring Languedoc and makes what are best described as more rustic wines, along with its own particular speciality, a port-like wine that comes under the French classification of *vins doux naturels*. The Banyuls, just north of the Spanish border, is the most famous of these semi-fortified wines, along with Maury. In the case of still wines, many are produced under the Côtes du Roussillon Villages *appellation*, with the majority of reds made from Grenache and the majority of whites made from Grenache Blanc, Roussanne and Marsanne. However, the vast majority of still wines are made as Vin de Pays.

 Major white grape varieties:
Grenache Blanc, Bourboulenc, Chardonnay, Picpoul.

 Major red grape varieties:
Carignan, Syrah, Grenache, Mourvèdre.

 Key areas to watch:
Fitou is making a comeback, Corbières is reliable and St Chinian and Faugères regularly overdeliver.

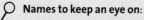

Names to keep an eye on:
La Baronne, Etang des Colombes, Meunier St Louis (Corbières),
Alquier, Moulin de Ciffre (Faugères), Cazal-Viel (St Chinian),
Casenove, Mas Crémant, Mas Segala, Cazes (Roussillon).

VIN DE PAYS

Because the Appellation Contrôlée system is so ingrained in France, most
of its inhabitants have a tendency to view the Vin de Pays classification as
somewhat inferior. Meaning literally 'country wine', it essentially says that
nothing but the most generic geographical description can be used, and
that the grape variety has to be the dominant indicator on the wine's
label. However, French snobbery and protectionism have resulted in a
better deal for those who buy other than French wines: because of the rise
of New World wines in recent years, grape varieties have become far more
prevalent in our minds than regions or subregions, so an average wine
buyer with a fiver or more in their pocket is far more likely to recognise
the word Chardonnay than, say, Banyuls. What it doesn't do is indicate
or guarantee a particular quality level, but then, with so many producers
abandoning the AC strictures in favour of the freedom of Vin de Pays,
there's quite a lot of good stuff floating around, and the supermarkets
do a good job of picking the best of it out.

Major grape varieties:
Virtually all the main varieties of France.

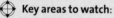
Key areas to watch:
Vin de Pays can come from anywhere in France,
but the Languedoc is particularly strong in this area,
so look out for Vin de Pays d'Oc on a label. Other regional
Vins de Pays to keep an eye on include, Vin de Pays d'Aude,
Vin de Pays de Jardin de la France (Loire), Vin de Pays du Gard
(Côtes du Rhône) and Vin de Pays de Côtes de Thongue.

Germany

Ah, Germany. An image problem that would tax even the most creative of creative agencies. Let's face it, it doesn't exactly help having tall, fluted bottles that, whatever the historical presence, still say one thing to us: '1970s Liebfraumilch'. I mean, that's what the vast majority of the public associate with Germany, unfortunately: sweet wines with naff labels. That's a shame, because Germany produces some of the finest dry whites, usually from Riesling, that you can find on the planet. But try persuading the average person to give them a go and, not surprisingly, they come over all shy and retiring. Various excuses, such as 'must wash my hair tonight' and 'dog ate my wineglasses', seem to pop out of nowhere. It doesn't help that the wine labels are about as clear as a pea-souper in nineteenth-century London. Nor does it particularly help that German Riesling is also the darling of most wine critics and aficionados, who every year trot out the same old claim: that this year will be the year for Riesling and the Germans will be leading the charge. It's an almost Canute-esque take on the reality of the situation. Yes, Riesling is a fantastic grape variety, but for the majority of people, even in its dry state, it just doesn't do it for them.

Still, that means there's a relatively plentiful supply for all of us who do like it. The best stuff isn't cheap, but, then, little in this life is, when you think about it. Germany does have some red wine production, but, like Austria's, it is fairly limited and very little makes it outside the country.

 Major white grape varieties:
Riesling, Gewürztraminer.

 Major red grape varieties:
Pinot Noir (known as Spätburgunder in German).

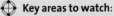 **Key areas to watch**:
Mosel-Saar-Ruwer, Nahe, Rheingau, Pfalz, Franken.

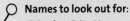 **Names to look out for**:
JB Becker, Fritz Haag, von Kesselstatt, Franz Künstler, Lingenfelder, Dr Loosen, Egon Müller, JJ Prüm, Selbach-Oster, Robert Weil.

Great Britain

I recently did a tasting of about forty or fifty English wines and managed to pick out only a handful that I would personally stick on my dinner table. My fellow tasters told me I was being a little harsh, but I don't think so. It would be lovely to have a thriving, humming, creative and successful wine industry, but generally we don't and never will have, because we don't have a terribly big history of growing grapes, and we don't have a particularly good climate for it. Perennial damp and wetness are not necessarily what a grape dreams about.

That said, there are one or two producers who are really flying the British flag high. The perfect example is Nyetimber, who make a sparkling wine that comes pretty close to rivalling some champagnes in the same price bracket. But the likes of Nyetimber are few and far between. Also, most wineries seem to have made a rod for their own backs by planting the most obscure of German varieties, with little regard for the fact that the *Germans* can't sell the stuff over here, let alone an English vineyard.

 Major white grape varieties:

Auxerrois, Chardonnay, Bacchus, Müller-Thurgau, Seyval Blanc.

 Major red grape varieties:

Cabernet Sauvignon, Pinot Noir.

 Names to look out for:

Chapel Down, Davenport, Nyetimber, Ridge View.

Italy

Italy is an immense source of variety, and yet more often than not on the shelves of a supermarket it is represented by two styles of wine: Chianti and Pinot Grigio. Both, when well made, are fabulous. Chianti in particular is one of Italy's finest gems. But, in the way that much of Spain is ignored while Rioja takes the full glory, so it is, in a way, with Italy. In particular, the other parts of central Italy, besides Tuscany – places such as the Marche and Umbria – tend to get brushed aside, but make some fabulous wines. And southern Italy, though still churning out a lot of bulk wine for cheap and cheerful exports, has come on in leaps and bounds in recent years. Likewise, the islands, Sicily and Sardinia, are currently providing masses of excitement.

The problem with Italy, however, is that such excitement comes at a price. It does have some heavy hitters in the under £5.99 bracket, but, in the main, the best Italian wines that make their way over to these shores are invariably above £7 or £8 and frequently in the £10–25 range. That makes it a hard sell for the average drinker, but for anyone who's beginning to get passionate about discovering new regions, and in particular new grape varieties, Italy really is the bee's knees.

Italy itself works on a rather complex system fashioned after France's Appellation Contrôlée system: it's known as the Denominazione di Origine Controllata (DOC) system. It's not terribly successful, and can be downright confusing, which is why I've concentrated on principal regions, styles of wines and a few recommended producers instead.

NORTHWEST

The northwest of Italy is dominated by two main regions: the Piedmont and Lombardy. The Piedmont, situated just south of Turin, is the most famous, as much for its gastronomy as for its wines. It produces the fantastically rich and intense Barolo and Barbaresco (made from the Nebbiolo grape) – both of which can command quite ridiculous prices. It is also the source of the more feminine and gamine-like red, Barbera, and of course the very famous, though not always quite so very chic, Asti Spumante, Italy's greatest sweet sparkling wine. Most importantly, though, grape varieties – rather than locale or predefined styles – are the key to the Piedmont. It would take a whole chapter to do them justice, so all I can recommend is that you just take a punt once in a while and see what you think. It will be several years before you've even begun to exhaust the possibilities.

Lombardy is far less well known than Piedmont, but it produces some stunning reds and wonderful dry sparkling wines, while the Valle d'Aosta to the east produces one or two interesting reds.

 Major white grape varieties:
Muscat, Arneis, Trebbiano, Vermentino.

 Major red grape varieties:
Nebbiolo, Barbera.

 Key areas to watch:
Piedmont as a whole, Valtellina, Lugana,
Franciacorta (all in Lombardy), Valle d'Aosta.

 Names to look out for:
Altara, Cà dei Frati, Ca' del Bosco, Ceretto, Aldo Conterno,
Fontanafredda, Angelo Gaja, Bruno Rocca, La Spinetta.

NORTHEAST

The northeast of Italy is divided into three main wine regions: the Veneto, Friuli, and Trentino-Alto Adige.

The Veneto is home to Soave and Valpolicella, two wines that have a poorer reputation over here than they truly deserve. That may be because we are sent an awful lot of the rubbish that is produced, but in both cases – when well made – the wines can be wonderful. It is also the home of one of Italy's most underappreciated wines – at least in the UK. Recioto and Amarone are the result of grapes picked and dried on special racks before being fermented – what emerges is some deliciously intense, powerful and alcoholic reds and whites that can be sweet or dry.

The Friuli region produces mainly aromatic styles of wine, with the best coming from the Colli (Goriziano) and Colli Orientali sectors. Grapes such as Tocai Friulano, Pinot Grigio (which can be very good), Sauvignon Blanc and Pinot Blanc abound, alongside Chardonnay and a few reds, mainly produced using Cabernet Franc or Merlot.

Last, the Trentino-Alto Adige region tends to produce more Germanic styles of wine in both red and white. Quality is mixed, and prices high, so it tends to be the most risky of the regions to experiment with.

 Major white grape varieties:
Garganega, Trebbiano di Soave, Chardonnay,
Tocai Friulano, Verduzzo, Traminer, Muskatellers.

 Major red grape varieties:
Corvina, Refosco, Lagrein, Schiava.

 Key areas to watch:
Veneto, Collio, Colli Orientali (both Friuli),
Trentino, Alto-Adige.

 Names to look out for:
Veneto: Anselmi, Pieropan, Allegrini, Quintarelli,
Maculan; *Friuli*: Jermann, Puiatti, Dario Raccaro,
Schiopetto; *Trentino*: Ferrari, Foradori, San Leonardo;
Alto Adige: Franz Haas, San Michele Appiano.

CENTRAL

This is home to Italy's most famous wine, Chianti, but a region that has more to offer than just that. Tuscany itself, for example, produces several wines other than Chianti, although most are made from the same grape variety, namely Sangiovese. Take, for example, Brunello di Montalcino, or Vino Nobile di Montepulciano; or the wonderful Carmignano subregion, which has done some fantastic work with Cabernet Sauvignon; or Vernaccia di San Gimignano – an often superb white wine from Tuscany. And there are also some very good wines made using Cabernet Sauvignon, although, thanks to the stringent classification systems, these tend to be known simply as *vini da tavola* (or table wines).

Then there's Emilia-Romagna, home to Lambrusco – some of which is terrible, but some of which is delicious. Then the Marche, which makes fantastic whites from Verdicchio but also some superb reds, principally from the Montepulciano grape variety. There's Latium and its famous Frascati, and, of course, Abruzzo and its wonderful Trebbianos. And last, but certainly not least, Umbria, which is one of the few Italian regions to be seriously producing Pinot Noir, Chardonnay and Cabernet Sauvignon alongside its most famous home-grown product, Orvieto – a white that can be variable, but is usually interesting.

However, Chianti is indeed central Italy's greatest export and, while there are seven different zones in Chianti (named after the seven hills surrounding the town of Chianti), there are a couple that tend to be more reliable than most: Chianti Rufina and Chianti Classico. The latter is the more important and the one you really want to see on the label when you next pick up a bottle to go with Jamie Oliver's latest little Italian-inspired kitchen creation.

 Major white grape varieties:
Trebbiano, Chardonnay, Vernaccia,
Malvasia, Verdicchio.

 Major red grape varieties:
Sangiovese, Montepulciano (the Marche only),
Cabernet Sauvignon, Lambrusco.

 Key areas to watch:
Chianti Classico, Vino Nobile di Montepulciano,
Emilia-Romagna, Latium, Abruzzo, Umbria.

 Names to look out for:
Tuscany: Castello di Brolio, Isole e Olena, Felsina Berardenga,
La Massa, Querciabella, Poliziano (Vino Nobile), Tenuta di Capezzana
(Carmignano), Il Borro, Ornellaia (VdT); *Marche*: Coroncino,
Umani Ronchi; *Umbria*: Caprai, Palazzone.

SOUTHERN ITALY AND ISLANDS

Southern Italy is a big-volume producer that's been lost in the shadows of its wealthy northern relations for quite a long time. However, areas such as Campania, Puglia, Basilicata and Calabria are all pulling their socks up and trying hard to project a higher quality image. And to some extent they're having some success. Campania, for example, is producing some fabulous reds from very obscure local varieties, while Puglia produces some great Chardonnays and lovely, spicy, very drinkable reds. Basilicata is making some fantastic reds from the native Aglianico del Vulture – not a big seller on name alone, but it does a roaring trade on the basis of its deep, dark chocolate and black-cherry fruit flavours.

And then of course there are the islands, Sicily and Sardinia. The latter is doing some great stuff with home-grown grape varieties such as Cannonau and Carignano, which produce wonderfully chewy, powerful reds, and making some delicious whites from the likes of Vermentino. As for Sicily – well it's no wonder that an island that regularly produces more wine than the whole of Australia (yup, that's right) should eventually start sending us over some of the good stuff. In particular they make some stunning reds from the Nero d'Avola variety, as well as some delicious whites – though these are usually from international varieties such as Chardonnay and Sauvignon Blanc.

 Major white varieties:
Greco, Chardonnay, Sauvignon Blanc, Vermentino.

 Major red varieties:
Cannonau, Carignano, Negroamaro, Primitivo,
Nero d'Avola, Cabernet Sauvignon.

 Key areas to watch:
Campania, Puglia, Basilicata, Calabria, Sicily, Sardinia.

 Names to look out for:
Puglia: Candido, Tenute Rubino, Cosimo Taurino;
Campania: Collio di Lapio, Feudi di San Gregorio;
Basilicata: D'Angelo, Paternoster; *Calabria*: Librandi;
Sicily: Abraxas, de Bartoli, Calatrasi, Inycon, Planeta;
Sardinia: Argiolas, Gallura, Sella & Mosca.

New Zealand

Tiny nation, relatively tiny production, especially in comparison with its enormous neighbour, Australia. The thing is, however, that, in general, New Zealand produces the goods – especially on the white side – which means it can often name its price.

Sauvignon Blanc has clearly helped establish the country's identity internationally, especially thanks to the likes of Cloudy Bay, though it makes fairly decent Chardonnay as well.

The problem comes when you turn to New Zealand's reds. The Cabernet Sauvignon and Merlot they've produced so far always tends to be on the young, raw and green side. It's a little like an adolescent who hasn't quite decided what she wants to do careerwise yet – though there are one or two wineries that seem to have brought things under control and are now producing Bordeaux blends that give great delight.

More recently, New Zealand has been producing Pinot Noirs that have even the most dedicated Burgundy aficionado taking a second look. The problem is that they have a fair idea that this is the case, and so, for the very best Pinots, the prices are reaching almost extortionate levels. And they've also been doing some sterling work with Riesling – a grape they stand more chance of marketing properly than the Germans currently do.

It's the cool climate more than anything else that makes New Zealand so well suited to the likes of Sauvignon Blanc and Pinot Noir, helping them achieve the zip and zing in fruit and structure terms that both these grape varieties so desperately crave.

Three wine regions dominate: Marlborough (South Island), Hawkes Bay and Gisborne (both North Island). But there are others, such as Central Otago on the South Island, that are beginning to emerge as strong competitors.

Main white grape varieties:
Sauvignon Blanc, Riesling, Chardonnay, Pinot Gris.

Main red grape varieties:
Cabernet Sauvignon, Merlot, Pinot Noir.

Key areas to watch:
Marlborough, Gisborne, Otago, Hawkes Bay,
Martinborough, Waiheke Island.

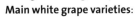 **Names to look out for**:
Ata Rangi, Cloudy Bay, Craggy Range, Dry River, Esk Valley, Felton Road, Forrest Estate, Hunter's, Jackson Estate, Palliser Estate, Seresin, Stonyridge, Te Mata, Villa Maria, Wither Hills.

Portugal

If Portugal could garner as much notice and fame for its whites and reds scattered throughout the country as it does for the fortified liquid it makes in the northern Douro region, it would truly be a force to be reckoned with. Sadly, however, most Portuguese still wines tend to stay that side of the border – and some, frankly, can stay there. The Douro itself, as well as being the source of port, is also the home for some increasingly classy reds, but the rest of the country is still lagging behind somewhat. Bairrada and Dão are the two regions that stick out uppermost in the mind when one is thinking of good, solid, basic reds and whites. Fortunately, however, there is a whole new breed of young winemakers emerging – people like Dirk Niepoort, who makes the fabulous Redoma range – who look as if they stand a good chance of kick-starting the country's still-wine regions out of their slumber and into the twenty-first century.

From the point of view of port, though, the country has the world eating out of its hand. Only one other fortified wine in the world comes close to matching the wonderful drink that port is – and that's Madeira, also the produce of Portugal.

Major white grape varieties:
Albarinho.

Major red grape varieties:
Touriga Nacional, Tinta Barroca, Touriga Francesa, Tinta Câo, Tinta Roriz.

Key areas to watch:
The Douro, Dão, Bairrada, Estremadura, Ribatejo.

Names to look out for:
Port: Dow, Fonseca, Graham, Quinta do Noval, Taylor, Warre, Quinta do Vesuvio; Nieport; *Madeira*: Blandy's, Cossart Gordon, Henriques & Henriques; *Bairrada*: Luis Pato; *Dão*: Quinta dos Roques, Conde de Santar; *Douro*: Niepoort, Quinta do Portal, Quinta do Crasto; *Estremadura*: Quinta da Boavista, Quinta de Pancas.

South Africa

It's very straightforward, really. In simple terms, South Africa is one of the most exciting, potentially exhilarating wine nations of the moment. It has spent the last decade bouncing back resiliently from the body blows of the apartheid regime that almost crippled its wine industry and is now poised to become a major player in the British wine market. And that is good for all wine punters, because what South Africa seems to be doing really well is not just providing a reasonable drop of juice at around the £4–5 mark, but increasingly giving us some fabulous value in the £5–8 bracket. And that's important because it is the bracket most people find difficult to shop in for fear of being ripped off.

In grape terms, South Africa covers all the bases as far as international varieties are concerned, but there are a few that it is not so hot on and a couple that it excels at. Sauvignon Blanc in particular is something that seems eminently suited to the country's climate, despite its being a little on the hot side. Chardonnay does well, too, as do Merlot and Cabernet. Best of all, though – and this is with a firm eye on the future because there are not that many making their way over here yet – Shiraz looks to have enormous potential, producing wonderfully robust, characterful wines with plenty of oomph. There are also one or two top-class sparklers emerging from the country's vineyards and, when they get it right with Chenin Blanc, they get it very right indeed. I am not, however, much of a fan of Pinotage. I think it's something of an acquired taste, and to date I have failed to acquire it.

The main wine-producing areas are situated around Cape Town, but drive quite far inland and along the coast. The oldest, Constantia, dates back to the late seventeenth century, when the first Dutch settlers landed in the Cape, but neighbouring Stellenbosch is just about the biggest and home to some of the Cape's best wineries.

 Major white grape varieties:
Chardonnay, Chenin Blanc, Sauvignon Blanc.

 Major red grape varieties:
Cabernet Sauvignon, Pinot Noir, Merlot, Syrah, Pinotage.

 Key areas to watch:
Constantia, Stellenbosch, Robertson, Franschhoek, Paarl, Simonsberg, Elgin.

 Names to look out for:
Beaumont, Graham Beck, Boekenhoutskloof, Bouchard Finlayson, Jean Daneel, Neil Ellis, Fairview, Ken Forrester, Glen Carlou, Hamilton Russell, Hartenburg, Iona, Jordan, Rustenberg, Spice Route, Thelema, Vergelegen, Warwick Estate.

Spain

Spain produces some of Europe's most delicious reds, and increasingly some of its most interesting whites. Yet it's famous for only one thing, really, and that's Rioja. That is a shame, because it has so much to offer.

Like the rest of Europe's winescape, however, Spain loves it wine laws and classifications. This can make it a bit tricky getting to know the rest of the county's wine regions outside Rioja. Their version is the Denominación de Origen (DO) and there are more than fifty of them. I'm not going to run through them all here, but it's fair to say that Spain, more than Italy perhaps, has managed to keep its DO system relatively well preserved. So it's still very much an indication of quality as much as of where the wine comes from.

NORTHWEST

The Ribera del Duero is northwest Spain's most dominant DO and it's the region that has managed to rocket most – in terms of reputation and price – over recent years. It harbours perhaps the most highly priced wines in Spain, including the fabled producer Vega Sicilia and a host of others that are catching up quickly, such the cult wine Pesquera and Pingus.

The main variety grown is Tempranillo, which produces the most deliciously sweet strawberry and cherry fruit flavours. The best producers in Ribera take this fruit character and intensify it, giving it structure, depth and complexity.

However, there are other equally impressive if less well-known DOs. Rías Baixas on the northern coast makes the most delicious dry whites from a grape variety called Albariño. The closest comparison is probably a Riesling from Australia, where the fruit is rich and in your face, but the wine is also crisp, zingy and very refreshing. Further inland Valdeorras also makes light dry whites from the Godello grape, along with some interesting reds.

Then there's Rueda, which is increasingly home to some of the country's most exciting whites, made in the main from Verdejo but also with increasing amounts of Sauvignon Blanc creeping in. Again, the whites are dry, with a deliciously peachy, lemony fruit character, a racy zing and slight nuttiness. To the west of Rueda is Toro, which produces some fantastically beefy reds from a local grape known as Tinta de Toro. Some are so deep, they almost seem like Australian Syrah when first opened, and it's no surprise that winemakers from across Spain are slowly but surely investing in the region. Last, and probably least, there's Cigales, which makes some fun reds and the odd rosé but nothing too special to write home about.

 Major white grape varieties:
Albariño, Godello, Sauvignon Blanc.

 Major red grape varieties:
Tempranillo, Tinta da Toro, Garnacha.

 Key areas to watch:
Ribera del Deuro, Toro, Rias Baixas, Rueda.

 Names to keep an eye on:
Alíon, Cillar de Silos, Pesquera, Dominio de Pingus, Vega Sicilia (*Ribera del Duero*), Alquiriz, Viña Bajoz (*Toro*), Marques de Griñon, Durius, (*Rueda*) lagar de Cervera, Pazo de Barrantes, Pazo de Señorans (*Rias Baixas*).

NORTHEAST

Rioja is the focus around which everything else in Spain flows. Based in the northeast, it is divided into three winegrowing areas: the Rioja Alta, the Rioja Alavesa and the Rioja Baja. Nearly all Rioja is made from a combination of Tempranillo and Garnacha grapes, with the former taking the lion's share of the blend. And nearly all is a blend from wines taken from the three aforementioned areas. What that means is that the producer, rather than the region, is all important in Rioja, almost as important as the oak treatment he or she decides to give the wine.

Nearly all Rioja is oaked – and often for a relatively long period of time. This gives it that characteristic sweet vanilla flavour, but can also dry the wine out and reduce the 'fruitiness' of the Tempranillo. However, tradition is giving way to modern methods and, while oak still plays a massively important part in the making of Rioja, many younger producers are taking their foot off the oak pedal, easing back, and producing much more fruit-led versions. You can find white Riojas, made mainly from Viura, but its not the region's strength.

While Rioja may still be the northeast's most famous export, it has strong competition in the popularity stakes. Neighbouring Navarre, for example, produces some great rosés, and its reds are increasingly popular, and good, especially now that more Tempranillo is being used alongside the traditional Garnacha grape variety. Similarly, Somantano is doing some promising work with international grape varieties (Cabernet Sauvignon, Chardonnay, Merlot etc.). At the moment it is still relatively unknown but several producers are beginning to help put it on the map.

Then there's Catalonia, in which the largest DO is Penedès, home to the only internationally known wine that gives Rioja a run for its money in Spain: Cava. This is Spain's sparkling wine, and while it isn't produced only in Penedès, that is where the majority of the best examples come from. Cava is traditionally made from a mix of Macabeo, Parellada and Xarel-lo, but increasingly there are versions featuring the classic Champagne grape varieties of Chardonnay and Pinot Noir.

For still wines, Catalonia most notably contains the DO of Priorato – perhaps the most talked-about DO in Spain. Traditionally the region has been using Garnacha and Cariñena as its main vine varieties, but over the last decade several producers have been blending in Cabernet Sauvignon, Merlot and Syrah to produce increasingly impressive wines, with depth, fantastic fruit and thrilling structure. Just north of Priorato is Conca de Barbera, mainly a DO devoted to growing grapes for Cava production. Other DO regions include Costers del Sagre (strong on Tempranillo- and Bordeaux-style blends), Alella (crisp dry whites) and Campo de Borja (increasingly fine reds aimed at the value sector of the market).

 Major white grape varieties:

Macabeo, Parellada, Xarel-Lo, Chardonnay.

 Major red grape varieties:

Tempranillo, Garnacha, Cabernet Sauvignon, Merlot.

 Key areas to watch:

Priorato and Navarre stand out as the big competitors to Rioja.

 Names to keep an eye on:

Jean Léon, Miguel Torres, Codorníu, Freixenet (*Penedès*),
Clos Mogador, Palacios L'Ermita, Finca Dofí, Mas Martinet (*Priorato*),
Artadi, Barón de Ley, CVNE, Marqués de Griñon, Muga, Remelluri,
La Rioja Alta (*Rioja*), Guelbenzu, Chivité, Ochoa (*Navarra*).

CENTRAL AND SOUTH

The central part of Spain, around the capital of Madrid, is dominated by the DO of La Mancha, which is actually Europe's largest demarcated wine region. Sadly, however, it doesn't match quantity with quality. The most planted grape variety is Airén, a fairly innocuous characterless white, and that's probably the best way to describe the wines that result.

However, La Mancha has been undergoing a quiet revolution in wine production over the last decade or two and there are now some producers making up for lost time. The most quality-led section of La Mancha is the enclave of Valdepeñas, which makes some intense, deep and very flavoursome Tempranillos. It's also doing some wonderful things with international varieties, so keep an eye out in the future for some decent Cabernet and Syrah.

To the south, running towards the coast, is the region known as the Levante. It's a rather peculiar mix of DOs, all of which are relatively small and bijoux compared with their central and northern counterparts. However, experiments combining traditional Spanish varieties with the likes of Cabernet , Merlot and Syrah are proving very fruitful.

The DOs to look out for include Utiel Requena, Yecla, Jumilla and Bullas. And for those snobs who consider Alicante to be the home of the worst kind of package holiday for Brits, it also happens to be capable of producing reasonably drinkable, if somewhat simple, wines. And the same goes for the Canary Islands and Majorca. The latter produces some enviable and deliciously deep fruity reds from the local staple grape, Manto Negra, while the Canary Islands are very adept at producing some excellent dry whites. You have to be a bit picky, especially since the islands contain as many as ten different DOs, but it's worth it on the occasional day that the beach and bar don't beckon.

 Major white grape varieties:
Airén, Malvasia, Chardonnay.

 Major red grape varieties:
Tempranillo (often in the form of Cencibel), Monastrell, Bobal, Manta Negro, Cabernet Sauvignon, Syrah, Merlot.

 Key areas to watch:
Valdepeñas, Utiel Requena, Jumilla.

 Names to keep an eye on:
Dominio de Valdepusa (*La Mancha*), Los Llanos (*Valdepeñas*), Enrique Mendoza, Gutierrez de la Vega (*Alicante*), Anima Negra (*Mallorca*), Casa de La Ermita (*Jumilla*)

ANDALUSIA AND JEREZ

Andalusia produces a variety of wines, but by a long chalk the best and most notable is sherry.

This may sound odd, but I can guarantee that there's a 50 per cent chance that, if you have tried sherry, you won't have liked it. But that's not because you don't like sherry, necessarily, rather that you've tried one of the sickly sweet versions known as British sherry that bear little relation to the true nature of the original stuff.

Jerez in Andalusia is the home of sherry. There are a variety of styles of sherry moving from bone-dry through to sweet. What they have in common is that at some point in their life they entered a unique system known as the *solera* – a process of ageing wines unique to Jerez and sherry. It works on the simple basis of keeping older wines in a barrel 'topped up' with younger wines so that the blend is nearly always 'fresh' and the style and flavour consistent. A rough basis is that for every third of each barrel taken off and bottled, a third of new, freshly made sherry is added.

The two most basic styles of sherry are Fino and Manzanilla – both of which are dry, fresh and fruity. They derive their unique nutty, tangy crisp flavours from the yeast or 'flor' that sits in the top of each wooden barrel as the wine ages (for around three years). It protects the wine from the air and imparts a distinctive tang to it. The difference between the two is that the Fino is aged in *solera* in Jerez, whereas the Manzanilla is aged in *solera* in Sanlúcar de Barrameda, just outside Jerez.

The other styles include Amontillado (which has been aged in the *solera* system for five years or more, past the time the flor naturally dies). It's bone-dry and usually and a darker colour because of the extra ageing period, although you can get versions that have been 'sweetened'. Oloroso is a sherry that has been fortified before the flor develops (the flor can only survive at around 15 per cent alcohol – anything higher and it dies), which means the wine ages with air contact. Hence an oloroso is much darker in colour, with a nutty, intense, raisin-laden fruit flavour.

If Fino, Manzanilla and to some extent Amontillado are ideal aperitifs before dinner, then the latter two styles are real winter warmers, capable of banishing the chills in an instant.

If you haven't tried sherry before, give it a go. You can only decide you don't like it, but there's every possibility you might love it.

Major white grape varieties:
Palomino, Pedro Ximenez (used in a reduced form to sweeten certain styles of sherry).

Key areas to watch:
Just look for Jerez or Sanlucar de Barrameda on the label, but it's the producers that really make a difference.

Names to keep an eye on:
Argüeso, Barbadillo, Domecq, Gonzalez Byass, Hidalgo, Lustau, Osborne, Valdespino, Williams & Humbert.

United States

In volume terms, the USA is really only one region, and the rest don't amount to much more than a hill of beans, as John Wayne used to say. California is that one region, with its rich subdivisions and many differing climates. It produces 98 per cent of all the wine made in the USA and knows exactly how to sell and market itself. And, as with most things American, there's a certain amount of gloss and glitz that needs to be wiped aside before you can tell what's really underneath.

Part of the problem with California is that it is extremely highly priced. There are some high street names, such as E & J Gallo, fighting at the £5–7 price bracket, but not that many more. Most Californian wines start at around £8–9 or above in the UK, and that makes them relatively uncompetitive. Part of the reason for this is that land prices in California are ludicrously high – thanks primarily to the Internet boom of several years ago and the presence of lots of computer nerds from Silicon Valley who retired on fortunes in the early 90s and decided to open a winery. But in recent years California has suffered something of a wine glut. This means we're seeing some more wines creep in under the £7 mark – and that's good, because California has an awful lot to offer, even if it is working with very familiar varieties such as Chardonnay, Cabernet and Merlot. One grape that is fairly exclusive to California is Zinfandel, which produces big, full-on fruity wines with a spicy, punchy nature. They're not to everyone's taste but they really are unique.

The most important wine areas in California are headed up by the Napa Valley, which has some of the highest quality-oriented wineries. Sonoma Valley, Russian River Valley, Dry Creek and Los Carneros are all also major sources for top-quality merchandise.

About the only significant place other than California where wine is produced in the States is in the Pacific Northwest, which comprises Washington and Oregon states. The latter is best known for its work with Pinot and Chardonnay, while Washington has been doing some fantastic stuff with Cabernet and some very interesting Rieslings, and also producing some stunning, world-class Syrahs. Sadly, though, by the time they make their way over here, the price has usually shot through the roof, making them a specialist wine for the dedicated (and probably slightly overpaid) enthusiast.

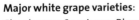 **Major white grape varieties**:
Chardonnay, Sauvignon Blanc.

Major red grape varieties:
Cabernet Sauvignon, Syrah, Merlot, Zinfandel, Pinot Noir.

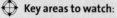 **Key areas to watch**:
California: Napa Valley, Sonoma Valley, Russian River Valley,
Alexander Valley, Los Carneros; *Washington state*:
Columbia Valley, Walla Walla; *Oregon*: Willamette Valley.

Names to look out for:
California: Arrowood, Au Bon Climat, Beringer, Cain, Caymus,
Dalla Valle, Diamond Creek, Domaine Chandon, Fetzer Bonterra,
Gallo Estate, Kistler, Robert Mondavi, Nalle, Rochioli; *Washington state*:
L'Ecole No. 41, Leonetti Cellar, Andrew Will; *Oregon*: Adelsheim,
Cristom, Domaine Drouhin, Evesham Wood, King Estate, Ponzi.

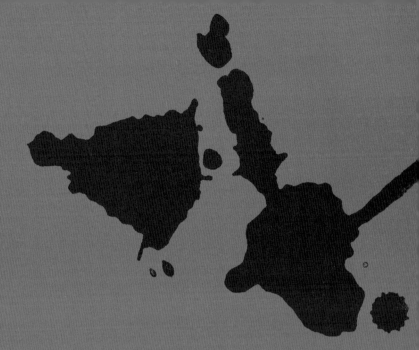

chapter fourteen
matchmaking

Most people think matching wine and food is about the combination of great wines with fine food: top-class champagne with river-caught smoked salmon, Sauternes with foie gras, Château Haut-Brion with rib of beef.

Poppycock. That's part of it. Don't get me wrong. Good food – especially *great* food – requires great wines. But the fact is we spend an awful lot of our time eating takeaways, fast food or comfort food. Few of us have three-course dining experiences twice a day, every day. So you'll find this chapter has several distinct sections, dedicated to the consumption of junk food, comfort food and what we might term ooh-la-la food.

It's also, unashamedly, one of the largest in the book. And that's because most of us don't sit around tasting wine and comparing notes. Most of have a glass of wine with our dinner, or with friends and food. Which is why I am always stunned by those TV shows where chefs spend three-quarters of an hour creating a beautiful dish, but then don't tell anyone what to serve with it.

Note, though, that these are handy hints, not the law! You can take 'em or leave 'em. It's up to you.

I'm sure we've all been in that position where we think we should drink one thing when we would rather drink another, because tradition says such and such goes with such and such. In truth, you can drink absolutely what you want with anything you want (see Chapter 9, 'Myths and Monsters', for more information). The following is just a helping hand to find a few combinations that might make watching TV or a celebratory dinner that bit sweeter and more special.

A few pointers to start with

GO FOR THE SAUCE
With the exception of Sunday roasts, a very large number of the dishes we eat, whether meat- or vegetable-based, end up smothered with sauce, or highly flavoured with herbs or spices. In a way, the meat and vegetables are often merely a handy way of conveying these flavours to our mouth and adding a little bit of added texture. So, when trying to work out what you're having with, say, coq au vin, it's the sauce that's important, not the chicken.

WEIGHTY SUBJECTS
It's not always the case, but it's a good rule of thumb that often light wines will go with light dishes, while richer, more intense wines will go

with heavier hitters in the flavours department. So try to match the weight of the wine with the richness or strength of the dish's flavours.

IT'S NOT ROCKET SCIENCE

Think about this. If you were given a pork chop baked in cider in the West Country, you'd be sorely tempted to have a nice cold pint of cider with it. So don't mess around when it comes to wine. Lamb roasted in Burgundy – bring on the Burgundy. Steak-and-ale pie – forget the wine and go for a nice pint of Adnams. As I say, it's not rocket science.

Everyday, comfort food

It's all very well knowing what goes with foie gras, caviar or truffles – or having the perfect match for a plate of yakitori or a Thai green curry, not to mention knowing the ideal combination for a plate of garden fresh, seasonal asparagus.

But the reality is that, especially during the week, our menus are a little more mundane and pedestrian. That doesn't mean you can't enjoy a decent glass or two of wine – or that it won't benefit from a little thought on the food-and-wine-pairing front.

BAKED BEANS

A nice rosé will do the job, but I really like a sweet, juicy, redcurranty red with baked beans that will work well with the rich, sweet tomato sauce – perhaps a Grenache from the South of France or a young Barbera from the north of Italy, or a nice Shiraz from South Africa.
My favourite match: Southern French Grenache.

BANGERS AND MASH

A classic dish that, if you're going for a straightforward banger, requires something soft, juicy, red and raring to go. Try a good Chilean Merlot, or a nice juicy, basic Aussie Cabernet – wines with lots of fruit and a nice whack of silky tannins that will slip down easily. If you've gone for a slightly more exotic sausage, such as a spicy Moroccan merguez, or perhaps wild boar, you might want something a little more substantial, such as a big Aussie Shiraz, or perhaps a red from the Douro region of Portugal, where there are lovely, deep fruit flavours but also a bit of a kick.
My favourite match: Chilean Merlot or a decent Shiraz.

BARBECUE

Pretty generic term, I know, but when it comes to barbecue, whether
it's fish, fowl or red meat, all have that one distinctive charred quality in
common. So that means you need to up the ante a little. With red meats,
it's got to be quite big, juicy, jammy reds, so Aussie Shiraz, South African
Pinotage or Argentinian Malbec are all in the frame. With seafood or fish,
it's big, oaked whites – perhaps Semillon or Chardonnay. Or quite tropical
styles of Sauvignon (from Australia and New Zealand) or a wide variety
of rosés. The trick, whether red or white, is to make sure they have lots
of body and fruit, but also good acidity.
My favourite match: Lots, literally. Aussie Shiraz and a good Semillon
cover most bases, though.

BUBBLE AND SQUEAK

Lovely basic dish that can be enlivened with bacon or ham. I like medium-
weight reds, so perhaps a southern French Syrah, a Beaujolais or a Chilean
Pinot Noir. But, if it's with bacon or ham, I think you can easily manage a
good Spanish rosé or get away with a nice clean, crisp, quality Chardonnay
from Australia.
My favourite match: Aussie unoaked Chardonnay.

CAESAR SALAD

Lightly oaked Chardonnays are very good with this – so a nice one from
Argentina or Chile, or perhaps the Languedoc Roussillon in France, would
all be perfect. Likewise, Sauvignon Blanc from any of these regions would
equally fit the bill, especially given the strong parmesan edge this dish has.
My favourite match: Chilean Sauvignon Blanc.

CHEESE

Don't believe the red-wine hype: there are lots of whites that go, too. With
gently flavoured hard cheeses such as mild Cheddar or Wensleydale, try a
Sauvignon Blanc, while a nice soft juicy Merlot from Chile would be a good
match with the likes of Edam or Jarlsberg. For stronger, tangier hard cheeses,
a mature Spanish, French or Italian is more appropriate. For something like
Brie or Camembert, again, Merlot works, but also a juicy Pinot Noir – both
have a sweet fruit that counters the sourness of the rind and cheese.

Goat's cheese is perfect white-wine territory, with Sauvignon Blancs
from the likes of the Loire in France or New Zealand working really well.
Blue cheeses are surprisingly good with sweet dessert wines such as
Sauternes or a nice Muscat, but also work well with tawny port. But for

most cheeses the old pairing of port is still one of the best, particularly a late-bottled-vintage (LBV) version.

My favourite match: LBV port.

COQ AU VIN

I like a nice oaked Chardonnay – a classic Burgundy, Meursault or Puligny-Montrachet, for example – but, given the rich sauce, many people prefer a red. A nice Grenache Mourvédre mix from the Languedoc-Roussillon is a good bet, or something nice and juicy from down under, perhaps a good Aussie Shiraz. But I think a classic Côtes du Rhône or a Gigondas from the Southern Rhône beats most things hands down.

My favourite match: Gigondas.

FISH PIE

If it's got a lot of smoked fish in it then you need a biggish oaked Chardonnay. If it has more shellfish, such as mussels, scallops and squid, then you probably want an unoaked Chardonnay. Either way, Chardonnay is your main choice, possibly a nice clean Italian version or a big Californian oaked number.

My favourite match: Californian Chardonnay.

GREEN SALAD

In these days of diets it's perfectly possible to end up at home of an evening chomping down a fancy green salad and little else. Personally, I go for the Italian option with this and definitely in the clean and crisp style, so Pinot Grigio, Orvieto, Italian Chardonnay or Arneis will all do.

My favourite match: Pinot Grigio.

HAGGIS

There's one grape variety that suits haggis's spicy, oatmeal-laden contents perfectly and that's Shiraz/Syrah. Whether it's the reserved but huge nature of a nice Côte-Rôtie or Châteauneuf-du-Pape, or the juicy, full-on character of an Aussie Shiraz, it will bring out the best in this dish.

My favourite match: Aussie Shiraz.

IRISH STEW

Ideally, a pint of Guinness goes best, but this is a wine book, so I'd opt instead for either a good Rioja from Spain, especially if it's quite a rich version, or a cracking raspberry-and-blackcurrant-laden heavyweight Valpolicella from Italy. A good, modern-style Bordeaux would probably do well, too.

My favourite match: Rioja.

LANCASHIRE HOTPOT

This can be quite 'claggy' in the mouth, so you need a red, ideally, and one that has a good, zippy acidity that can cleanse the mouth. A New World Pinot Noir would be good, or perhaps a nice taut red from the Marche region in Italy, with its spicy leanness. Also suitable, though, would be a Sicilian red.

My favourite match: New Zealand Pinot Noir.

LASAGNE

Classic Italian dish calling for some classic Italians. Most people go for red, which is fair enough, and there's enough choice in Italy to last a lifetime. A good, simple Barbera would be great, as would a Chianti Classico or indeed a Montepulciano d'Abruzzo, with its deep, cherry fruit flavours. But you can go white – preferably something on the light, spritzy side: a Sicilian Chardonnay, for example.

My favourite match: Chianti Classico.

LIVER AND BACON

I'm going for red, but the choice is endless. A good claret always works well, Rioja can make a dream team, and Shiraz from down under or South Africa, because of its soft juicy flavours, can make very sweet music together with a plate of liver and smoked bacon.

My favourite match: Rioja, preferably a Gran Reserva.

MEATBALLS

Depends on whether they're spicy or not, but if they are then you need something with a bit of punch. Perhaps a California Zinfandel, or a nice zesty, peppery Aussie Shiraz. You could also try a nice chewy Portuguese red, from the Douro or Dão regions.

My favourite match: California Zinfandel.

MOUSSAKA

Great Greek dish, and you might try putting a Greek red on your wine list, but I'd tend to go with some more easily pronounceable creations. Southern Italian reds go great, as does the lovely produce of Priorato in northern Spain. I also think the Douro in Portugal makes some reds that contribute a ridiculous amount to even the worst-baked Moussaka.

My favourite match: Primitivo (southern Italy).

NOODLES

Noodles are a bit like chicken in that it all depends on what you're serving them with, or how you are serving them. I think most noodles, certainly in Thai or Japanese dishes, end up with a bit of natural chilli spice added to them, so it's wise to watch out for you drink. I'd tend to plump for a white, unless it's obvious to do otherwise, and would go for a New World Riesling, a Gewürz from Alsace, or perhaps a nice Verdelho from Spain. **My favourite match**: Gewürztraminer.

PASTA

If it's a cream-based sauce, with anything from smoked bacon to a bit of broccoli, you ideally need white – preferably unoaked or lightly oaked, but with quite a lot of fruit character. A good New Zealand Sauvignon usually does the trick, too. But without a doubt Verdicchio, particularly from the Marches on the east coast of Italy, is great. When the sauces are more tomato-based or exceptionally highly spiced, you obviously need reds, so Sangiovese (not necessarily from Italy), is great, as is Chianti or Merlot (preferably a soft one from the New World).
My favourite match: Australian Riesling for whites, good Merlot for reds.

RABBIT STEW

Rabbit's more difficult than you think, but generally it's like a rich, rich chicken. A Fitou from the South of France or perhaps a nice Grenache will always be a great match – and, if you prefer a white, then a heavily oaked Chardonnay from Australia or California will work well. If it's been made into a rich terrine, it's probably a good idea to take the champagne route, especially one with decent bottle age.
My favourite match: A southern French Grenache.

RAVIOLI

It's probably no surprise that one of Italy's most famously exported dishes should be suited very much to Italian wines. A good Soave from a decent supplier will be a very good mix, as will a Sicilian white, preferably a Chardonnay. However, a relatively young light Pinot Noir works well, too.
My favourite match: Soave.

SALMON

It's quite fatty, so you need to go for something with good acidity, but also relatively strong flavours. A good classic white Burgundy works well, as does a nice crisp Chilean Chardonnay. If it's a seared or barbecued, then you might try a light red, perhaps a young Sangiovese from Italy or a light red from the Loire.
My favourite match: Chilean Chardonnay.

SEAFOOD SALAD

With any salad, it depends greatly on what the content is and, importantly, what the dressing is. Most dressings have a vinegar base, which usually destroys most wines, so it doesn't really matter what you actually drink with it. For a seafood salad, however, the flavours of the main ingredients are usually so strong it is possible to match. I'd go for something very crisp and clean – perhaps an Italian Pinot Grigio, or a crisp unoaked Chardonnay from somewhere like Argentina, or the classic and undeniably good pairing, a decent Chablis.
My favourite match: Chablis.

SHEPHERD'S PIE

I like a nice creamy strawberry-laden Rioja with this, but a basic claret is also very good, as is a nice Aussie Cabernet or Merlot. A basic hearty dish, which requires basic hearty wines.
My favourite match: Rioja.

SPAGHETTI BOLOGNESE

Straightforward, no-nonsense pasta dish that requires the same of its wine. Think Barbera, Chianti, or a decent Valpolicella – all wines with lovely, sweet, juicy fruit characters but plenty of tartness to cut through the rich, oily Bolognese sauce. Equally, a good Rioja or a southern French simple red will do.
My favourite match: Barbera (Piedmont).

STEAK

A lot of people would pair a classic claret with a good steak, but I think most steaks, because of their savoury, sanguine nature, need a richness of fruit that you don't always get from Bordeaux. I'd plump for an Aussie Shiraz or Cabernet any time. If you've got deep pockets a decent Barolo from Italy is always nice.
My favourite match: Aussie Cabernet.

STEAK-AND-KIDNEY PUDDING

Like Irish stew, this sort of dish cries out for a pint of Guinness or real ale, but in wine terms it's red – and the simpler and juicier the better. So a South African Shiraz or Chilean Cabernet are just right.
My favourite match: South African Shiraz.

TROUT

When it's just plain grilled I'd go for a light, crisp Chardonnay, or perhaps a Chenin Blanc from South Africa. If it's in an almond sauce you need something a little richer, so perhaps a Pinot Blanc from Alsace or a Chilean Chardonnay. An Aussie Riesling will also be a good match, as will German Riesling.

My favourite match: Pinot Blanc (Alsace).

TUNA

If it's been seared on a barbecue or griddle, you've got several options. Perhaps a strongly flavoured Sauvignon Blanc from New Zealand or South Africa, or alternatively a light red, perhaps a Pinot Noir, or a light red from the Loire – both of which can be chilled just a little. Personally, I like a good southern French rosé.

My favourite match: Southern French rosé.

TURKEY

Ah, the Christmas favourite, often spoiled by being washed down with dodgy claret. If you want red with your turkey, you're much better off with a decent Châteauneuf-du-Pape or frankly a good, simple Chilean Merlot. I like a rich Riesling or a wonderfully spiced Viognier, from Condrieu, with my turkey.

My favourite match: Viognier.

Sunday roasts

We all love 'em, and they are beautifully simple to match wine with. Assume that you'll have parsnips, peas, roast potatoes and Yorkshire puddings included on the menu – but it's still the meat that needs to be matched when it comes to a good old-fashioned Sunday roast.

ROAST BEEF

Claret is usually the one picked as the classic pairing for roast beef, but I think a Merlot from Bordeaux usually works much better. For me, though, a good Châteauneuf-du-Pape is actually best with a big roast rib of beef, or a lovely Côte-Rôtie. Alternatively, a really top-class Aussie Shiraz will always show well, as will a really good Barolo from Italy.

My favourite match: Châteauneuf-du-Pape.

ROAST CHICKEN

As with all chicken, it depends on what you flavour it with, but, for your common-or-garden, straightforward chicken roast, I think a good Chardonnay, oaked, or a really nice Pinot Noir is just perfect, whether from Burgundy or somewhere more far-flung such as Australia.
My favourite match: Basic red Burgundy.

ROAST DUCK

Pinot Noir, either New World or Old World, works fantastically well with duck, but also Italy provides some very good matches in the guise of top-class Chianti, Barbera and Barolo. Also, a Valpolicella Ripasso (much better than your bog-standard Valpolicella) is a great match.
My favourite match: Barbera.

ROAST GOOSE

As with duck, Pinot Noir from around the world is usually a great match, but I actually prefer a powerful white to match what is a less dark, more subtle meat than duck. I'd go for a good German Riesling or a wonderfully rich and intense Alsace Gewürztraminer. A classy Viognier from Condrieu in France is an exceptional match, too.
My favourite match: Gewürztraminer from Alsace.

ROAST LAMB

I think that classic good red Bordeaux, i.e. claret, is as good a mix for lamb as it is for beef, if not better. But what does go fantastically well with roast lamb is a nicely aged, top-class Rioja. Pinot Noir can also be lovely, though, as long as it's a biggish version of the grape, so classic Burgundy would work.
My favourite match: Rioja Reserva.

ROAST PORK

You've got to love it, and you've got have something that can cut through the fattiness of the meat, but not overpower its relatively mild meat flavour. If it's white, a good southern French Chardonnay, or a nice Californian Viognier works well, and with reds a slightly chilled Beaujolais or juicy Chilean Merlot is perfect. I also like a good unoaked Aussie Chardonnay.
My favourite match: A nice juicy Morgon (Beaujolais, France).

Ooh-la-la dishes

There's always the opportunity to spoil ourselves, whether it's in a restaurant or in our own kitchen with a copy of Jamie Oliver's latest tome propped up in front of the kitchen scales. This is a dipping of the toe in the lake of the luxury food that's around, but hopefully it'll give you a few ideas to help find a good wine match.

BEEF CARPACCIO

Beef served this way actually has quite a subtle flavour. So don't overpower it with an over-the-top red. Go for something juicy and mid-weight, such as a good basic Pinot Noir from Burgundy, or a lightish Cabernet Sauvignon from the South of France. A nice young Chianti is pretty impressive, though you could actually get away with a nice deep, rich rosé if you wanted.
My favourite match: Chianti (Italy).

BEEF WELLINGTON

The thing about beef Wellington is that it is wrapped not only in pastry, but in a reasonably thick layer of rich, intense pâté. So you've got quite a few flavours going on there. You need a powerful, ideally red, wine to cope with all that. A good Shiraz from Australia with a couple of years of age on it would be great, but the classic would be a Cabernet Sauvignon from Bordeaux, or a nice Châteauneuf-du-Pape from the Rhône.
My favourite match: Châteauneuf-du-Pape (Rhône).

CAVIAR

On the rare occasion I've been lucky enough to blag some of this, I have found that the classic champagne and caviar match is actually pretty unbeatable – especially if you go for an extra-dry drop of fizz. As for iced vodka – I've never understood the pairing, but the Russians go mad for it.
My favourite match: Champagne.

DOVER SOLE

There are a variety of choices to make. You can go for a top-class Chablis, or if you like a little oak on your Chardonnay then perhaps a very traditional Puligny-Montrachet. Alternatively, Sauvignon Blanc is a very good match and I think the more tropical style from New Zealand tends to go better than Sancerre.
My favourite match: New Zealand Sauvignon Blanc.

DRESSED CRAB

If you love seafood, you usually adore crab. But it's not easy to match with wine. Half of it is delicate white flesh, the other half a rich intense pâté-like meat. I think a good Chablis, or an unoaked Aussie Chardonnay, is about the best match you can find. But there's also white Burgundy, Sancerre, Riesling and Pinot Blanc to consider, as well as Viognier. A drop of decent Italian Soave doesn't go amiss, either, and a good Muscadet is an excellent partner.

My favourite match: Chablis.

FOIE GRAS

Many find this an offensive dish to serve and I can understand why. But I'll be honest, it is delicious. The classic combination is actually a Sauternes, so a sweet wine, but I think a nice rich Gewürztraminer from Alsace is a pretty good equivalent.

My favourite match: Gewürztraminer.

LANGOUSTINES

Ooh, lovely! What you want with a plate of these is a nice, lightly oaked but very good Chardonnay. So either classic Burgundy, say Montrachet, or a decent St-Véran – or a new world Chardonnay, perhaps from Australia or California.

My favourite match: St-Véran.

LOBSTER

Depends on how it's served, really. Champagne is a great match, particularly a rich style. But Chardonnay and Sauvignon Blanc are both very good when it's served cold with mayonnaise or as a lobster salad. If it's in a rich sauce and cooked, as with lobster thermidor, for example, you need something a little more substantial, and with more punch. An oaky Aussie or California Chardonnay would be good, as would a French Viognier.

My favourite match: Classic white Burgundy – take your pick.

MONKFISH

Quite a meaty texture, so you can go a bit more full on with a fish like this. I think Albariño from northern Spain and Gavi from Italy are two very good matches, although again a classic Burgundy also works well. What's great is that you can go for a light red, say a Beaujolais or a nice light Grenache, perhaps even slightly chilled.

My favourite match: Beaujolais on the reds or Gavi if white.

OYSTERS

A century ago raw oysters would never have made it into the ooh-la-la list. Now they're a staple. I think Chablis is a great match – or a crisp, clean, unoaked Chardonnay from New Zealand. Champagne is good, but unnecessarily expensive, as a good New World sparkler will do just as well.

My favourite match: New Zealand Chardonnay.

PARTRIDGE AND PHEASANT

With game, I think a good Pinot Noir – one from its homeland, Burgundy, or a really decent one from down under, or perhaps from the Pacific Northwest (US) – is without doubt one of the best matches you can find. It has a meatiness of flavour, combined with a sweetness of fruit and sharp tang that brings out the best of things like partridge and pheasant. However, a top-class Chianti Reserva, or a juicy, fresh Merlot from the likes of Chile or Australia would be just as good. Alternatively, a nice Barolo from the Piedmont will work pretty well.

My favourite match: Nuits-St-Georges, Burgundy (Pinot Noir).

QUAIL

Fiddly to eat, and usually best when chargrilled, so you need something that can stand up to quite rich flavours and a lot of fiddling around. Pinot Noir is good, but I like a decent basic Syrah or Shiraz with mine – say a Shiraz from the Barossa, or a Côtes du Rhône. Nothing overly heavy, but big enough to matter.

My favourite match: Côtes du Rhône (Syrah).

SMOKED SALMON AND GRAVADLAX

If it's just plain smoked salmon, then I'll always go for champagne, even if it is a little too predictable. If you can afford to splash out a bit, then vintage champagne is best because it has the acidity to cut through the fattiness of the salmon but also quite a rich fruity character that combats the fishiness. If it's gravadlax, with that sweet, dill and mustard sauce, you'd be better going for something like an off-dry version of Riesling or perhaps a Vouvray.

My favourite match: Champagne.

SQUID

It's on the ooh-la-la list because it's one of those dishes that people tend to eat in restaurants rather than at home. Most of the time it's fried with spring onions and chilli, which makes it a tough match. A classic

Sauvignon Blanc is the ideal, but a good rosé can do really well, too.
My favourite match: Sancerre (Sauvignon Blanc).

SUSHI AND SASHIMI
Not the easiest, because there are so many textures and flavours, but, leaving the obvious combination of sake (rice wine) to one side, there really is quite a wide variety of options. Riesling is a good one, again, but make sure it's a very young fresh one, preferably from Australia or New Zealand. Likewise, Muscadet is a great match. Basically, you want whites that are crisp and dry. Champagne is also suitable, especially if it's blanc-de-blancs.
My favourite match: Muscadet.

TRUFFLES
They are unique and so pungent – and so very expensive – that it's difficult to know what to match, although reds usually have it. A good red Burgundy or a mature medium-weight Rhône is a good match for black truffles, as are a host of Italian reds, in particular Barbera, Barolo and a good Valpolicella. With white truffles, you can opt for white – a good Italian Chardonnay or an Arneis is a good pairing.
My favourite match: A decent Barbera from the Piedmont, in Italy.

VENISON
Because it's got the same texture as beef, though a richer, more intense, gamy flavour, a lot of the same wines go. Good claret with a couple of years' bottle age works, as does a decent Rhône, perhaps an Hermitage. I like to match top-quality Spanish reds myself. A good Gran Reserva Rioja or a fine Ribera del Duero is a good choice.
My favourite match: Gran Reserva Rioja.

And for dessert …

With desserts, the only real thing to bear in mind is that ideally the wine you choose should be sweeter than the dessert, otherwise it will taste bitter and less refined. It should also have a good acidity, so that it leaves the mouth feeling clean and refreshed even after the most indulgent dessert.

BANOFFEE PIE

Quite a difficult one, this. I like a good sweet tawny port, with its orange peel and nutty flavours, which works well with the toffee in the pudding. Another good match is a sweet Tokaji from Hungary or an Australian Liqueur Muscat.

My favourite match: Tawny port.

BREAD-AND-BUTTER PUDDING

This is a classic pudding, but actually relatively light – if it's made correctly. I like a simple sweet Muscat from the South of France, or a sparkling Moscatel from Italy. A crisp, tart, late-harvest Semillon from down under is also an excellent match.

My favourite match: Muscat.

CHEESECAKE

A very rich dessert, this needs top-of-the-range sweeties to carry it off. A Beerenauslese from Germany (I know it's a mouthful) will have the right level of sweetness but also really clean, sharp acidity. Or you could try a late-harvest Riesling from Alsace.

My favourite match: Beerenauslese.

CHOCOLATE CAKE

Chocolate is actually very good with richer, sweet reds. In particular there's an Italian wine called Recioto, which is made in a dessert style, but is also a big, cherry-laden wine. It's a great match for most chocolate dishes but for a rich, gooey cake it's perfect. Also, port is a wonderful match, particularly vintage or late-bottle-vintage (LBV).

My favourite match: Recioto (Italy).

CHRISTMAS PUDDING

I think the best match is one of Italy's most underrated wines and yet it's absolutely delicious – and that's a Moscato d'Asti from the Piedmont. It's a lightly sparkling sweet wine with great charm and raciness – and it's delicious. If you can't get hold of a bottle, try a southern French Muscat instead.

My favourite match: Moscato d'Asti.

ICE CREAM

Ice creams are difficult because of the many varied flavours, but for simple

vanilla ice cream the best match I know is a sweet sherry called PX, which is thick, deliciously rich and works very well whether it's drunk alongside or poured generously over it like a sticky brown sauce.
My favourite match: PX Sherry (Jerez, Spain).

JELLY
Simple semisweet or sweet sparkling wines are the best match for jellies of all flavours. Again Moscato d'Asti is the obvious one, but you might try one of the richer styles of champagne that are produced with a little more sugar in them, making them ideal for this sort of dessert.
My favourite match: Moscato d'Asti.

LEMON MERINGUE PIE
You need big rich intense sweeties for this dessert. So we're talking late-harvest Rieslings, Beerenausleses from Germany or Botrytis Rieslings from the likes of Australia. They all have the right level of rich, honeyed sweetness, but with a good tart kick on the finish.
My favourite match: Late-harvest Riesling.

STRAWBERRIES
It all depends on what they're with or how they're prepared. For straightforward strawberries or cream it's back to Moscato d'Asti, or a demi-sec champagne. For strawberry mousses or gateaux, these would do again; but, if it's a richer, pastry-based dish, such as a tart, you want to up the ante a bit. Try a Sauternes or a Muscat de Beaumes-de-Venise.
My favourite match: Demi-sec champagne.

SUMMER PUDDING
It's worth trying an Australian Sparkling Shiraz with this dish, because the berry-dominated pudding needs something big, red and sweet to bring out the best in it, and you don't get much better than a fizzy red from down under. If that sounds a step too far for your taste buds, try an Italian Recioto or Black Muscat from Australia.
My favourite match: Sparkling Aussie Shiraz.

Fast food, fast wine

How often do we get home and find ourselves too tired to cook? Hence out comes the junk food or a takeaway. Well, believe me, you can drink wine with a burger, KFC, pizza, Chinese, Indian or Lebanese and add to the pleasure by picking the right bottle out of the wine rack. The combinations may not be as overtly impressive as caviar and champagne but they do work.

BURGERS

If it's a McDonald's you're going for, I'd suggest you stick with the milkshake, but, if you've got yourself a proper American-style hamburger, then it's akin to having a nice bit of ground steak with a smattering of extras. You need something soft, juicy and red, with a good whack of acidity. Most whites will get killed off by the ketchup/mayonnaise concoction. If your hamburger isn't sporting this, then I would genuinely question why you've bought a burger in the first place.

Likely reds: Rioja, southern French Grenache, Shiraz (South Africa), basic red Burgundy (Pinot Noir).

Possible whites: A good oaked Chardonnay from the New World will do.

CHINESE TAKEAWAYS

The difficulty with Chinese takeaway is that there is such a variety of dishes that it's difficult to know what to go for. But in general you want something to combat the natural (and sometimes unnatural) sweetness a lot of the dishes have. So you need tangy, zesty reds or whites, which is why the likes of Beaujolais, Riesling and Sauvignon Blanc work so well. With the richer, more meaty dishes, such as spare ribs or beef with black-bean sauce, you may want to up the stakes a bit, but not too much. And don't forget: rosés are fantastic with Chinese.

Likely reds: Beaujolais, Grenache (southern France, Spain), Pinot Noir, Shiraz (Australia, South Africa).

Possible whites: Champagne, Sauvignon Blanc, Riesling (Australia, Alsace).

A drop of rosé? Bordeaux or southern French.

DONER KEBABS

Most people eat doner kebabs that look as if they've been made from the minced-up nasty bits of a variety of animals that once led a wretched life before being put out of their misery. A proper doner, though, is anything but. Because it's quite fatty, however, you probably don't want a red, but rather a white with a peppy spice to it.

Likely reds: Would give them a body swerve, but if you have to a decent Rioja would do.
Possible whites: Southern French Chardonnay or Viognier, Aussie Riesling.

FISH AND CHIPS

Champagne goes fantastically with fish and chips. You want a white that has enough acidity to cut through the fattiness of the batter and the fries – and champagne does that very well. Other good matches are unoaked but fruity Chardonnays or a nice crisp Sauvignon Blanc. If you fancy a red, I'd go for a light Pinot Noir or perhaps a Gamay (say from Beaujolais).
Likely reds: Pinot Noir (southern French), Gamay (Beaujolais).
Possible whites: Champagne, New World fizz, unoaked Chardonnays (southern France, South Africa, Italy), Sauvignon Blanc (New Zealand).

INDIAN TAKEAWAY

Always a challenge. There's no doubt that an ice-cold Cobra beer is more or less the ideal match. But in wine terms some of the best matches are usually spicy whites, such as Riesling, Viognier and Gewürztraminer. Again, a nice rosé is good and for the richer, more spicy dishes, you might want to try a red. Something with a sweet fruit but good tangy finish would be preferable, so perhaps a juicy Pinot Noir or good Rioja. However, for the hottest dishes you might want to try a big Shiraz or a Zinfandel.
Likely reds: Pinot Noir, Rioja, Shiraz (Australia) and Zinfandel (California).
Possible whites: Riesling (Australia, Alsace, Germany), Gewürztraminer (Alsace), Viognier (South of France).
A drop of rosé? Try some Tavel (France), or Aussie pinks with a slightly richer character.

JERK CHICKEN, RICE AND PEAS

One of my favourite dishes, this, but very spicy. And that's the problem, really: finding something to stand up to the chilli-and-garlic-infused mesh of spiciness that gives your taste buds such a good kicking. In the main you want a big, juicy red, with a good whack of tannin and perhaps a bit of spice of its own – so basically something big and ballsy.
Likely reds: Zinfandel (California), Shiraz (Australia), Syrah (Rhône).
Possible whites: You must be joking.

KEBABS

We're talking skewered, flame-grilled kebabs here. If it's lamb or beef you want a mid-weight red, something with lots of plum and currant fruit

flavours that will stand up to the 'charred' flavours. With the chicken, a nice oaked white is probably the best, or perhaps a really rich Viognier.
Likely reds: Go for a New World Shiraz, a nice chewy Cabernet from the South of France or a decent Rioja.
Possible whites: Oaked Chardonnay (Australia, California, South Africa), Viognier (Aussie or southern French).

KENTUCKY FRIED CHICKEN
When the time is right KFC is one of the world's most comforting foods. But it's very greasy. Champagne or a good fizz work a treat, stopping the grease from clogging up the taste buds. Soft and juicy reds with a nice tang to them work well, too.
Likely reds: Rioja, Chianti, Cabernet Franc (Loire).
Possible whites: Champagne, New World fizz.

MEXICAN
If you think carefully about Mexican, then you quickly realise that it's not usually as spicy as, say, an Indian or perhaps a hot Thai dish, so you don't need to be too aggressive in your choice of wine. A lot of chargrilled chicken and ground beef is used, often in a tomato sauce or spicy salsa. What you really want is something in the middle ground – a good Cabernet or a juicy Syrah or powerful Pinot Noir. Most whites won't go, but an oaky Chardonnay may just get away with it.
Likely reds: Cabernet Sauvignon (California, southern France, Australia), Pinot Noir (Australia, New Zealand), Syrah (South Africa).
Possible whites: Basic white Burgundy, Chardonnay (Chile, Argentina, California).

PIZZA
Because of the doughy nature of the dish, and the wide variety of ingredients, you need something tangy and usually red, thanks to the tomato sauce that covers most pizzas. The reds you choose should be of light to medium weight with lots of juicy fruit. If you prefer whites, then go for something fairly zippy, fresh and uncomplicated. And it's worth considering a nice raspberry-flavoured rosé while you're at it.
Likely reds: Sangiovese (Chianti), southern French Gamay or Grenache, Tempranillo (Rioja), Pinot Noir (Australia or South Africa), Pinotage (South Africa).
Possible whites: Unoaked Chardonnays, Semillons (Australia), Gavi (Italy), Pinot Grigio, Muscadet (France).

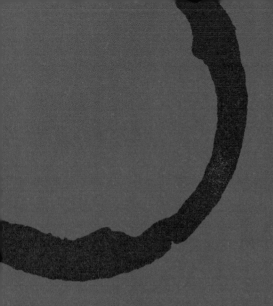

chapter fifteen
troubleshooting

Most wines are delivered to your door, dinner table or wine rack in pretty much tiptop condition, but there are times when it goes a bit pear-shaped.

Most of the time, it's because a wine is corked – which means either the cork has failed to work or it has reacted with the wine to produce an unpleasant taste and smell.

However, there are other faults that can affect wine, some of which are easy to detect, others less so. Here are the top ten faults that can affect wine – and a few hints on how to spot them.

1 WHAT IS CORKED?

Pure evil. The big, bad boy of wine faults. If you've seen Ray Winstone in *Scum*, then you'll know what I'm talking about when I compare faulty corks and their ability to destroy a decent wine with Ray's wonderfully vicious juvenile delinquent.

Basically, cork is a natural product, and it's been used to seal wine for hundreds of years – mostly successfully. However, there is one small problem. It can be contaminated by a little substance called trichloroanisole or TCA, which can be detected in cork at concentrations as low as a handful of parts per trillion. This causes the wine to smell and taste mouldy, corky and off.

How do I spot it? Well, as I say in Chapter 9, 'Myths and Monsters', not because there's cork floating in your glass. Some cork taint is so slight that you'll never spot it. But when it's obvious it's like a cross between a dank cellar and mouldy cork. Essentially, if you think you can smell it, it's probably there.

What should I do? Send it back if you're in a restaurant. Cork it up and take it back to the shop otherwise. Both should give you a refund if they agree with you.

2 IS MY WINE PAST ITS SELL-BY DATE?

Some wines are simply past it. They've stayed in the bottle too long and have lost the will to live. Most wine spoils over time because it has too much contact with air. Perhaps the cork is faulty or loosens up after a while. Sometimes, though, it simply is just too old.

How do I spot it? Fairly easily, really. The fruit will be dull if not nonexistent. There will be no zing, and the wine may taste like a cross between vinegar and sherry.

What should I do? In a restaurant, if it's a very old vintage, usually you'll have been warned that it's at your own risk. If it's at home, curse Uncle Montague for not having bought a longer lasting vintage of Latour.

3 WHAT IS MADERISATION?

It's similar to oxidation (see below), but the main reason why a wine may be maderised is that it has been exposed to heat, either over time or in the extreme sense (i.e. left out in the sun for days on end). Some wines, like Madeira (note the word stem), are meant to be that way – it's actually part of the winemaking process. However, Madeira is a fortified wine. Most wines aren't, and the effect of severe heat on them essentially 'bakes' the wine, giving unpleasant flavours.

How do I spot it? Pretty straightforward, really. A wine that has been maderised looks quite brown rather than red, and has essentially a cooked taste. The fruit will taste burned and baked.

What should I do? Buy another bottle and stop storing them by the hot-water tank.

4 WHEN IS A WINE OVEROAKED?

The problem with overoaked wines is that it's not the oak that's necessarily at fault. Some wines are big on oak, and that's because the winemaker has chosen that style. Others, however, have a big oak flavour because there are fundamental faults in the wine and a big splash of oak is one of the ways of disguising it.

How do I spot it? Oak is easy to spot. Overoaked, however, depends on what the rest of the wine is doing, but, fundamentally, if oak is the dominant flavour by a long way and puts the fruit flavours in the shade, then you're probably looking at an overoaked wine.

What should I do? Take a note of the wine and producer – and stay clear in future.

5 WHAT IS OXIDATION?

Oxidation is very simple. It's when a wine has had continued or overt exposure to air and the wine has absorbed too much oxygen. There are obviously differing degrees, however. If significant amounts get into the wine in the winemaking process, or during its bottled life, perhaps through the cork, then it's usually bad, causing the wine to age too rapidly. If it's done in a controlled way, i.e. by decanting and allowing a wine to breathe, it can be beneficial to the wine.

How do I spot it? Usually in young wines it results in a dullness of fruit but sometimes the wine can take on an almost sherry-like feel, especially with whites. There will also be a loss of aroma and fruit, especially in reds.

What should I do? Not a lot you *can* do, although buying wines with a screw cap will probably help.

6 WHAT IS RE-FERMENTATION?

Re-fermentation is essentially when fermentation starts again in the bottle, once the wine has been shipped or sold. It can happen for a variety of reasons, but usually occurs most in wines with a lower alcohol level. This is because they have residual sugar that, given the right temperature or situation, can be forced to start the fermentation again.

How do I spot it? If you have a still white or red wine, and notice a slight spritz to it, which may well appear slightly cloudy, this is probably a re-fermented wine.

What should I do? In a restaurant, send it back. At home, pour it down the sink – a re-fermented wine will cause bad gut rot.

7 IS SEDIMENT GOOD OR BAD?

Let's get this straight, in fine wines sediment is a good thing. But if poured out with the wine, the sediment will result in a cloudy liquid that can often taste more like soup than the fine, beautifully balanced wine that it probably is. However, with cheaper wines – in particular those under £5 – sediment often means the wine has been subjected to extreme temperature fluctuations, which is not good for it.

How do I spot it? With a wine older than around five or six years and costing £10 or above, you can more or less assume there will be some sediment. With younger wines that shouldn't, technically, have sediment, you often spot it only once it's been poured into the glass.

What should I do? With older wines, decant (see page 40). With younger wines, pop the cork back in and take it back to the shop. Sometimes it's a simple bit of natural sediment and the wine is fine. Other times the wine will be spoiled, and they should refund your money.

8 WHAT'S THE DEAL WITH SULPHUR?

When people talk about sulphur in wine they're talking about sulphur dioxide (SO_2), which is a disinfectant and, most importantly, an antioxidant. In the case of many wines, a little sulphur is added, usually in the bottle neck, to prevent oxidation. Theoretically, it is in tiny amounts and usually evaporates very quickly. Sometimes too much is added, though, and it causes a fault in the wine, not to mention a fairly unpleasant odour. It can also discolour the wines, particularly reds.

How do I spot it? Easy. Sulphur smells like freshly burned matches and causes a prickly sensation in the nose. In large quantities it can also contribute to asthmatic symptoms.

What should I do? Sulphur tends to 'burn' off fairly easily. So leave the bottle for ten minutes or so. Even better, decant it and let it breathe properly. If it is still really strong in odour, don't drink it – it won't do you any favours.

9 AND THOSE WHITE CRYSTALS?

Ah, you mean tartrate crystals. In a white wine, in particular, there is usually a fairly high concentration of tartaric acid (which helps give it freshness). Sometimes this can form into crystals, which then fall in tiny quantities to the bottom of the bottle. Often this is caused when the bottle of wine undergoes an extreme temperature fluctuation from warm to very, very cold.

How do I spot it? Tiny crystals in the bottom of the wine and also sometimes on the base of the cork, which has been in contact with the wine. The crystals often look like tiny bits of dandruff suspended in the wine. How nice.

What should I do? Drink it. Unless the wine is packed with them, which is unlikely, they are completely harmless.

10 WHY CAN SOME WINE BE VINEGARY?

This is when a particular type of bacteria has attacked the wine and essentially turned it into a vinegar in your wine. Often the bacteria have got in to the bottle or tank, with air, meaning that often there is evidence of oxidation as well.

How do I spot it? Open a bottle of ordinary malt vinegar and sniff deeply. Any whiff of malt vinegar and you want to plug that baby up again.

What should I do? Take it back. Something's gone wrong somewhere along the path from winery to wine shop and it certainly isn't your fault, so you shouldn't pay for it (unless it's a bottle of Bulgarian wine you've saved from the late 60s, in which case it *is* your fault!).

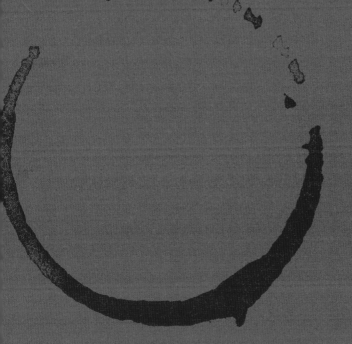

chapter sixteen
wine course

I've called this a mini-course or wine game, but in reality it is actually little more than an excuse for a bloody good party with a few nice mates who are also interested in learning a little bit about wine and having a laugh while they do it. You'll see below a list of wines, laid out in 'rounds'. The idea is that you should take this list into your local wine merchant and present it as a shopping list in the same way that you would give a butcher a list of cuts you want for the weekend. Explain what you're planning to do – or just show him or her these pages of the book. It should all become pretty clear soon enough.

I've designed it so that the least you'll spend is £75, which is just over £6 a bottle, but remember that you'll be buying some classic varieties and regions, hopefully some that you've either never tried before or never tried *together* before. The maximum you should be spending is around £95–100, but only if you spend the upper level of each bracket and splash out an average of around £8 per bottle. Even then, if there are six or seven friends, it shouldn't cost you more than around £10–15 each to get completely hammered, learn a bit about wine and have a lot of fun. So not a bad deal, really.

Any decent wine merchant should easily be able to put this case together for you. Once you get it back, I suggest you take a few saved supermarket plastic bags, and wrap each of them up, numbering them 1–12 and taping them up to the neck so no one can read the labels or see what's in them. If you do it a day or two before you taste them, the likelihood is that even you will have forgotten which is which, so you can enjoy it just as much as your fellow participants.

Then simply photocopy Pages 184–6 – or, alternatively, act as master of ceremonies yourself, and follow pages 187–92, reading the riot act to your chums where appropriate.

Other than that, my only advice is to make sure you have a bit of giggle and a lot of wine.

The wines

ROUND 1
A. New World Sauvignon Blanc (preferably New Zealand) (£7–9)
B. Sancerre (£8–10)

ROUND 2
C. Chablis (£7–9)
D. Aussie oaked Chardonnay (£5–6)

ROUND 3
E. New World Viognier (£6–8)
F. German dry Riesling (£6–9)

ROUND 4
G. Classic Bordeaux Claret (£7–10)
H. Chilean/Californian branded Cabernet (£5–8)

ROUND 5
I. Côtes du Rhône (£6–8)
J. South African Shiraz (£5–7)

ROUND 6
K. Burgundy Villages (£8–9)
L. Rioja (£6–7)

The rules

Well, there are only four, and they're not really rules but rather simple advice.
► Be honest – tell everyone what you think about the wines and why.
  I repeat again, for the umpteenth time in this book, there's no right
  or wrong with wine, just personal opinion.
► Don't peek.
► Try to write everything down as well. It'll feel nerdy at first, but next
  time you go to buy some wine you can always refer to your notes and
  think, Did I or didn't I like Riesling? or Was Pinot Noir for me?
► At no point should you attempt a handstand. If you feel like doing so, it
  means you've not been tasting: you've been gulping and are inebriated.

The questions

ROUND 1

- Have a sniff at wine A. Then write down what the first smell is that hits your nasal passages. Once you've done that, write down anything else you can smell.
- Have a sip of A. What's the first taste that hits your tongue? Do you like it? Or is it not your kind of thing? Either way, write down why.
- Have a sip of wine B. Is it sharper, more fruity, less fruity? What would you say are the primary flavours? Are they the same as or different from those of wine A? If different, why?
- Do you prefer it to wine A?
- Have a crack at giving it a rating – the simplest way is to go back to schooldays. Is it a one-star or a five-star wine as far as you're concerned? Do the same with each of the wines you taste from now on. And feel free to come back and revise one if you think you've found a better one further on.

ROUND 2

- If you can, line up two glasses, one with C one with D in. Swirl and sniff each of the wines. Then taste them. What's the most noticeable difference?
- Write down which you prefer and why.
- With wine C, what's the most noticeable characteristic?
- How would you compare the fruit flavours in wine C to wine D? Are they the same or different?

ROUND 3

- Have a look at the colour of these two wines. What's the main difference?
- Take a sniff of the first wine E, then have a quick sip and write down the first fruit that comes to mind.
- Take another sip and tell the group what other fruits you think you taste. Have a crack at describing the texture, too.
- Do exactly the same with wine F.
- Have a crack at describing the texture of both.
- Which one do you prefer? Do you like either of them?

ROUND 4

- ▸ Take a sip of each of these wines, both G and H. Which would you call the more fruity? Which do you think is from the Old World and which from the New World?
- ▸ Which would you pay more for and why?
- ▸ If you had to liken these wines to two people, either in the room or someone whom everyone in the room may know, describe why and write the people's names down on a piece of paper. Fold it up and put it in a glass.
- ▸ What food do you think these wines are most suited to?
- ▸ Again, which do you prefer and why?

ROUND 5

- ▸ Take a look at the colour of both wines. Which is the more intense?
- ▸ How would you describe the fruit flavours of each wine? Write it down
- ▸ Which of these wines do you prefer, I or J? Do you prefer them both to the previous two wines?
- ▸ As well as fruit, what else can you taste in these two wines?
- ▸ Which would you guess to be French and which would you guess to be New World, wine I or wine J?

ROUND 6

- ▸ Take a sniff and a sip of wine K and name the first three things that come into your head – no matter how bizarre you may think they are.
- ▸ Do the same for wine L.
- ▸ Which wine do you prefer?
- ▸ Which wine do you think is from the Old World and which from the New World?
- ▸ Which do you think would be the better food wine and why?
- ▸ If you haven't done so already, pick out your favourite wine, pour a large glass of it. Tease the person next door to you for being a thickie (unless of course you're the thickie) and get your host either to read out or circulate the 'notes'.

COPY SHEETS

ROUND 1:

Wine A ....

Wine B ....

ROUND 2:

Wine C ....

Wine D ....

ROUND 3:

Wine E ....

Wine F ....

ROUND 4:

Wine G ....

Wine H ....

ROUND 5:

Wine I ....

Wine J ....

ROUND 6:

Wine K ....

Wine L ....

The 'notes'

I call these 'notes' as opposed to 'answers', because, with the exception of what the actual wines are (and you'll find that question doesn't appear), there is little that's right or wrong in wine, as I have been at pains to point out. The aim of the above has simply been to get you to try a range of different grape varieties and compare them in different settings, and to make you think about what it is that you do or don't like about them. Hopefully, you'll have discovered something new, something different and something you'll experiment with again next time you walk into your nearest wine shop.

You'll also have it all written down – so there's no excuse not to remember.

ROUND 1

If your wine merchant has done his/her job properly, then wine A should be a New World Sauvignon Blanc. It could be from South Africa, but with any luck it'll be from New Zealand. Wine B should be a Sancerre. Obviously both come from different sides of the globe, but both are made from the same grape variety.

When you first sniffed wine A, you probably found a very distinctive smell. Most probably it would have been gooseberries, or freshly cut grass. There may have been a little of what is so charmingly called 'cat's pee'. Either way, it would have been distinctive. When you tasted it, the gooseberry fruit flavours should have jumped out, along with a tingle on the tongue – that's what's known as acidity, and Sauvignon Blanc usually has it in buckets.

When you compared it with B, did you find that the Sancerre has a slightly less fruity, perhaps sharper aroma? Did you get a whiff of asparagus? And, when you tasted it, you may have found even more of a tingle on the tongue, but not as fruity or rich a set of flavours in the mouth. All of this is possible. Importantly, though, did you clock that both were made from the same grape variety? If you did, stick a gold star in the corner of your tasting sheet.

If you preferred wine A to wine B, then essentially you probably prefer the New World style of Sauvignon to Old World. You prefer your Sauvignons a little richer and a bit more luscious. If you preferred wine B, then you're clearly a classical person, perhaps preferring a more reserved, less in-your-face style of Sauvignon Blanc.

Where did you get with your rating? Was that useful? Lots of people score wines, but their scoring systems aren't always useful. However, we've all stayed in enough hotels to understand the difference between two-star, three-star and four-star. The confusing and difficult thing about wine is that it is possible to pay the same price for three wines, and find that one is maybe a two-star, another a three-star and another a four-star.

ROUND 2

When you compared the smell of wine C with wine D, what was the most noticeable thing. Was the fruit different? Was one creamier than the other? Most importantly, did you spot that the first wine, which was a Chablis, was clean and crisp, whereas the second wine, which was an Australian Chardonnay, was bigger, fatter, rounder – and, crucially, had been oaked? In other words, did you spot that the second smelled of wood?

When you tasted them you may have found it easier to tell the difference. The Chablis more than likely had a very lemon-filled fruity flavour, while the Australian Chardonnay would have perhaps been a little more like lemon and pineapple – and it would have had a creamy, or possibly buttery, edge to it, two flavours that are often imparted by oak. And of course there will have been the oaky taste, too.

Which did you prefer? If you liked the fruit on the Aussie, but not the oaky flavours, it's perfectly possible that you like a New World style of Chardonnay, but just didn't enjoy the oak side of the wine. Don't worry, that's perfectly all right, and you can get some great unwooded Chardonnays from Australia, South Africa and Chile these days. If you preferred the Chablis, but would have liked a little bit of oak, you sound as if you'd quite like a good classic white Burgundy and prefer more of a European edge.

When you tasted the Chablis, did you find what's often described as a minerally or steely quality to it? The best way to illustrate this is to take a silver spoon and suck it, without anything on it. That's the sort of edge you can get with classic Chablis and with European Chardonnay. You may have also tasted a slightly stony flavour – again, get yourself a decent sized pebble off the beach next time you go. Wash it thoroughly, then give it a lick. It all sounds ridiculous but it's often the best way to illustrate the added flavours that you might have got in this wine.

ROUND 3

If you compared the colour of the two wines you probably found the Viognier was more of a goldy colour, while the Riesling, if it's a very recent vintage and properly dry, will have more of a light straw colour, with an almost green tinge to it. Different grapes produce different intensities of colour. You probably noticed the same with the Chablis and the Aussie Chardonnay in the last round. And oak ageing can add a little extra colour, usually turning a white slightly more golden rather than light yellow.

When you sniffed wine E, did you get a very heady, perfumed aroma? You'll probably have got the same with the Riesling, although that will have been more of a lemon-fresh scent, while the Viognier will be more like sniffing freshly squeezed peach juice. And with both you'll probably have got exactly the same fruits coming through in the mouth. When you tasted both, what did you think about the texture? Did it feel slightly more viscous, almost oily? This is classic for both these varieties. Some people love it. Others hate it.

Which of the two did you prefer? If both, then you are probably the type of person who loves fragrant, fruity wines, in which case you should also give Gewürztraminer a go. You may have preferred the Riesling because it will have had a cleaner, crisper style. Riesling is never oaked, but it's possible that the Viognier was. Did you get a creamy oaky taste from the Viognier? If you did and you preferred that style, then great.

If you didn't like either variety, then move on. But next time you're in the local wine shop remember that these aren't the grapes for you. However, don't let that stop you from experimenting with a new, different variety.

ROUND 4

Again, both the same grape variety: Cabernet Sauvignon. And, again, one from the New World and one from the Old World. Did you manage to guess that G was the Old World while H was New World?

Which did you pick as the one you would pay more for? If your wine merchant has given you a decent claret, it should be at the top end of the price bracket (unless he has some great deals on), while the Chilean or Californian Cabernet, especially if branded, may well be nearer the bottom of the price bracket. Would you pay extra for the claret, though? Essentially it's the same variety, but it probably isn't as fruity, sweet and immediately attractive as the Chilean or Californian. Sometimes, however, it's because Bordeaux Cabernet can take a while to 'open up'. One way to test this is to pour a large glass of it, put it to the side, and have another taste in an hour. You might find it a bit softer, a bit less harsh, and the fruit may well have opened up a lot. However, it's likely that the claret was the more expensive of the two. Did you think it was worth it? Again, there's no right or wrong but at least you know what you're prepared to pay for either style now.

I would describe most clarets as I would your typical banker: reserved, a little fruity, but only when really pushed; quite handsome in a very classical way, but not very giving to begin with; opens up eventually, but can be quite an expensive date and an acquired taste.

With most Chilean or Californian Cabernets I'd describe them as pretty full-on. Not a shrinking violet and definitely up for a bit of fun. Could be a little too loud on occasion, but thoroughly trustworthy and reliable. Quite good for getting you out of awkward scrapes – and back into them as well.

By this stage, I've probably offended half your party. Now it's time to find out if you have, too. Take the names out and read out your explanations as to why you've named whom you have.

Once you've stopped laughing, give a little thought to which you preferred. Was it the upfront fruity style of the New World? Are you a classicist or up for something a little different on occasion? And what food would you most like to drink this with? Most of you will perhaps pick a decent steak, but both wines are probably more suited to a joint of lamb, or alternatively a nice big bowl of spicy cannelloni. Or just a big hunk of strong cheddar. The point is, it is worth giving a little thought to what food you want to drink it with.

ROUND 5

What we have here are two wines from essentially the same grape variety. In the Rhône they call it Syrah, in South Africa and Australia it's known as Shiraz. Nothing new to some of you, I'm sure.

Did you notice one was perhaps more intense in colour than the other? More likely it was the South African Shiraz, which always has a little more depth of colour at this price level. Also, the Côtes du Rhône may well have been blended with one or two other varieties, possibly giving it a slightly less intense colour. The Shiraz was also probably a dark purple while the Côtes du Rhône is more likely to have been a deep, dark crimson red. Again, it's not something that always makes a difference – but the more you look at the colour of a wine, often the more you can tell instantly if you're dealing with an older or younger wine. If it's dark and intense, almost inky, it's likely to be a very young wine. If it's more opaque, perhaps with a touch of brown as opposed to pure red or purple at the edges, then perhaps it's several years old.

In flavour terms, which did you prefer? The Shiraz was probably a lot sweeter, richer and jammier than the Syrah, but you might have got a bit more 'complexity' from Rhône, perhaps a smokiness and spiciness from the oak used. Also, the South African wine will probably have had more plum and prune fruit flavours, perhaps almost raisiny ones. The Côtes du Rhône, on the other hand, will have had more blackberry or black cherry fruit flavours, perhaps with a touch of sweet liquorice.

What this illustrates, as do a lot of the pairings in this exercise, is how different the same grape can be in different contents, at the hands of different winemakers. You may have enjoyed one more than the other. Perhaps you preferred the slightly less brash style of the Côtes du Rhône, or perhaps you liked the full-on fruit bomb experience of the South African. Or perhaps you liked both.

By the way, did you guess which was French and which was New World? Was it the fruit that gave it away, or the overall structure and style? If you have a classic Côtes du Rhône and typical South African Shiraz, you should be able tell the two apart fairly easily – now that you know which is which, that is.

ROUND 6

This time there are two different varieties. When you tasted the first wine, the Pinot Noir from Burgundy, what did you get? Most probably the first was fruit – red and black cherries, perhaps, with a little raspberry or strawberry thrown in. Second, probably oak, some creamy wood flavours and aromas. And for the third, well, it could have been several things. You may have got liquorice, or perhaps a touch of smoky bacon. You may have just thought it was a bit more 'meaty' than some of the previous reds you've had.

You will probably have got a lot of the same in the second wine as well, although the oak or wood flavour and aromas would probably have been more pronounced. This is a Rioja, from Spain, and, although you may have written very similar notes for each, you can see that they are completely different wines, made from different grapes (the Rioja is made mainly from Tempranillo). The Rioja will probably have had a lot more oak used in it than the Burgundy – which is why you get a much stronger aroma and flavour with it.

Which is Old World? Well, obviously both of them. But it's possible that the Rioja you have in your glass is a 'new'-style Rioja, which follows the fruit-driven style of the New World – so you may well have picked this one as New World.

Which is the better food wine? Well, without tasting the specific wines in front of you, I wouldn't know, but both should have a good whack of what is known as acidity. Think back to that tingle and sharpness that you got tasting the Sauvignon Blanc earlier, then see if you can sense a little of the same in these wines – more obvious than in the Cabernets and the Shiraz and Syrah, for example. That makes them both very good food wines, because a lot of dishes (especially the naughty but ever so nice ones) involve a degree of oil or butter – greasiness if you like. Acidity helps a wine cut through this and leaves the palate clean and ready for the next mouthful of food or wine. It also stops the greasy texture from killing the fruit in the wine dead.

Now get on and choose that favourite wine – and make sure you grab whatever's left in the bottle.

chapter seventeen
essential reading

So you want to know more?

It is possible that, having read this book, you will be enthused enough to read more about wine, get more involved and become more passionate about the subject. If that's the case then I direct you to Chapter 18 first, where you should take the test to see whether you're at risk of becoming a wine nerd. If you pass with flying colours, then the books below may be useful in your quest for better wine.

BUYING GUIDES

The Wine List 2005, Matthew Jukes (Headline)
This lists Jukes's top 250 wines currently in the country, ranging from as little as £3.99 up to 'use your imagination'. The tasting notes are written in a way that makes all the wines sound totally delicious.

Oz Clarke's Wine Buying Guide 2005 (Websters)
The great beauty about Oz is that not only does he exhaustively taste the majority of wines in the country to give you a fair and accessible breakdown of each of their pluses and minuses, but he does it in a way that is thoroughly engaging and entertaining.

Jancis Robinson's Wine Course (BBC Books)
This is a great book for learning more about a grape and region, as well as getting to grips with the basics, such as tasting wine or learning the ropes with wine etiquette.

The Oxford Companion to Wine, Jancis Robinson (Oxford University Press)
This is the world's most authoritative wine book. It has in its hundreds of pages on everything you ever wanted to know about wine but were too afraid to ask. If you are serious about learning more about wine, you can't live without this book.

The New Sotheby's Wine Encyclopaedia, Tom Stevenson (Dorling Kindersley)
A little dry but into its umpteenth edition, Stevenson's book still has all the necessary information on the world's major wine regions, splitting them into easily absorbed slices of wine knowledge.

The World Atlas of Wine, Hugh Johnson and Jancis Robinson (Mitchell Beazley)
The 'daddy' of all wine writers, Hugh Johnson first penned this guide more than two and a half decades ago, and it's no less relevant or helpful now than it was then. Responsible for converting a whole generation of wine lovers and delightfully unpretentious.

Vintage Wine, **Michael Broadbent (Little, Brown)**
I love this book because it appeals to the real spod in me. It's a fascinating read for anyone who wants to get a feel for the flavours of wines that we mere mortals can only ever dream of.

Parker's Wine Buyer's Guide **(Dorling Kindersley)**
The US wine market is more or less dictated to by the statements included in this doorstep of a book. It's not made the author, former lawyer Robert Parker, particularly popular, but, if you're loaded and you want to get a handle on what you should be splashing your cash on, this is definitely the book for you.

Sniff, Swirl and Slurp, **Max Allen (Mitchell Beazley)**
Max Allen is the *enfant terrible* of Aussie wine writing and this book is a fine example of his informative yet irreverent and punchy style. A book for beginners who have a tendency to fall asleep during the first haltering steps of an explanation of carbonic maceration. Boring it is not.

Drink: Never Mind the Peanuts, **Susy Atkins and Dave Broom (Mitchell Beazley)**
Fantastic book, which breaks wine and other types of booze down into flavour terms. It is aimed at those who want to find out a little bit more about alcohol in general but is particularly good on wine.

The New France, **Andrew Jefford (Mitchell Beazley)**
If you want to know more about the wines of France, then this book is one to buy. Andrew Jefford is one of the most gifted wine writers around, and it shines through in what is a very classy and accessible summation of the great wines that France has to offer.

ON THE WEB

www.wine-pages.com
Tom Canavan, the site's creator, is passionate but realistic about the world of wine. There are sections dedicated to those more complex matters that make the aficionados and wine geeks come over all funny, but equally there's a lot there for beginners who simply want to know more and have a little bit of fun at the same time.

www.wine-anorak.com
This site is unashamedly for wine nerds, although its author, Jamie Goode, is pretty tongue-in-cheek about it all, and provides lots of info for novices to get started with before ploughing into the slightly more complex and perhaps less scintillating discussions about corks and closures.

www.superplonk.com
Great site from the *Guardian*'s Malcom Gluck, who encouraged a whole
generation of us to get involved in wine with his fantastically practical
and down-to-earth book of the same title as the website. Malcolm can
be scathing, passionate or indifferent when reviewing wines on this site –
all of which makes it as much fun to read as it does informative.

ON THE MAGAZINE RACK

Decanter
This was the UK's first ever consumer wine magazine and it remains as
highly regarded today as it did when it first came out. Be warned, though:
it is only really for those who have seriously caught the wine bug and with
relatively large wallets. However, there are some very good interviews
with some of the world's greatest winemakers.

Wine International
More down to earth than *Decanter* and a little more populist, this
magazine is attempting to reach an international audience as well
as UK readers. It has very good tastings pages that cover everything
from low-price Rioja to top-class claret, always written in a really
easy-going, easily understood manner.

The Wine Spectator
This is on an American magazine rack rather than a UK one, but that's
OK because they do international subscriptions. This is a magazine for
those who take themselves and the subject of wine very seriously.
However, the writing is always of a high standard, and the writers are
allowed to express their sometimes very vehement opinions.

chapter eighteen
am I a wine nerd?

If you've got this far, it's quite reasonable that you may well have caught the wine bug. I hope so, because there are some great wines out there to enjoy and you don't have to spend a fortune to get hold of them. Nor do you have to treat them like objects of worship. It's just pressed grapes at the end of the day – an important thing to remember. However, there are always some people who take it to anorak proportions. There are people who get obsessive – sometimes frighteningly so. Well, here's a checklist that you should do every so often, just to ensure you haven't crossed the line.

- If you were offered tickets to watch England play in the World Cup final, would you give them up to make sure you were present at the opening of a bottle of Mouton-Rothschild 1945?
- Are you rescheduling your holidays around the world's wine hotspots?
- Do you get excited by dust?
- Do you fondle your bottles?
- Do you get nervous and vaguely sweaty if a friend brings round a bottle of Blossom Hill to dinner?
- Do you wrap white napkins around the neck of your wine bottle, just like in your favourite restaurant?
- Do you start referring to your wines using the pronoun 'she' and hence end up sounding like a grapey version of Swiss Tony from *The Fast Show*?
- Have you logged where you bought each wine, for what price and given each an ideal drinking date?
- Are you studying to become a master of wine? If so, why?
- Look around you. Is something missing? Perhaps a partner, some children? Can you remember when you last saw them?

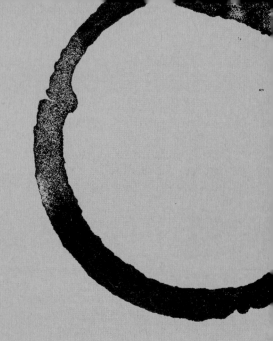

chapter nineteen
don't do drunk

'Wine', said the great seventeenth-century poet George Herbert, 'is first a friend and then an enemy.' How true, and yet anyone who knows me well will think the notion of my writing an entire – albeit succinct – chapter on taking it easy when it comes to drinking hypocritical and will be hurling accusations at me at speed. But, then, with the exception of the abstemious and the teetotal among us, there's probably a point, if not many, in our lives where we wish we had behaved a little more responsibly and drunk just a wee bit less. We have, to use a hackneyed phrase, all been there.

But from time to time it's good for us all to remember that, essentially, wine is a drug – a legal and thoroughly nice one but a drug all the same. It's also a toxin, and when overindulged in can have long-term and very damaging effects.

Let's look at it this way, the total alcohol industry in the UK is worth £30 billion. The total cost to the NHS and government of alcohol-related accidents, illnesses and deaths in the UK is £20 billion. That's about the most unfair business deal I can think of and the only justification for the government to tax the hell out of a bottle of wine. But it also makes you think about the cost to our bodies as well as the chancellor's war chest.

Anyway here are four fairly obvious tips for keeping the enjoyment factor up and the wooze factor and liver damage as near to zero as dammit.

TIP 1: YOU CAN NEVER DRINK ENOUGH WATER
As a general rule, match a glass of wine with a glass of water. Dehydration is directly related to the amount you drink and the level of illness you feel next day. Apart from anything else it helps you pace yourself.

TIP 2: YOU CAN NEVER EAT ENOUGH FOOD
Drink on an empty stomach and you're asking for trouble. Also, the more you munch, the fuller you feel, the fuller you feel, the less likely you are to be throwing the booze back. But avoid salty snacks – they make you more thirsty. And if there's no water around? That's right, you'll drink more booze.

TIP 3: LEAVE MIXING IT TO THE BARTENDER
I don't mean you can't treat yourself to a few cocktails at home now and again. What I mean is don't mix your drinks. I don't know of any scientific explanation that shows this is a bad idea, but I do know from personal experience that it is an *extremely* bad idea. Apart from anything else, nine times out of ten, when you start mixing your drinks, it's because you've finished every bottle of wine in the house and have to move on to spirits, which means you're already in trouble.

TIP 4: PACE YOURSELF

It's not a competition. And if you're a macho beefcake of a male I am going to say that again so that it sinks in. *It's not a competition.* Take it easy, sip, don't glug – you'll appreciate the wine more and you absorb the alcohol more slowly.

And for all of us who conveniently forget the recommended, maximum number of units of alcohol we should be consuming each week – especially when being questioned by the doc at our yearly health check-up – please see the table below.

Remember: the word 'recommended' doesn't mean you *have* to drink them all.

RECOMMENDED UNITS

	Maximum per day	Maximum per week
Male	4	21
Female	3	14

So in practical terms that equals:

	Maximum per day	Maximum per week
Male	2 pints lager (4.2%)	10 pints lager
	or	or
	4 glasses wine (small)	21 glasses wine
	or	or
	4 measures spirit	21 measures spirit

	Maximum per day	Maximum per week
Female	1–1.5 pints beer	14 pints beer
	or	or
	2–3 glasses wine	14 glasses wine
	or	or
	2–3 measures spirit	14 measures spirit

chapter twenty
merchant guide

Going mainstream

The following is a list of the major supermarkets and high street retailers that are around at the moment, with a few words on what's hot and what's not when it comes to their wine selection.

ASDA
Head office number: 0800 068 6727.
Number of stores: 270.
Website: www.asda.co.uk.
What's hot: Asda are pretty big on the everyday-low-price (EDLP) policy – which basically means they spend a lot of time and effort making sure they're extremely price-competitive. Which is good for you, but tough for some of the other retailers.
What's not: The choice is decent, but not abounding for a supermarket.

EH BOOTH & CO.
Head office number: 01772 251701.
Website: www.booths-supermarkets.co.uk.
Number of stores: 27.
What's hot: It's like having an independent wine merchant, but across 27 stores, and you can buy your food there as well. So basically it's great. Very nifty website, too.
What's not: It's found only in the North, which is a bit of a bummer if you live in Penzance.

CO-OPERATIVE GROUP (CO-OP)
Head office number: 0800 068 6727.
Website: www.co-op.co.uk.
Number of stores: 1,763.
What's hot: Pretty accessible range and, if you're spending under a fiver, then there are some good deals to be had.
What's not: Used to be quite strong on Italy, but have become a little bit bland of late.

MAJESTIC WINE WAREHOUSE
Head office number: 01923 298200.
Website: www.majestic.co.uk.
Number of stores: 104.
What's hot: Majestic are undoubtedly the best high street wine retailer currently around, in my opinion. They offer a great range, from a very

decent £3.99 Rioja, up to ... well the sky's almost the limit. Also, they tend to have the best deals on the market when it comes to champagne. The staff are exceptionally knowledgeable and very helpful.

What's not: You have to buy by the case – but there's always plenty of space for parking, so it's not that much of a grumble, really.

MARKS & SPENCER

Head office number: 020 7935 4422.
Website: www.marksandspencer.co.uk.
Number of stores: 332.

What's hot: Good old Marks & Sparks. Until two years or so ago their wine list was a little weak and fairly unimpressive. But there's new blood in the wine department and they are putting some cracking wines out there, with some particularly nice Italian and Spanish numbers making it to the shelf.

What's not: The breadth of choice is still not as good as somewhere like Tesco or Majestic. But they do have all the classics, so, if you want a bottle of Chablis that's reliable, they're the place to start.

WILLIAM MORRISON

Head office number: 01924 870000.
Website: www.morereasons.co.uk.
Number of stores: 115.

What's hot: They've just bought Safeway, so will no doubt be expanding significantly across the country. Great range of wines under £5, with some genuine bargains.

What's not: Not as wide a choice as one might hope, and not great in the £6–10 department.

ODDBINS

Head office number: 020 8944 4400.
Website: www.oddbins.co.uk.
Number of stores: 234.

What's hot: The Fine Wine Stores (of which there are eight) are great, with a great selection of really top-notch wines. The main stores always have a cracking whisky range.

What's not: Oddbins has lost some of its sparkle in recent years. It used to have one of the most innovative ranges around, but it's become rather boring of late. And the service isn't a patch on what it used to be.

SAINSBURY'S

Head office number: 0800 636262.

Website: www.sainsburys.co.uk.

Number of stores: 489.

What's hot: A lot of the wines in store are also available on the website, though it is a bit clunky. The wine aisles are always pretty well stocked (which is not always the case for supermarkets) and the choice, in country and brand terms, is always wide, if not exactly inspiring. They often have good offers on champagne at key times of the year.

What's not: A little bit lacklustre with its traditional areas, such as France, but makes up with it in Australian and New Zealand sections.

SOMERFIELD

Head office number: 0117 935 6669.

Website: www.somerfield.co.uk.

Number of stores: 600.

What's hot: Nice range of Old World wines at decent prices, with a few stars dotted about.

What's not: Website is pretty poor and it needs to be stronger in areas such as Australia etc., but it's getting there.

TESCO

Head office number: 0800 505555.

Website: www.tesco.co.uk.

Number of stores: 737.

What's hot: The range is pretty wide for a supermarket. They claim to have around 700 wines on their list, although most stores only ever see between 250 and 400 appear on the shelves – however, that's still very good. They also run some of the best bargains around, pretty much year-round.

What's not: While wide, the range can be a little boring and is very brand-dominated. However, try the website because it really does have some spectacularly good offers from time to time.

THRESHER GROUP (INCLUDES BOTTOMS UP, THRESHER, WINE RACK)

Head office number: 01707 387200.

Website: www.threshergroup.com.

Number of stores: 2,105.

What's hot: Ranges can be quite limited, but the new Origins and Ratcliffe ranges in the Thresher shops in particular are showing that the group is trying to make a strong comeback after a few unfocused years. **What's not**: Shops can be a bit impersonal and the assistance a little bit lacking.

UNWINS
Head office number: 01322 272711.
Website: www.unwins.co.uk.
Number of stores: 432.
What's hot: Not a lot, to be perfectly honest, although they do have a decent little French section from which to pluck some good Chablis. **What's not**: Unwins has lost its way in recent years and the range has become quite boring. It needs a bit of a kick up the backside.

WAITROSE
Head office number: 01344 825232.
Website: www.waitrose.com.
Number of stores: 142.
What's hot: I'm a big Waitrose fan. They've got one of the most interesting ranges of any of the supermarkets, with a great little fine-wine section in most stores to spoil yourself with from time to time, and some real little gems to discover, at both the cheap and expensive ends of the scale. Good organic selection, too.
What's not: Can be a little more highly priced on major brands than their competitors but they make up for it with other interesting, well-priced stuff, and a good website to boot.

On the Internet trail

There's only a handful in this section, because, while a lot of stores do Internet business on the side, few use the medium as a major way of communicating with their customers – or indeed their only way. Those that use it as a bit of a sideline are mainly listed in the independents section.

However, here I've recommended the top five that I think will have you relaxing in your Parker Knoll extendable armchair, with foot rests and drinks holders of course, playing with your laptop to your heart's content.

BERRY BROTHERS & RUDD

Website: www.bbr.com.

Why surf? Because if you want one of the best selections of 'fine wines' then this is the place to come. It really does have it all. They may be listed in the independent section, because they have only a couple of shops in London, but the Internet site has taken them worldwide now and they are doing tremendous trade.

What should I snap up? For basics, the Berry Brothers' own range of classics is difficult to beat. For fancy stuff, the sky is the limit.

LAITHWAITE'S

Website: www.laithwaites.com.

Why surf? Laithwaite's is part of the company that owns the *Sunday Times* Wine Club. However, I think the laithwaites.com website offers much better choice than the STWC, and it's a lot more convenient being online. The 'Webdeals' cases aren't the best you can find from quality point of view, but the bin-ends section is excellent, with some really good wines at very decent prices.

What should I snap up? The Grant Burge Barossa Sparkling Pinot Noir Chardonnay is a steal for under a tenner.

MAJESTIC

Website: www.majestic.co.uk.

Why surf? I'll admit that I prefer shopping in store at Majestic than I do on the company's website, because you get more interaction with the very good staff that populate the company's shops. But the website is the next best thing. In particular you get some very good deals and some great bin-end offers, especially when they're changing over lists.

What should I snap up? Great deals on champagne, and you don't have to move from your computer screen to get hold of them.

TESCO

Website: www.tesco.com.

Why surf? Lots of reasons, really, the first being that they have one of the best delivery services around. The second is that they do monumental offers through their 'web warehouse' – sometimes much better than you'll find in the store. There isn't the most enormous choice, of course, but that's the price you pay in order to get some proper bargains. The site is easy to use, but, because it is the most popular grocery site in the UK, it can sometimes be a bit of grind getting through the ordering process.

What should I snap up? Whatever looks like the best bargain that suits your tastes. It's not rocket science, you know.

VIRGIN WINES

Website: www.virginwines.com.

Why surf? I'll admit I am biased, having worked for them in the past, but I do genuinely think they are one of the best wine websites around. They don't do the fine wine that someone like Berry Brothers do, but then that's not their bag. What *is* their bag is being genuinely relaxed, entertaining and completely unpretentious about buying wine. So, for example, you have wines laid out by style, rather than country or grape. This makes it easier to discover a wealth of wines from different countries, but all in a similar style. Apart from anything else, it gives you more of a desire to experiment and makes you less nervous about doing so.

What should I snap up? The 'exclusives' ranges are of excellent quality and value and the mixed cases are not only fun but also very pennywise.

The independent route

I am a big fan of independent wine shops. They may not always offer the best bargains, but the good ones offer sound advice, great choice and most of all the opportunity to discover some cracking new, different and exciting wines.

The following list is simply the ones I can, with hand on heart, recommend highly. There are plenty of others, though, and I'm sure many are just as good. However, because of the limits of space, I've picked mainly those that also do mail order or Internet sales as well as shop sales.

LONDON

JOHN ARMIT WINES

5 Royalty Studios, 105 Lancaster Road, London W11 1QF

Phone: 020 7908 0600 / Fax: 020 7908 0601

Email: info@armit.co.uk / Website: www.armit.co.uk

What's hot: A great Italian specialist, listing some of the Piedmont and Tuscany's best. Also some top wines from New Zealand and South Africa.

What's not: Not cheap. However, that's because many of the producers are the best from their particular region. Also only does mail order for retail customers (so no actual shop) but the service is good, and they know what they're talking about. Very cool, fashionable wine list that covers a lot of the key countries.

What to look out for: Cracking champagne, Beaumont des Crayéres, and, if you're feeling in the mood to spoil yourself, try the wines of Angelo Gaja, one of northern Italy's best producers.

BERRY BROTHERS AND RUDD

3 St James Street, London SW1A 1EG
Phone: 020 7396 9600 / Fax: 020 7396 9611
Email: orders@bbr.com / Website: www.bbr.com

What's hot: The UK's oldest-established wine merchant, Berry's is on the face of it a pinstripe-suited and rather imposing establishment. However, it's got the lot, with one of the widest choices of fine wine available in the UK.

What's not: It is very-old school in image terms and the shop in St James's is very intimidating.

What to look out for: There's a great website (see the Internet entries above) and the Berry's Own selection range provides good-quality stuff at a relatively reasonable price.

CORNEY & BARROW

12 Helmet Row, London EC1V 3TD
Phone: 020 7539 3200 / Fax: 020 7608 1373
Email: wine@corbar.co.uk
Website: www.corneyandbarrow.com

What's hot: Very strong on top Bordeaux and Burgundy, so, if you're thinking of investing, this is a good stop.

What's not: Quite dominated by France, so if you're thinking about experimenting with the New World, or are a big Aussie fan, you need to look elsewhere.

What to look out for: Quite tidy little Spanish section. Small but perfectly formed. Good website, and efficient mail-order service.

EL VINO

Vintage House, 1 Hare Place, Fleet Street, London EC4Y 1BJ
Phone: 020 7353 5384 / Fax: 020 7936 2367
Email: elvino.wines@btopenworld.com
Website: www.elvino.co.uk

What's hot: Good all-round list, but the French section is probably the best. Its buyer's own list, however, which includes port and Armagnac, is actually pretty good value.

What's not: Do mail-order and web sales, but the website isn't really what it could be and is pretty slow.

What to look out for: They also have a series of wine bars across London, which are pretty cool if you want a decent wine by the glass.

FORTNUM AND MASON

181 Piccadilly, London W1A 1ER
Phone: 020 7734 8040 / Fax: 020 7437 3278
Email: info@fortnumandmason.co.uk
Website: www.fortnumandmason.co.uk

What's hot: Strong Bordeaux section, with a great selection of older vintages if you feel like splashing the cash on something traditional but can't be bothered to wait for it to age in the cellar.

What's not: You are paying a premium for the Piccadilly location.

What to look out for: The F&T Champagne is pretty good, and they run a mail-order service for those who fancy getting in a booze order to go with the Christmas hamper.

HARVEY NICHOLS

109–125 Knightsbridge, London SW1X 7RJ
Phone: 020 7235 5000 / Fax: 020 7235 5020
Email: wineshop@harveynichols.com
Website: www.harveynichols.com

What's hot: I'd have to say virtually everything, but, if you wanted something a little more precise, they've got a very good and well-priced German section, so if you like Riesling this is for you. Also a very eclectic but really enjoyable mix from the New World.

What's not: It's only in London and Manchester.

What to look out for: It does do mail order. The Harvey Nichols nonvintage champagne is very good, too.

JEROBOAMS

8–12 Brook Street, London W1S 1BH
Phone: 020 7629 7916 / Fax: 020 7495 3314
Email: sales@jeroboams.co.uk
Website: www.jeroboams.co.uk

What's hot: Good wine list that's particularly hot on fine wines from old vintages but has a very tidy Spanish section and some interesting stuff from the New World, in particular Australia.

What's not: Can occasionally be a little overpriced, but its mail-order side is very good and it makes up for it with an excellent website.

What to look out for: You can also order the most fantastic cheeses to go with your nice juicy reds.

JUSTERINI & BROOKS

61 St James Street, London SW1A 1LZ
Phone: 020 7484 6400 / Fax: 020 7484 6499
Email: info@justerinis.com
Website: www.justerinis.com
What's hot: Very good selection of the classics, particularly Bordeaux
and Burgundy – as long as you've got the bucks to match.
What's not: Less imposing than St James's neighbour Berry Brothers,
but still quite old-school.
What to look out for: Fantastic German range, particularly from the
Mosel, plus their famous whisky brand, J&B Rare, which is handy if
you feel like making a break for the hard stuff from time to time.

LEA & SANDEMAN

170 Fulham Road, Chelsea, London SW10 9PR
(they have a branch in Notting Hill, too)
Phone: 020 7244 0522/ Fax: 020 7244 0533
Email: sales@leaandsandeman.co.uk
Website: www.leaandsandeman.co.uk
What's hot: Strong on France, with a nice little selection from the Loire
and the Rhône, which are often overlooked, even by independents.
Very good on Italy as well.
What's not: Could do better when it comes to the New World.
What to look out for: They have a nice selection of ports, and some
good older vintages to boot. Also some nice sherries, in particular
those from Valdespino.

MORENO WINES

26 Macroom Road, Maida Vale, London W9 3HY
Phone: 020 8960 7161/ Fax: 020 8960 7165
Email: sales@moreno-wines.co.uk
What's hot: Without a doubt one of the best selections of Spanish wine
in the UK. In fact they're nuts about Spain and it shows in a great wine list.
And most of it is also available via mail order.
What's not: If you don't like Spanish wine, then there's little else to really
grab your interest.
What to look out for: Try the Cuvée 21 – it's a brilliant Cava (and you can't
say that about too much Cava). Also worth splashing out a bit and trying
the wines of Guelbenzu from Navarra in Northern Spain.

PHILGLAS AND SWIGGOT

21 Northcote Road, London SW11 1NG
Phone: 020 7924 4494 / Fax: 020 7924 4736
Email: contact@philglas-swiggot.co.uk
Website: www.philglas-swiggot.co.uk
What's hot: Wonderful Australian range of wines, especially if you're willing to invest a few bucks. Some very good-value French as well as top-notch Burgundy. A really delightful list overall.
What's not: You can see it all on their nice clean, fast website, but you can't order from it. It's mail order only.
What to look out for: Their subscriber's club is great, even if you do get your arm twisted to spend more than you planned – it is worth it, though.

ROBERSON

348 Kensington High Street, Kensington, London W14 8NS
Phone: 020 7371 2121 / Fax: 020 7371 4010
Email: wines@roberson.co.uk
Website: www.roberson.co.uk
What's hot: Roberson has one of the best selection of wines in London – full stop. And it's strong in most areas, perhaps with the exception of the Crimea. Particularly good on New World.
What's not: The fact that they've never opened up anywhere else in the country is a little disappointing. But they do have a mail-order service, which kind of makes up for it.
What to look out for: The Argentinian selection is very good, particularly the Bodega Lurton wines. I'd give the bizarrely named Marquis de Sade Champagne a body swerve, though.

SELFRIDGE & CO.

400 Oxford Street, London W1A 1AB
Phone: 020 7318 3730 / Fax: 020 7491 1880
Email: info@selfridges.co.uk
Website: www.selfridges.co.uk
What's hot: Excellent range of champagnes, and pretty good on the New World, too.
What's not: Again, tends to be a little overpriced and could be better on everyday drinking styles of wine. Very friendly service, though.
What to look out for: If you've come into the cash and you want to spoil yourself, you may enjoy their excellent range of Prestige Cuvée champagnes (Dom Pérignon, Cristal etc.).

SWIG

188 Sutton Court Road, London W4 3HR
Phone: 020 8995 7060 / Fax: 020 8995 7069
Email: imbibe@swig.co.uk
Website: www.swig.co.uk
What's hot: Excellent Italian and South African ranges of wines, the latter of which is particularly good and has won them many awards in the past, and no doubt will continue to do so.
What's not: French section is a bit thin, and the website can be a little clunky.
What to look out for: Try the Vergelegen wines. You won't be able to pronounce it, but you will love the wine, especially the Sauvignon Blanc.

SOUTHEAST

BACCHUS FINE WINES

Warrington House Farm Barn, Warrington, Olney, Bucks MK46 4HN
Phone: 01234 711140 / Fax: 01234 711199
Email: wine@bacchus.co.uk
Website: www.bacchus.co.uk
What's hot: Excellent range of Austrian wines.
What's not: Prices aren't always as competitive as they could be and New World choice isn't overly exciting.
What to look out for: Before you roll your eyes about the Austrian bit (and trust me, I normally do too), try a Grüner Veltliner. It's very similar to Chardonnay, but often more enjoyable and worth a punt.

BUTLERS WINE CELLARS

247 Queen's Park Road, Brighton, East Sussex BN2 9KJ
Phone: 01273 698724 / Fax: 01273 622761
Email: henry@butlers-winecellar.co.uk
Website: www.butlers-winecellar.co.uk
What's hot: Good mail-order service within the East Sussex area. Very personalised service. Quite an extensive Spanish range with some nice Italian stuff, too.
What's not: Quite eclectic choice and highly individual – sometimes to the point of eccentricity, but then that's part of the fun.
What to look out for: The bin ends and the very good selection of organic wines.

ETON VINTNERS

47 St Leonard's Roard, Windsor, Berks SL4 3BP

Phone: 0800 056 0770 / Fax: 01753 790189

Email: sales@etonvintners.co.uk

Website: www.etonvintners.com

What's hot: Excellent French and Italian ranges, which have some really undiscovered gems lurking within their depths.

What's not: Could be a lot better on the New World. Some nice Australian wines, but overall it's more of a nod to the New World, rather than being truly representative.

What to look out for: Nice website, clearly laid out. Everyday drinking cases are particularly interesting and good value to boot.

VINTAGE ROOTS

Farley Farms, Reading Road, Arborfield, Berkshire RG2 9HT

Phone: 0118 976 1999 / Fax: 0118 976 1998

Email: info@vintageroots.co.uk

Website: www.vintageroots.co.uk

What's hot: It is one of the few wine merchants to specialise almost solely in organic wines, but, if you have an impression of them as sandal-wearing hippies selling really bad wines, nothing could be further from the truth. Very good French selection and some interesting stuff from Chile and Argentina and very honest about how organic the wines really are.

What's not: In some cases you do pay a premium – but, hell, no one said saving the planet was cheap.

What to look out for: The Albet I Noya wines from Spain are stunning.

SOUTHWEST

AVERYS OF BRISTOL

Orchard House, Southfield Road, Nailsea, Bristol BS48 1JN

Phone: 01275 811100 / Fax: 01275 811101

Email: averycellars@dialstart.net

What's hot: Very good French assortment and strong on most of the classics, though a little weaker when it comes to the likes of Australia and New Zealand.

What's not: No website to speak of yet, but does do good mail-order service.

What to look out for: Their Avery's own selection range is very good, particularly the champagne.

GREAT WESTERN WINE COMPANY

The Wine Warehouse, Wells Road, Bath, Somerset BA2 3AP

Phone: 01225 322800 / Fax: 01225 442139

Email: post@greatwesternwine.co.uk

Website: www.greatwesternwine.co.uk

What's hot: Amazingly strong French list, particularly when it comes to the southern French appellations as well as the Loire and the Rhône. Nice Aussie selection, too.

What's not: Doesn't do sales over the Web, but does have good mail-order service and very readable wine list in paper format. Just ask.

What to look out for: If you like discovering some great Southern Rhône reds, then this is the shop for you.

HICKS & DON

4 Old Station Yard, Edington, Westbury, Wiltshire BA13 4NT

Phone: 01380 831234 / Fax: 01380 831010

Email: mailbox@hicksanddon.co.uk

Website: www.hicksanddon.co.uk

What's hot: If you want good, solid, traditional French fare, from a decent Sancerre to a top-flight Bordeaux, or perhaps just an everyday drinking claret, then this is the place for you.

What's not: The rest of the world doesn't really get much of a look in.

What to look out for: Very good basic reds from Bordeaux that are easy on the wallet, and very kind to the taste buds.

LAYMONT & SHAW

The Old Chapel, Millpool, Truro, Cornwall TR1 1EX

Phone: 01872 270545 / Fax: 01872 223005

Email: sales@spanish-wine-specialists.co.uk

Website: www.laymont-shaw.co.uk

What's hot: Laymont and Shaw are pretty difficult to beat when it comes to getting the best out of Spain. They cover virtually every square inch of the country in wine terms and dig out some real bobby-dazzlers.

What's not: if Spain isn't your bag, you are in big trouble.

What to look out for: The Rioja list is impressive, but try some of the Los Santos organic wines: they're cracking good value.

PETER WYLIE FINE WINES

Plymtree Manor, Plymtree, Cullompton, Devon EX15 2LE

Phone: 01884 277555 / Fax: 01884 277557

Email: peter@wylie-fine-wines.demon.co.uk

Website: www.wyliefinewines.co.uk

What's hot: Great Bordeaux and Burgundy section for those prepared to splash the cash and vintage ports that go back as far as 1904 – which is quite useful for Uncle Monty's hundredth-birthday present.

What's not: Virtually no New World producers. Not great on everyday drinking.

What to look out for: If you like Cognac, you'll like the great vintage selection. The title says fine wine and it means it.

YAPP BROTHERS

The Old Brewery, Mere, Wiltshire BA12 6DY

Phone: 01747 860423 / Fax: 01747 860929

Email: sales@yapp.co.uk

Website: www.yapp.co.uk

What's hot: Without a doubt one of the best French-oriented lists in the land, although instead of being packed with Burgundy or Bordeaux it's lined with the very best that the Loire and the Rhône can offer.

What's not: Well, if you're a New World fan, you'll find quality but slim pickings.

What to look out for: Good mail-order service and a wonderful couple of Muscadets that defy the wine's traditionally naff image.

MIDLANDS

BAT & BOTTLE

9 Ashwell Road, Oakham, Rutland LE15 6QG

Phone: 0845 108 4407 / Fax: 0845 458 2505

Email: post@batwine.com

Website: www.batwine.com

What's hot: Fantastic Italian list, with some very decent stuff in the £5–7 range, as well as some lovely little 'discoveries' to be made.

What's not: If you're not an Italian wine fan (you should be, though), this is not the one for you.

What to look out for: Quite simple but effective website. Some great stuff from the often overlooked Franciacorta DOC in Italy.

BENNETTS FINE WINES

High Street, Chipping Camden, Gloucestershire GL55 6AG

Phone: 01386 840392 / Fax: 01386 840974

Email: charlie@bennettsfinewines.com

Website: www.bennettsfinewines.com
What's hot: Strong on France, nice tidy Australian section and some very, very good Italians – all of which cross a good range from the very affordable to the ludicrously expensive.
What's not: Sadly, can't buy online.
What to look out for: Try the Pieropan wines from Italy. Wonderful.

ANDREW CHAPMAN FINE WINES

14 Haywards Rod, Drayton, Abingdon, Oxfordshire OX14 4LB
Phone: 01235 550707 / Fax: 0870 136 6335
Website: www.surf4wine.co.uk
What's hot: Great website as well as shop, and a wine list that is not only strong on France, Italy, Spain and Germany but also has a cracking Aussie section.
What's not: Chile and Argentina get a bit neglected but otherwise it's a great selection.
What to look out for: Try any of the Dr Loosen wines from Germany – at either end of the price scale they'll make you change any misconceptions you have about German wine.

GAUNTLEYS

4 High Street, Exchange Arcade, Nottingham NG1 2ET
Phone: 0115 911 0555 / Fax: 0115 911 0557
Email: rhone@gauntleywine.com
Website: www.gauntleywine.com
What's hot: Strong on France, particularly the Rhône, with a nice offering from Alsace as well. All pretty well priced, too.
What's not: Virtually no Aussie or New Zealand wines, which is a shame.
What to look out for: The Domaine Schoffit wines from Alsace. Sublime.

NOBLE ROT WINE WAREHOUSE

18 Market Square, Bromsgrove, Worcestershire B61 8DA
Phone: 01527 575606 / Fax: 01527 823434
Email: info@nrwinewarehouse.co.uk
Website: www.noble-rot.co.uk
What's hot: A good all-rounder, really, with a little bit of everything, from everywhere, most of it pretty good. Their 'off the beaten track' selection has some lovely stuff from a variety of up-and-coming areas such as Ribera del Duero in Spain and Puglia in Italy.
What's not: Sadly, deliver only locally and within a defined area, and don't sell over the Web.

What to look out for: Look out for the wines from Australia's very odd-sounding region, Wrattonbully – they're the hot tickets down under at the moment.

SELFRIDGES

The Bull Ring, East Mall, Birmingham B5 4BP
Phone: 0121 600 6842
What's hot and **what's not** (see Selfridge & Co. under London)

TANNERS

28 Wyle Cop, Shrewsbury, Shropshire SY1 1XD
Phone: 01743 234500 / Fax: 01743 234501
Email: sales@tanners-wines.co.uk
Website: www.tanners-wines.co.uk
What's hot: Great Australian range and a nice mix of southern French reds and good Bordeaux. They have quite a nifty website, too.
What's not: North American range is a bit skimpy, so, if you're a California fan, look away now.
What to look out for: Tanners champagne at under £15 a bottle is really good.

EASTERN COUNTIES

ADNAMS WINE MERCHANTS

Sole Bay Brewery, Southwold, Suffolk IP18 6JW
Phone: 01502 727222 / Fax: 01502 727223
Email: wines@adnams.co.uk
Website: www.adnams.co.uk
What's hot: A great list, strong on the Old World, but particularly good on the likes of Australia and New Zealand. The 'buyer's own pick' cases are good value and of top quality.
What's not: Sadly, they're based all the way out on the coast by Southwold, but they do have a very good website.
What to look out for: I'd opt for Alistair Marshall's (the buyer) 'personal choice' case. It works out around £6.50 a bottle and is great.

LAY & WHEELER

Gosbecks Park, 117 Gosbecks Road, Colchester CO2 9JT
Phone: 01206 764446 / Fax: 01206 560002
Email: sales@layandwheeler.com

Website: www.layandwheeler.co.uk
What's hot: Lay and Wheeler is another strong all-rounder, with a great selection of New World and Old World. Very nice website, and their everyday drinking wines are very good value, and can be delivered regularly to you if you want to pay by standing order.
What's not: They don't have an English wine on the list – but I'm not entirely sure that's a bad thing.
What to look out for: The Lay and Wheeler nonvintage champagne is cracking.

NOEL YOUNG WINES

56 High Street, Trumpington, Cambridgeshire CB2 2LS
Phone: 01223 844744 / Fax: 01223 844736
Email: admin@nywines.co.uk
Website: www.nywines.co.uk
What's hot: Noel wins awards for his wine list because it's simply one of the most comprehensive around. It even has decent wines from Switzerland, and that's saying something!
What's not: There are some wines that are too 'out there' even for me – the Greek ones are a good example.
What to look out for: I am not sure how he does it but he does some great mixed cases for as little as £50 – I mean really, really great.

SECKFORD WINES

Dock lane, Melton, Ipswich, Suffolk IP12 1PE
Phone: 01394 446622 / Fax: 01394 446633
Email: sales@seckfordwines.co.uk
Website: www.seckfordwines.co.uk
What's hot: Great selection of Bordeaux with a strong *en primeur* section – an intense mix of stuff.
What's not: Website is good, but quite complicated.
What to look out for: Nice selection of Australia's greatest wine, Penfold's Grange – if you've just won the lottery then you might be interested.

NORTHWEST

LOVE SAVES THE DAY

Smithfield Buildings, Tib Street, Northern Quarter, Manchester M4 1LA
Phone: 0161 832 0777 / Fax: 0161 834 1144
Email: service@lovesavestheday.co.uk

Website: www.lovesavestheday.co.uk

What's hot: Some good Italians and nice New World wines, not to mention some great deli food to match.

What's not: The range is relatively small, and the website needed a bit of a revamp at the time of writing, although apparently this was on the way, and it may well be a lot slicker by the time you read this.

What to look out for: The Tasmanian sparkler called Pirie – awesome.

PLANET WINE

126 Northenden Road, Sale, Cheshire M33 3HD

Phone: 0161 973 1122 / Fax: 0161 973 2121

Email: paul.sherlock@planetwine.co.uk

Website: www.planetwine.co.uk

What's hot: Fantastic stocks of vintage champagne that will make any fizz fan go weak at the knees.

What's not: Bubbles are their speciality and the website is sadly quite clunky and slow.

What to look out for: Their hot list. When I hit the website, they had Laurent Perrier nonvintage brut on at £15.27 a bottle. It's normally around £23.

SELFRIDGES

1 Exchange Square, Manchester M3 1BD

Phone: 0870 837 7377

What's hot and **what's not** (see London entry)

NORTHEAST

GREAT NORTHERN WINE COMPANY

The Warehouse, Blossomgate, Ripon HG4 2AJ

Phone: 01765 606767 / Fax: 01765 609151

Email: info@greatnorthernwine.com

Website: www.greatnorthernwine.com

What's hot: Again, good all-round selection, with some interesting stuff from both the New and Old Worlds.

What's not: Website is a little difficult to navigate.

What to look out for: Nice little champagne selection and good regular bin-end offers (real ones – not 'created' ones).

MARTINEZ FINE WINES

35 The Grove, Illkley, West Yorkshire LS29 9LU
Phone: 01943 816515 / Fax: 01943 816489
Email: martinez@illkley.co.uk
Website: www.martinez.co.uk
What's hot: Really good Spanish and Portuguese selection and a very good spread across most other wine-producing countries, including such rarities as the Lebanon.
What's not: Bit skimpy on France and the website, while easy to use, is a little on the slow side.
What to look out for: Try some of their pricier Portuguese – they are an eye opener to say the least.

VINCEREMOS

74 Kirkgate, Leeds LS2 7DJ
Phone: 0113 244 0002 / Fax: 0113 288 4566
Email: info@vinceremos.co.uk
Website: www.vinceremos.co.uk
What's hot: Another great specialist in organic wines (and, like Vintage Roots, they're very clear about the 'level' of organic for each wine). Also have decent range of vegan and vegetarian wines.
What's not: Australian selection is a little light and the website is clunky, but they do good mail-order service.
What to look out for: They do some really interesting mixed cases. Not cheap, but good. And remember: you are helping to save the world. (Birkenstock sandals are not included apparently.)

SCOTLAND

RAEBURN FINE WINES

21–23 Comely Bank Road, Edinburgh EH4 1DS
Phone: 0131 343 1159 / Fax: 0131 332 5166
Email: sales@raeburnfinewines.com
Website: www.raeburnfinewines.com
What's hot: Pretty comprehensive selection of wines from around the globe, but particularly good on French and Italian. Very good on fine wine and past vintages, especially ports.
What's not: The website can be a little difficult to navigate and quite slow.
What to look out for: Great bin-end offers.

VALVONA & CROLLA

19 Elm Row, Edinburgh EH7 4AA
Phone: 0131 556 6066 / Fax: 0131 556 1668
Email: sales@valvonacrolla.co.uk
Website: www.valvonacrolla.co.uk
What's hot: They have an Italian section to die for, with the most
amazing selection of wines you can imagine from the likes of the
Piedmont, Trentino, Tuscany.
What's not: The rest of the range is not as comprehensive, but then
they are an Italian specialist, so you kind of expect it.
What to look out for: You can buy via the website, but the store is something
else to behold. It's half deli, half wine shop, so great wines but also fantastic
fresh pasta, sauces, charcuterie – the lot, basically. It's like an Aladdin's cave.

VILLENEUVE FINE WINES

1 Venlaw Court, Peebles EH45 8AE
Phone: 01721 225000 / Fax: 01721 729922
Email: wines@villeneuvewines.com
Website: www.villeneuvewines.com
What's hot: Great New World selection and particularly strong
on Australia and New Zealand. Who would have thought Peebles
would have such a gem hiding in it? Good website, too.
What's not: French selection suffers a bit.
What to look out for: Their mixed cases. Perhaps some of the
best-value mixed cases around, and always carrying some interesting
little new discoveries.

WALES

BALLANTYNES OF COWBRIDGE

3 Westgate, Cowbridge, Glamorgan CF71 7AQ
Phone: 01446 774840 / Fax: 01446 775253
Email: sales@ballantynes.co.uk
Website: www.ballantynes.co.uk
What's hot: Very strong French section but also some top names from
the New World, including Australia's very expensive, but oh so worth it,
Mount Mary wines. But when I say expensive in this case, I really mean it.
What's not: A shame they haven't really branched out of Wales.
What to look out for: As well as the Mount Mary they stock Lopez de
Heredia, which is one of Rioja's finest.

TERRY PLATT WINE MERCHANTS

Council Street West, Llandudno LL30 1ED

Phone: 01492 874099 / Fax: 01492 874788

Email: plattwines@clara.co.uk

Website: www.terryplattwines.co.uk

What's hot: Good all-rounder again, but the French list is very strong. Look out for some interesting wines from Argentina and Chile.

What's not: Website is informative but quite clunky.

What to look out for: Very good bin-end section that lists some unusual but worthwhile wines as well as the usual run-of-the-mill stuff.

NORTHERN IRELAND

JAMES NICHOLSON WINE MERCHANT

27a Killyleagh Street, Crossgar, Co. Down DY30 9DQ

Phone: 028 4483 0091 / Fax: 028 4483 0028

Email: shop@jnwine.com

Website: www.jnwine.com

What's hot: More or less everything. They've got a great Aussie selection, but are also strong on places such as Bordeaux and Burgundy. They give many English wine merchants a real run for their money.

What's not: Spain is a bit weak, though they've got some nice Riojas.

What to look out for: Quinta de la Rosa from Portugal – great reds well worth the extra couple of quid – and Domaine Drouhin from the Oregon in the Pacific Northwest.

Index